PEACE, RECONCILIATION AND SOCIAL JUSTICE LEADERSHIP IN THE 21ST CENTURY

In all my years as a public servant, I have always looked for guideposts to help me better understand a fractured world. This outstanding interdisciplinary volume provides an excellent roadmap to piece together the mosaic of peace, reconciliation, and social justice not just from a leader's perspective, but from the voices and actions of followers. This book forms an essential praxis through the lens of gender, diversity, spirituality, inclusiveness to better deal with global restoration of a more beloved community.

Ambassador Eric M. Bost (Ret), Former US Ambassador to the Republic of South Africa, Deputy Director of the Borlaug Institute for International Agriculture and Development at Texas A&M University

In this ambitious interdisciplinary volume, the authors seek to understand the concept of peace and reconciliation through leadership and followership theories and practice from the current generation's perspective in the midst of today's turbulent and unsettling times. The immediate need for this global analysis of peace and reconciliation from a trans-disciplinary lens is crucial. The authors of this volume provide a solution through the concept of decolonization by first giving a voice to those most impacted by conflict and then by listening to those voices in order to bring about social justice.

Raida Gatten, Associate VP of Academic Affairs, Woodbury University

At a time when the global order founded by liberal democracies is in retreat, beset by authoritarian rivals on one side and failing states on the other, academia might be ready for the tonic of a "peace and conflict studies" approach to the study of leadership — leading to an understanding of the moral, spiritual, and political roles of leaders in healing a divided society. This book lays the groundwork.

Michael Woo, Dean, College of Environmental Design, California State Polytechnic University, Pomona

Social oppression, civil war, and state genocide are often a direct product of leadership failures, but recovery from them can be facilitated by other leaders and even followers who appreciate and exercise the powers of truth telling, community reconciliation, and national rebuilding. H. Eric Schockman, Vanessa Alexandra Hernández Soto, and Aldo Boitano de Moras have gathered a host of penetrating and informative accounts of just that in *Peace, Reconciliation, and Social Justice in the 21st Century*, which serves as both an inspiration and a roadmap for those whose wish to apply their own leadership to recovering and coming back from human calamities.

> Michael Useem, Professor of Management, Wharton School, University of Pennsylvania, and the author of *Leadership Dispatches: Chile's Extraordinary Comeback from Disaster*.

An excellent view of the study of leadership and a just world order, the book provides a trans-disciplinary approach to issues of equity, inclusion, and trust. The building of sustainable peace is basic to the text as each chapter examines the themes of reconciliation, community building, international law, and social justice. This book is important and I give it my highest recommendation.

> Dr June Schmieder-Ramirez, Chair, PhD in "Global Leadership and Change Chair of Leadership Studies," Pepperdine University

PEACE, RECONCILIATION AND SOCIAL JUSTICE LEADERSHIP IN THE 21ST CENTURY: THE ROLE OF LEADERS AND FOLLOWERS

Edited by

H. ERIC SCHOCKMAN
Woodbury University, USA

VANESSA ALEXANDRA HERNÁNDEZ SOTO
United Nations Human Rights, Geneva, Switzerland

and

ALDO BOITANO DE MORAS
International Leadership Association, Chile

United Kingdom — North America — Japan — India — Malaysia — China

Emerald Publishing Limited
Howard House, Wagon Lane, Bingley BD16 1WA, UK

First edition 2019

Reprints and permissions service
Contact: permissions@emeraldinsight.com

British Library Cataloguing in Publication Data
A catalogue record for this book is available from the British Library

ISBN: 978-1-83867-196-9 (Print)
ISBN: 978-1-83867-193-8 (Online)
ISBN: 978-1-83867-195-2 (EPub)

ISSN: 2058-8801 (Series)

ISOQAR certified
Management System,
awarded to Emerald
for adherence to
Environmental
standard
ISO 14001:2004.

Certificate Number 1985
ISO 14001

INVESTOR IN PEOPLE

We dedicate this volume to the peacebuilders, social justice activists and survivors of mass atrocities around the world. Your courage and inspiration give us hope for the future.

ACKNOWLEDGMENTS

This endeavor has been a labor-of-love from the start and we were blessed by the amazing synergies of efforts of many individuals who provided unconditional support.

The editors owe a huge debt of eternal gratitude to Debra DeRuyver, Communications Director of the International Leadership Association (ILA). Debra is really the backbone for ILA/Emerald publications and she was with us every step of the way – offering advice and critique and overall was the consummate professional cheerleader for the editorial team. We also wish to thank the staff at ILA for their unflinching support and faith in our work. Megan Scribner also worked closely with us and kept us on task. Kudos go out in particular to Cynthia Cherry, CEO; Shelly Wisley, COO; and Bridget Chisholm, Director of Conferences. They and the rest of the ILA staff, interns, and volunteers were the cementing blocks and foundation that enabled us to construct the architecture of this book. An additional shout-out goes to Charlotte (Charlie) Wilson of Emerald Publishing for all her support and encouragement.

The editors wish to thank our readers who are leading every day by example in fighting discrimination, inequality, and hatred in their respective multiple arenas. We want you to know you are not alone. We also wish to recognize and relish the diligent efforts from those authors who have contributed chapters to this volume. We have collectively learned much from each author and it was a sheer joy to work together to produce this endeavor. We thank the authors for their openness, pushing the inter-disciplinary boundaries to purse intellectual rigor and truth-telling. Taken together, we hope that in our small way that we have moved the 'arch of moral justice' bending it toward some categorical imperative when justice, brotherhood, and sisterhood will deliver us to the promised land of peace.

Additionally, Vanessa would like to thank her grandparents whose sacrifices, courage, and unconditional love inspired her to become an advocate for justice and human rights. Vanessa is also deeply grateful for the support of her colleagues and friends for their generous insights and wisdom. Aldo would like to thank his colleagues and co-editors for their incredible hard work and thank ILA for their support for allowing him to be part of this second book volume of *Building Leadership Bridges*. Aldo especially wants to thank his family for giving him time for this important project and in particular his wife Claudia and his son Matteo. Eric would like to thank his co-editors Vanessa and Aldo for providing the intellectual comradeship that bonded them forever. Eric would also like to thank his distinguished colleagues: Will McConnell, Douglas Cremer, Randy Stauffer, Richard Matzen, Reuben Ellis, Raida Gatten, Matthew Bridgewater, Ofelia Huidor, Elizabeth "Lisa" Cooper, Seta Javor, Matthew Cahn, Henrik Palasani-Minassians, Mylon Winn, June Schmieder, Seta Khajarian, Farzin Madjidi, Kerri Crissna-Heath, Christie Dailo, Scott Beckett, Cody Thompson, Eric Bost, Frederick D. Barton, Satinder Dhiman, Michael K. Woo, Linda Daly, Scott Sveslovsky, Leslie Thurman, Edwina Pio, Jason Miklian, Rebecca Marsh, and finally Eric's family and loved ones: Marlene Noonan, Steven Henry Crithfield, Michael Brett Mason, Deborah Lamberton, Valerie Crithfield, James Pinnick, and his chocolate lab Brixton, who served as his comfort writing partner always at his side.

CONTENTS

PART II: COMMUNITY BUILDING: TO MAKE, BUILD, AND MAINTAIN PEACE

PART III: INTERNATIONAL LAW AND SOCIAL JUSTICE

ABOUT THE CONTRIBUTORS

Miznah Omair Alomair, PhD, obtained her doctorate degree in Education, with an emphasis on Leadership Studies, from Chapman University in California. She focuses her research on the areas of leadership and leadership development of women and youth in the Gulf Cooperation Council states, with particular focus on the context of Saudi Arabia.

Ambassador Rick Barton is the author of *Peace Works: America's Unifying Role in A Turbulent World*; now Senior Fellow at the Woodrow Wilson School @ Princeton; former Assistant Secretary of State and founder within the US State Department of the Bureau for Conflict and Stabilization Operations; US Ambassador to the Economic and Social Council of the United Nations; Co-director for the Center for Strategic and International Studies; Board Member: Alliance for Peacebuilding and the Institute for Sustainable Communities.

Aldo Boitano de Moras has 25 years of experience in top management, technological, educational, marketing, and sales positions with a strong leadership and team work emphasis. He received a Bachelor's and Master's in Engineering in December 1992 (Universidad de Chile) and an MBA in December 2006 (University of North Carolina-Charlotte Belk School of Business). He recently finished his first year of a doctoral program in Organizational Leadership at Pepperdine University. Aldo has broad international experience and is a world-class mountaineer and an active philanthropist. As a seasoned lecturer to companies and world forums, he has taught in the United states at Wharton and UNCC and in Chile in International Business, Leadership, and Building High Performance teams. Aldo serves on the board of Pleiades and the International Leadership Association and acts as an honorary "Ambassador" of "Hay Mujeres" a women leader in Latin-American association.

Sylvester B. Maphosa, a Fulbright S-I-R Fellow alumni, is a Chief Research Specialist and Head, Governance, Peace and Security, Africa Institute of South Africa, in the Human Sciences Research Council, Pretoria, South Africa. He is also an Adjunct Professor, University of Venda.

Douglas de Castro is the Visiting Scholar in the Foundation for Law and International Affairs (USA). Post-doc in International Economic Law — FGV São Paulo Law School; PhD in Political Science; and Master of Law, University of São Paulo; LL.M. in International Law, BYU-J. Reuben Clark Law School; Professor of International Law and Relations.

Sarah Chace is an Assistant Professor of Leadership Studies at Christopher Newport University. She has studied, taught, and conducted research on leadership for nearly 20 years, working extensively with the Adaptive Leadership framework, as well as various constructs of group relations incorporated within this framework. Professor Chace recently published a book with Routledge: *Advancing the Development of Urban School Superintendents Through Adaptive Leadership.*

Ira Chaleff is the Visiting Leadership Scholar at the Møller Institute, Churchill College, University of Cambridge in England. He is the founder of the International Leadership Association Followership Learning Community, author of the book *The Courageous Follower*, and co-facilitator of the Northern Shenandoah Valley chapter of "Coming To The Table."

Douglas Cremer, PhD, Professor of History and Interdisciplinary Studies at Woodbury University in Burbank, California, studies religious social and political engagement, religious and political violence, and philosophical and theological reflections on these issues. He also serves as an ordained permanent deacon in the Archdiocese of Los Angeles.

Benjamin Dürr is an International Lawyer and Policy Expert. He has experience as a policymaker in government and worked at the Dr. Denis Mukwege Foundation of the Congolese Nobel Peace laureate on advocacy and communications strategies against conflict-related sexual violence. As an award-winning journalist, he reported from ten African countries and wrote extensively about conflicts, peace, and humanitarian affairs. He studied political science and diplomacy at the London School of Economics (LSE) and holds an LL.M. in international law from the United Nations Nations Interregional Crime and Justice Research Institute (UNICRI) in Turin, Italy.

Vanessa Alexandra Hernández Soto is an International Criminal Lawyer with a special interest and expertise in international criminal law, human rights law, and international humanitarian law, with years of experience in the judicial and criminal field domestically and internationally. She holds an advanced LL.M in Public International Law, specialization in International Criminal Law from Leiden University, The Netherlands, a Law degree from the Pontifical Catholic University of Chile, and is a member of the International Criminal Court Bar Association. She was worked on a wide range of human rights and international criminal law issues at the International Criminal Court Chambers and the Office of Public Counsel for Victims, United Nations Mechanism for International Criminal Tribunals, United Nations OHCHR, and Oxford Reports, Oxford University Press. Vanessa is currently working at Office of the United Nations High Commissioner for Human Rights in Geneva, Switzerland, and as a Senior Editorial Reviewer at the *Groningen Journal of International Law* at the University of Groningen, The Netherlands.

Edin Ibrahimefendic is an Attorney at the Institution of Human Rights Ombudsman of Bosnia and Herzegovina in Sarajevo. A popular speaker at conferences, he focuses on the promotion and protection of human rights, rule of law, and good governance. His publications include "The Cellist of Sarajevo," a chapter in *Grassroots Leadership and the Arts for Social Change* (2017). He graduated from the Law Faculty of Sarajevo.

Chantal Marie Ingabire works as a Senior Researcher at Community-Based Sociotherapy program in Rwanda. She holds a master's degree in Medical Anthropology from the University of Amsterdam and a PhD from Maastricht University, the Netherlands. She has coordinated various programs and research projects with a particular focus on health, social, and behavioral aspects. She is interested in exploring the interlinkage between mental health, psychosocial support, and peacebuilding processes in postgenocide Rwanda with a particular emphasis on youth. She is involved in a research exploring the mechanisms of intergenerational transmission of memories and its impact on second generation. She has authored various scientific publications.

Alphonse Keasley, Jr serves as the Associate Vice Chancellor in the Office of Diversity, Equity and Community Engagement (ODECE) at the University of Colorado Boulder. He is also a Visiting Scholar at the Africa Institute of

South Africa, a division of the Human Sciences Research Center, in Pretoria, South Africa.

Mike Klein, Ed.D, is an Associate Professor in the Department of Justice and Peace Studies at the University of St Thomas. He teaches undergraduate courses on leadership for social justice, qualitative research, and art for social change; and graduate courses on social justice pedagogy, critical education in social movements, and the pedagogy of Paulo Freire. His research, publishing, and consulting focus on democratizing leadership, intersections of art and social justice, and peacebuilding. He develops the agency of students and communities to transform social structures and advance social justice.

Malini Laxminarayan, PhD, currently works as a Program Officer at The Mukwege Foundation, where she coordinates SEMA: The Global Network for Victims and Survivors to End Wartime Sexual Violence. She also teaches Human Rights at the University of Amsterdam. Her research areas include victimology, transitional justice, survivor empowerment and access to justice, primarily from a socio-legal perspective.

Lisa Liberatore Maracine holds a Master's in Public Diplomacy from the University of Southern California and is a current PhD candidate in Global Leadership & Change at Pepperdine University. Her work centers on the intersection between business, government, and education to create sustainable social enterprise for women's empowerment.

Sandra Marić, CWWPP's Deputy CEO, has worked extensively with children and young people. She has been with the Coalition for Work with Psycho-Trauma & Peace (CWWPP) since 2006.

Josephine R. Marieta is a Lecturer at the Faculty of Psychology, Universitas Indonesia, and Universitas Pertahanan, Indonesia. Currently, he is completing a doctoral program at the Faculty of Psychology, Universitas Indonesia. She also became a consultant at companies in the field of Community Development and Conflict Reconciliation.

Fátima Esther Martínez Mejía holds a Master's degree in Latin American Studies and Law degree from the Autonomous University of the State of Mexico. Her line of research focuses on human rights and transitional justice. In 2016, she developed as a Visiting Researcher at the Institute of Advanced Studies of the University of Santiago de Chile.

Whitney McIntyre Miller, PhD, is an Associate Professor of Leadership Studies at Chapman University who centers her scholarship on peace leadership and community development and leadership. She has experience in community and international development, refugee resettlement, nonviolence, and elections monitoring. She has served as the co-convener of the International Leadership Association's Peace Leadership Affinity Group and as a Community Development Society board member.

Katleho Mohono is a leadership development facilitator, coach, and community builder with over seven years of experience in youth leadership development, corporate education, coaching and training. A founding member of the African Leadership University, Katleho helped shape the culture and leadership development ethos of the institution.

Ziyana Mohamed Nazeemudeen is a Lecturer at the Faculty of Law, University of Colombo and PhD candidate at the School of Law, University of Aberdeen. Her major research interests are in the field of private international law and human rights concerns in cross border disputes.

Nelson Andrés Ortiz Villalobos holds a law degree from the Pontifical Catholic University of Chile and currently develops as a coordinator of legislative advisors in "Centro Democracia y Comunidad."

Bruce C. Pascoe, principal of Bizthinking, is a leadership and personal development consultant in Brisbane, Australia. He has worked in business, taught at Queensland University of Technology's School of Management, and spent 12 years in the United Arab Emirates, developing and teaching courses in Management and Leadership for Arab students.

Gavin Michael Peter joined the African Leadership Group as an inaugural faculty member in 2008 and has enjoyed working with all areas of the group as a community and culture builder. He is passionate about Africa, and building communities, using communication to encourage and strengthen connections.

Lyndon Rego consults, teaches, writes, and speaks at the intersection of leadership, innovation, and change. He has worked in Asia, the Americas, and Africa on individual, organization, and community transformation efforts. At the African Leadership University, he was the founding director of the Center for Entrepreneurial Leadership.

Corina D. Riantoputra gained her doctoral degree from University of New South Wales, Australia. Currently, she serves as an Associate Professor at the Faculty of Psychology, Universitas Indonesia. She utilizes her research in the area of leadership, diversity, and proactivity to bring betterment for individuals, organizations, and societies.

Annemiek Richters is Emeritus Professor in culture, health and illness (Leiden University Medical Center) and a staff member of the Amsterdam School for Social Science Research (University of Amsterdam), the Netherlands. From 2005 onward, she has been affiliated with community-based sociotherapy Rwanda, contributing in particular to its research.

H. Eric Schockman a Professor of Politics and International Relations and Coordinator of Humanities and the Center for Leadership at Woodbury University. He also teaches in the MPA program at CSU Northridge, and the PhD program in Global Leadership and Change at Pepperdine University. A public policy expert Schockman previously served as Associate Dean and Associate Adjunct Professor at the Sol Price School of Public Policy at the University of Southern California. He is the President and the founder of the Global Hunger Foundation, dedicated to helping women in the developing world brake the chains of poverty by funding projects designed to provide sustainable development and organic farming. He served as the CEO and the President of a prestigious international anti-hunger organization for over a decade pumping some $60 million in grants into the field.

Lorraine Stefani is a Professor Emerita, University of Auckland, New Zealand, and an independent higher education consultant and leadership coach. Her 2017 edited book *Inclusive Leadership in Higher Education: International Perspectives and Approaches* includes chapters from colleagues in Saudi Arabia, Hong Kong, Canada, South Africa, the USA and the UK, reflecting the global reach of her work. Her research focus is new models for building leadership capacity and capability in complex organizations.

Patrick Sweet is the Co-director of the Geneva Leadership Alliance. He was raised in the industrial Midwest of the USA and immigrated to Sweden where he lives with his spouse and two children. His education, research, and practice experience spreads across North America and Europe, and most economic sectors (public, private, civil, military, government, and transnational).

Bagus Takwin is an Associate Professor at the Faculty of Psychology Universitas Indonesia. He gained his doctoral degree from Faculty of Psychology, Universitas Indonesia. He utilizes his research in the area of self and identity, philosophy of psychology, well-being, and positive institutions.

Charles David Tauber, MD, CEO, Coalition for Work with Psychotrauma and Peace (CWWPP), has worked with traumatized people since 1988. He has worked with peace processes and non-governmental organizations since 1966.

Randal Joy Thompson is a scholar-practitioner who served as a Foreign Service Officer in international development. She recently edited the award-winning book *Leadership and Power in International Development: Navigating the Intersections of Gender, Culture, Context, and Sustainability*. She has published several chapters in other ILA volumes as well as articles in academic journals.

FOREWORD

Setting out to make the world more peaceful is ambitious. The work is hard. When neighbors start to kill neighbors, the fabric of a society is shredded. War mongers, spoilers, historic, and perverted arguments hover everywhere – resisting change, insisting on familiar and destructive paths. Oftentimes, the institutions that might help are misaligned. Success is rare.

When I started working on Bosnia, Rwanda, Haiti, and Angola in the 1990s, a wise boss cautioned that we should approach these places as "venture capitalists." Lacking experience in both peacebuilding and high-level investment, I took that to mean several things: high risk; open to new ideas; early and catalytic funding; unconventional partnerships; and accepting of the occasional positive results with a big payoff. That mindset allowed us to accept long odds and minimize the feeling of failure.

A favorite phrase became a staple: "If it works, it is a precedent; if not, it was an experiment." In over 40 war-torn places in the next 25 years, working for the United States, the United Nations, and as a scholar/practitioner, I felt that we had the license to find the local people, listen to their stories and voices, encourage them to pursue their own creative paths, and promote hope and trust. With that attitude, we pursued fresh approaches and built original offices, bureaus, and strategic relationships. We began to address the "gap" between humanitarian response and development assistance, always keeping "people first."

Taking on the big ideas of global peace expansion in a book is also ambitious. As a practitioner and a student, I am delighted that the editors have seized upon: leadership and followership; reconciliation; international law and social justice; and peacebuilding. As a reader, I welcome the mix of high principles and practical examples. As a recent author, I appreciate the rigor and persistence required.

From the outset, this volume establishes several fundamental truths. There is a broad recognition that complex crises and effective peacebuilding require inclusive and interdisciplinary approaches; that a first rule of leadership is to have followers – for more than just a minute; and that colonization and paternalism scar societies for decades.

Modern antidotes are offered. Building trust, advocating, and speaking out, and embracing others are the grounding. "Democratic and inclusive" leadership is defined as "based on a leader's behavior and performance" and not limited by tradition or history. "Followership is a new means to decolonizing leadership." Women, youth, and the gender oppressed are seen as promising innovators and change agents.

Throughout the book there is a disruptive tone but with a vision, a plan, and a follow-thru – not for the sake of an ideology but with a broader ambition: to make us more effective in the growth of peace. Anchoring those practical thoughts is the wisdom of prior leaders and followers.

"Transformational leadership occurs when one or more persons engage with others in such a way that leaders and followers raise one another to higher levels of motivation and morality", is the foundational thought of James MacGregor Burns.

Ira Chalaff's concept of *courageous followership* is cited: "assuming responsibility while also serving others, challenging leadership while also participating in transformation, and taking moral action while also speaking directly to the hierarchy."

Leadership is described "as a fluid process of 'stepping up and stepping back' […] which implicitly calls for a holding environment, speaks to the question of how to encourage people to access their innate power, as distinct from 'empowering' them" from without.

Addressing genocide, mass suffering, and structural bigotry, we are told to "look the beast in the eye." Without that necessary step:

> it is reasonable to speculate that racism will continue to erupt in
> episodes of both micro and macro-aggression. The boundaries of an
> intentional holding environment such as a sanctioned arena for
> truth-telling may be the only way out of this dilemma.

From the Geneva Leadership Alliance (GLA), we learn that there is a traditional over emphasis on "individual leader-centered competencies, values, behaviors to the neglect of common, collective practices required to address tensions between groups, tribes, regimes." In the search for "common self-evident humanity […] there is a growing recognition of diversity (often compensating for traditional, core- or unicultural dominance)." The authors refer to

> the paradox of commonality that emerges from diversity [...]. When family, security, stability, community bonding, justice, equity, religious freedom, etc., become aspirational due to existential threat, we also know these common human values provide the core of community re-building, reconciliation, and rejuvenation [...].

From their years of leadership training, GLA recognizes:

> People and communities under stress lose sight of these; yet, bringing them back into focus, provides social cohesion to reconstruct shared humanity. Desire for self- and interpersonal respect is universal. Everyone, in every collective, generation, tribe or culture values respect — we just define and express it in different ways. Trust is essential. By and large, trust is valued at every level. Polarization is powerful. The destructive power of polarization is easily negatively leveraged under stress, while leveraging polarity as a positive collaborative tactic is virtually absent.

"Leadership's ontology is mainly person-centered. Leading as a set of learned 'practices' is rarely separated from the concept of leader," the GLA concludes.

> Leaders are often seen as special and a scarce resource. Collective capability to lead is intuitively understood, but rarely developed. Integrity is desired to be a pre-requisite for power. Corruption becomes prevalent the more that power is separated from integrity, and the loss of integrity in leaders and institutions undermines the realization of most all of the points above.

This book invites "us to pay greater attention to the roles of those who with little or no formal authority initiate, give momentum and deeply influence critical changes in their communities."

When success appears in peacebuilding, it is most often due to "bottom up, community led" efforts. This book suggests that we all have a broader responsibility to play a role. It also makes clear that "history matters." Humility is indispensable.

These pages brim with a greater wisdom applied to real life cases, from Rwanda, South Africa, and Bosnia to Sri Lanka, Uganda, and beyond. The authors of each chapter are expansive in their thinking and methods, using film and art, or whatever is available to empower women and others as they address their grim post-war realities, the threat of climate change, or the dagger of oppression.

A survey conducted in 2008 by the Pew Research Center, "A Paradox in Public Attitudes Men or Women: Who's the Better Leader?" is cited as we seek to improve our performance in global climate negotiations. Of eight important leadership traits in the public arena:

> women ranked higher than men in honesty, intelligence, compassion, creativity, and outgoingness. Thus, the concepts that are lacking in the international climate regime are exactly the ones present in the leadership traits of the women in both government and civil society dimensions.

The book offers numerous revelations and insights as it seeks to transform perspectives, definitions, rulemaking, and long-held attitudes with inclusive, expansive, and democratic thoughts. My own experience confirms this necessity.

Ambassador Rick Barton was the first Assistant Secretary of State for Conflict and Stabilization Operations, a former U.S. Ambassador, a past UN Deputy High Commissioner for Refugees, a Senior Advisor and Co-Director at the Center for Strategic and International Studies and the founding Director of USAID's Office of Transition Initiatives. He is a Lecturer at the Woodrow Wilson School and Co-Director of Princeton University's Scholars in the Nation's Service Initiative. His book, *Peace Works − America's Unifying Role in a Turbulent World* (Rowman & Littlefield 2018) is in its third printing.

By Ambassador Rick Barton (ret.)

INTRODUCTION: ON PEACE, RECONCILIATION, AND SOCIAL JUSTICE

H. Eric Schockman, Vanessa Alexandra
Hernández Soto and Aldo Boitano de Moras

This interdisciplinary volume examines the conditions and the ethical, foundational basis for leaders and followers in negotiating for peace in pre- and post-conflict situations around the world, as well as how and why reconciliation and forgiveness can ensue. Our aim is to draw together the best contemporary theories and practices within the study of leadership and followership to apply for a more peaceful and just world order. As opposed to the traditional literature in the field that operates from disciplinary silos, this volume provides a cutting-edge, trans-disciplinary approach to fill the intellectual vacuums and practices for peacemakers and peace-seekers in every sector of our global society.

We start off this volume with a series of critical weighty questions: Is a discussion and analysis of peace oxymoronic in today's turbulent times? Has the next generation given up on peace and conflict studies and succumbed to the prevailing realpolitik of a disintegrating post-WWII liberal global order? Has the human capacity for compassion and justice been numbed in the wake of daily accounts of the slow-moving global humanitarian crisis impacting at-risk populations and our searing collective remembrance of past failures such as in Rwanda, Somalia, Afghanistan, Iraq, Yemen, Palestine, and Syria? Has global development and sustainability over the past several decades produced an unprecedented gap between the global "haves" and "have nots" which predestines a Hobbesian state of nature at constant war and divisive struggles? How can we better understand followership in the manifestation of leadership when it comes to peace, reconciliation, and social/restorative justice? Is there some prevailing over-arching paradigm that can weave through the chapters in this book that advances contemporary knowledge as well as underpins leadership, follow-ership, and peace studies? We have at least one answer to the last question: decoloniality.

The importance of "decolonization" of our thinking around peace, conflict resolution, reconciliation, and social justice, especially as it pertains to leader-ship (and followership) theory and practice, is the praxis of this volume. The logic of decolonization is simple, yet complex: It involves the intense lived experiences of those on both ends of the modernity/coloniality complex. It challenges the dominant global capital world order — from the voyages of the fifteenth-century European explorers to the ossification of post-Cold War "neoliberal globalization" — that has left its scarred legacy in post-colonial classification of class, gender, sexuality, masculinity, femininity, gay/straight/ transsexual identities, and power relations between the Global North (GN) and Global South (GS). Behind this veil of the struggles between development vs underdevelopment, exploited vs exploiter, decolonization puts a laser-focus on the intersectionality of war, genocides, and a system that creates "epistemi-cide" (the annihilation of indigenous knowledge for a GN-centric new real-ity). Decolonization offers a counter-narrative to the GN-centric hegemonic social, political, and economic structures and might just be the juggernaut preventing a lasting peace. It also allows us to overcome stigmatization, polar-ization, and resentment and moves us closer to promote relationships of trust, inclusion, and equity. If the narratives of those most impacted by conflict are not brought into the post-healing process can we ever move past pseudo-peace? As chapters in this book demonstrate, bringing forward the strength and resilience of survivors, peacemakers, and human rights defenders can bring agency for healing and empowerment.

An older *coloniality of economics and gender* still permeates eternal divi-sions in the bastions of the GN and is especially prevalent in many former imperial colonies or capitalist economic pockets of exploitation in the GS. Challenging the heterosexuality of oppressive patriarchal machinations that deny people to determine whom they love has produced new grass-roots mass movements for social justice that support peace. The seeds of conflict reside in realteration of power and the distortion of the human spirit. The role of women who make up more than half of the world's population and indigenous minorities from the GS must be elevated in peace and security matters. They are most often the victims of war and conflict but left out of peace negotiations. They often are at the forefront of leading peaceful reforms and should be at the origins of post-conflictual community recovery. Women's agency, voice and capacities, as well as a real gender perspective, are critical to local dialogues, better inclusive policies and more equitable peace deals. As evidenced in this book, decolonilization cannot be defined as simple tokening of inclusion. Conflict "management" and the demonization of the "other" can only go so far in distracting us from the real essence of ending epistemic violence and persecution. Decolonizing peacebuilding is a new discourse that speaks throughout the chapters of this volume.

For countries and communities that have seen the depths of vicious violence, rebuilding relationships of trust and restoring its social fabric is key. Furthermore, transforming ethical, political, and institutional dynamics will take the work of generations and a great array of actors across the spectrums of societies. To build sustainable peace, it is essential that *all levels of society* come together in addressing the roots causes of conflict. Peace in the aftermath of violent conflict cannot be sustained without addressing the grievances of victims and historical social justice. In dealing with the past, justice plays a key role in building and sustaining peace. And in synergy with accountability mechanisms, the manifestation of transitional justice anchors such entities as "truth and reconciliation commissions" that can foster greater acknowledgment and condemnation of atrocious crimes, as well as overcoming narratives of denial which can infect the views of future generations. Broader dimensions of recovery, as well as the moral reconstruction of societies that had abetted atrocities, require that society as a whole, and in particular elites and those in leadership and influential positions, confront their own political and moral responsibility. Truth-seeking processes can help us to look deeper into the root causes of conflict and social unrest, often predicated on past systemic corruption and a culture of impunity, to take significant steps to address systemic issues of marginalization and inequality. Massive violations of human rights occur with the complicity of many actors, including the complicity of followers. Most conflicts are not only about victims and perpetrators but also about those who benefit from a prevailing unjust political and economic order. The chapters herein remind us that to cultivate and entrench a culture of respect for human rights, of respect and tolerance for another, we need democratic and inclusive leadership for a long-term commitment in building peace that *involves everyone.*

The prevailing realist school of international relations based on the hierarchical structure of hegemonic power of the GN has for decades rigidified the global agenda of what constitutes peace and who should benefit or who should not. Perhaps, the reason we saw no "peace dividends" from the collapse of the former Soviet empire was that we equated peace with some financial tool as if the global citizens of the world were invested collectively in a peace stock market. This metaphoric terminology really is the convolution of decolonizing sustainable peace. This fits well into the Kantian notion of "perpetual peace" which serves as the "greatest good" of the universal moral law and is built on the establishment of justice. As Kant believed as more "citizens of the world" begin influencing their own nations toward a republican form of governments, this would give birth to a greater world federation which would expand a system that discourages war and strive for universalist values of perpetual peace. Kant's vision of a world of independent states moving toward peace, foresaw in truth the decolonization efforts of the United Nations. In 1945 when the UN was founded, 750 million people, nearly a third of the world's population, lived under colonial powers. The wave of decolonization has meant that today fewer than two million people still live under direct colonial rule. In 1990, the UN General Assembly proclaimed the *International Decade for the Eradication of Colonialism* and since the creation of the UN over 80 former colonies have gained independence. Sounds all well and good, except decoloniality does not necessarily equate to decolonial construction. Decoloniality brings further disruption to the social, cultural, and political hegemonic capitalist hierarchies. Unless we find the legitimacy for example of what Rego, Mohono, and Peter's chapter on *Ubuntu* addresses, or why we need an *African Young Graduate Scholars Development Program* outlined in the chapter by Maposa and Keasley, we lose a critical "third-space" for Afro-centric episteme. Decoloniality is not just a phenomenon of the GS but permeates structures of the developed GN. Unless we address the social amnesia of 250 years of legalized enslavement of blacks in America, as the chapter by Ira Chaleff details, we will never find true reconciliation. Or as Lorraine Stefani's chapter posits that unless we deconstruct the toxicity of racism and xenophobia behind Brexit, the narrative of the "leadership industry" reveals an emperor-with-no-clothes. Within this context and by calling out gross injustices, we see the potential of perpetual peace flourishing.

Kant would be comfortable with the concept of the "decolonizing of thought" which in essence brings erased ontologies into their own categorical imperative (a moral end in itself) and the debunking of the modernity/coloniality complex. This is not some cosmic consciousness but a very intentional pursuit to right past wrongs and peel away the scars of exploitation, plunder, hegemonic patrimony, and enslavement.

Further, this leads us full circle to the issues of leadership and follower-ship which this volume is predicated upon. We find that "decolonizing of leadership theory" is an essential element that needs further examination. In retrospect, leadership scholarship has come a long way from the old para-digm of the leadership traits, skills, and attitudes of the "great men" theory (read: white, male heterosexual). Despite in large measures to post-feminist, post-queer, post-Marxist theorizing we are still in a void of understanding contemporary leadership and how it impacts peace, reconciliation, and social justice. Is there then any formative body of work to reexamine decolonizing leadership theory and practice? Actually, there is. From a long line of distin-guished thinkers dating back over 50 years from George Homas, to Mary Parker Follet, to James Gardner and James MacGregor Burns, we can con-nect the dots to the trailblazing work of Edwin P. Hollander (aka the "father" of inclusive leadership). Recasting the field of leadership studies from a less "leader-centric" top-down formula, Hollander begins to con-struct the principles of leadership inclusiveness as a symbiotic relationship between leaders and *followers*. Followers are critical for the success of the leader, and in the long run they too can become leaders. Hollander speaks of a two-way, interdependent relationship and developed a term to describe this as "idiosyncrasy credits." Think of these credits as a metaphoric "fol-lower's investment account" where deposits of additional credits are made based on a leader's behavior and performance. Legitimacy of leadership ergo is dependent on the reserves accumulated. But just as followers give leaders the latitude to venture from the followers-base, abuse, and the arrogance of power works as a double-edge sword (think: Arab Spring Awakening). Thus, what we see in Hollander's advancement of building inclusive and diverse organizations is a direct segue to how we view *followership* as a new means to decolonizing leadership.

Another remarkable approach evidenced throughout the chapters of this book is the testimonies of leaders and followers who invite us not to remain passive nor silent in situations of injustice when human dignity and lives are in jeopardy. At times when leadership with vision, integrity, and commitment to the rights of all humankind stumbles, we should ask ourselves how our individual actions can either alleviate or worsen toxic political climates and human rights abuses. This maybe a groundbreaking volume in analyzing leadership through the lens (and permission) of followers, especially as applied to peace and restorative justice. Decoloniality is a positive disruptor with new voices of indigenous followers giving us hope for a perpetual peace.

PART I

RECONCILIATION

H. Eric Schockman, Vanessa Alexandra Hernández Soto and Aldo Boitano de Moras

Reconciliation is often regarded as an elusive and at times controversial concept. Nevertheless, reconciliation does occur in fractured societies arising from conflict, repression, and widespread human rights violations. Reconciliation starts with the acknowledgment of our shared and common humanity and dignity. Forgiving means that we are acknowledging that the other side is also human and that their children and ours deserve to live safely and peacefully. It involves building or rebuilding relationships toward a peaceful coexistence and an ongoing healing process as we will explore in the ensuing chapters, for example in the context of post-legalized slavery, post-apartheid, the trauma of the Balkans War, and the first signs of change in the Catholic Church tackling widespread and systematic clerical abuses. Reconciliation may take the form of a set of complex processes that could take generations, and which depends not only on the state, social organizations, but also on the agency and inclusive leadership and courageous followership of individuals.

Reconciliation may involve the processes based on acknowledgment of past wrongs, political and social customs reforms through economic and educational transformations, dealing with the structural causes of marginalization and discrimination. More so, it will take the preservation of memory spaces, and the eradication of negative stereotypes and attitudes such as the dehumanization of groups of individuals. Reconciliation is a massive undertaking and a long journey, which if successful may result in living a more secure environment, dealing peacefully with differences and reaching compromises based on the common consensus of a community.

To achieve sustainable peace, it is essential to reflect on the conditions of reconciliation. Can conflict be transformed without reconciliation? How should we work with the most traumatized vulnerable groups to ensure a bottom-up, community-led rather than a top-down healing process in creating viable communities?

Reconciliation can take place through the work of many different actors at several levels, and approaches will largely depend on the particular context. At the nation-state level, it may require putting policies in place to address structural issues that led to prior violations and injustice such as weak and corrupt institutions, a long history of impunity, as well as memory initiatives through memorials, monuments, ceremonies, education, the media, and social discourse and agreements aimed at non-repetition of past human right transgressions, among others. Reparations schemes for victims of past atrocities should aim to recognize and address the harms suffered by victims of human rights violations, restoring victims to their position as rightful bearers and members of a community. Another layer in which reconciliation can take place it is at the sociopolitical level, between groups – social, political, ethnic, religious, or others – manifested in social organizations, trade unions, churches, professional associations, and voluntary associations. Whenever possible reconciliation approaches should incorporate trust-building at the grassroots level. At the inter-personal level, reconciliation often focuses on the relationship between victims and perpetrators. When perpetrators face their victims, acknowledge the harm done and ask for forgiveness; when victims face their torturers and forgive, and each of them as individuals reconcile themselves with their past experiences, this may contribute to rebuild their lives and relationships with one another and find ways to live peacefully side by side.

Psychological wounds and trauma arising from conflict and violence can have long-lasting negative effects on victims, when a person is paralyzed by the fear caused by what they experienced, the shame and guilt of not being able to do anything in the face of the loss of relatives and the social stigmatization. Add hatred and rage resulting from the injustices perpetrated on them and sometimes with the impunity of the perpetrators going unaccounted for their crimes. The question is: What we can do?

The ensuing chapters explore several strategies and experiences capable of fostering reconciliation among those once divided in the aftermath of conflict or violence. Can the emotions and feelings victims be left with be transform into forgiveness that allows the violent experience to be reconceptualized and redefined to find a new perspective on life? The journey toward reconciliation and lasting peace is fraught with peril, challenges, and many setbacks; however, we argue that is not a utopian aspiration, and we can all play a meaningful role toward it. We hope these four chapters invite the reader to reflect on the role in leading and nurturing peaceful communities where reconciliation can flourish.

Reconciliation across generations has a very special meaning in Ira Chaleff's chapter as he takes some concepts from his lifetime work and from his renowned book *The Courageous Follower: Standing Up to and for Our Leaders* (2009). Chaleff applies it to examine the growing awareness of the impact of the historic institutions of slavery and racial apartheid on current generations of those classified as "white" or "black" and how courageous leadership and followership contribute to the interracial healing process. Through this lens it examines the work required of all members of societies in which there are structurally advantaged and disadvantaged groups. Douglas Cremer's chapter looks into Pope Francis brave leadership role as a papal leader in highlighting significant global crisis such as climate change, poverty, and the plight of refugees. Cremer also addresses in a revolutionary inclusive way, the internal turmoil at the center of the Catholic Church with a deep analysis of the widespread clerical sexual abuses and how reconciliation and forgiveness can play an existential healing role. Cremer astutely offers that these reforms and global stances cannot occur without the active participation of courageous followership in transparent alignment with new networks of local pastoral laity driven by the core aegis of the church: mercy. Charles David Tauber and Sandra Marić's chapter addresses the often forgotten and overlooked role of psychological trauma in the healing and reconciliation process, the reintegration into society during and after conflict and working with vulnerable groups in the relapse to violent conflict due to unprocessed trauma. Sarah Chace in her chapter looks through the lenses of a "Holding Environment as Container" into the leadership process that took place in post-apartheid South Africa when the Truth and Reconciliation Commission (TRC) was formed. Chace argues and makes a strong case that a similar commission can bring dialogue and reconciliation in the United States around racial issues.

On this long journey toward lasting and sustainable peace, there are often many setbacks and disappointing events. However, as long as there is a historical memory of how terrible the violence was, people will understand that you cannot go back. We hope these four chapters will reflect for the reader to not stand idly by and motive us all never to forget.

1

LEADING AND FOLLOWING FOR TRANSFORMATION IN A RACIALIZED SOCIETY

Ira Chaleff

ABSTRACT

The roots of racial injustice in the United States precede its formation as a nation and continue to send up shoots that bear toxic fruit. Leadership and followership are intrinsic both to the continuation of this condition and to its resolution. The brutality of 250 years of legalized enslavement resulted in generations of children forcefully fathered by white enslavers and their black "property" and disowned by the masters and their white families and communities. The current popularity of genealogy has ripped off the social masks of denial and documented significant numbers of "white" and "black" families who clearly share the same ancestry. This has presented a new challenge and opportunity for truth-telling, reconciliation, healing, and repairing the social injustice engendered by structural racism. This chapter explores the work of a group committed to this process. Through this lens, it examines the work required of all members of societies in which there are structurally advantaged and disadvantaged groups. The requirement is to step beyond the roles of perpetrator, victim, or passive bystander, into the roles of courageous follower and inclusive leader, in mutual service to personal and societal transformation.

Keywords: Racism; slavery; justice; reconciliation; trauma; followership; healing

11

In this chapter, I will examine the growing awareness of the impact of the historic institutions of slavery and racial apartheid on current generations of those classified as "white" or "black" and how courageous leadership and followership contribute to the interracial healing process. My focus on this European-American and African-American dynamic does not imply that other historic dynamics such as those between indigenous peoples and European-Americans is less problematic; rather, it is a function of my direct experience with the European-African dynamic, which I will bring into this essay. I will begin with a brief historical outline. It is imperative to keep this history in mind to understand and transform racial tensions and inequities today.

A central point for understanding why history matters comes from the field of chaos or complexity theory. One of the tenets of complexity theory, as introduced to the world of leadership studies by Margaret Wheatley (1999), is that small changes in the early conditions of a system can lead to dramatically different and magnified outcomes over time. In contemporary race relations, the practice, begun by the early sixteenth century, of capturing, enslaving, and selling Africans to work on the plantations of the Caribbean islands and the British colonies in America (Thomas, 1997), set in motion dynamics that continue to reverberate and dismay today.

This slave trade, and the institution of slavery it spawned, is now recognized as a crime against humanity of the first order of magnitude. Millions of people were ripped forcefully from their lives, shackled, and transported in brutal, traumatizing conditions, and sold to "owners" to use as they pleased. Being given the legal status of property, these enslaved people had not even a patina of protection against wanton sexual abuse of women or disfigurement and murder as instruments of terror to keep a potentially rebellious population under control (Feinstein, 2019).

This predatory state was further reinforced when the 13 colonies on the Atlantic coast of North America declared and waged war against Britain for their political independence. When the newly independent Americans worked through their process for organizing a government of free people, they wrote a constitution that did not directly name the inherently contradictory institution of slavery, but preserved it through a compromise that allowed the "importation of such persons as any of the States now existing shall think proper to admit" (US Constitution, Article I, Section 9) for

20 years, and counted enslaved people as three-fifths of a person, for purposes of representation and taxation (US Constitution, Article I, Section 2).

When the Southern states broke away from the larger Union in 1861, Southerners wrote their own short-lived constitution, in which the institution of slavery was explicitly named and protected. Only the wrenching American Civil War brought an end to these sovereign laws that sanctioned treating human beings as property to be used, abused, or disposed of with no regard to the dignity of individuals or the sanctity of family bonds. The ripples of these early conditions continue to roil the waters today. One can hardly characterize the relationship of enslavers as leaders and those enslaved as followers, any more than one can characterize a rapist as a leader and a rape victim as a follower. Nevertheless, if placed in the leader-follower continuum, slaveholders would undoubtedly see themselves as the leaders, whom the enslaved better damn well follow, or else! This is a brutal distortion of what we consider the bounds of legitimate leadership and followership, yet a distortion found all too commonly in history and in contemporary autocratic and dictatorial regimes.

When these power-imbalanced and values-corrupted regimes collapse, a reckoning must occur. In the case of the collapse of the apartheid regime in South Africa in the late twentieth century, many feared that the oppressed black "followers" would exact revenge on the deposed white "leaders." Instead, the world witnessed an extraordinary act of restraint and an institutionalized process of forgiveness through the Truth and Reconciliation Commission, initiated by the former oppressed "followers" and skillfully guided by Bishop Desmond Tutu (Tutu & Tutu, 2014). Using its hard-won and tenuous power, the first black majority-elected officials, headed by Nelson Mandela (1994), demonstrated a generosity in leadership, based on high moral principles that black South Africans had never been accorded when in the oppressed followership role. Their approach became a model for post-conflict situations around the world.

No such reconciliation occurred in the United States after its fratricidal Civil War, from 1861 to 1865. The sudden emancipation of four million slaves from plantations that had been their only source of livelihood left a mass of destitute "followers." Their immediate need was to survive in a war-devastated economy. The planned restitution of providing forty acres to freed black families per Union General Sherman's Special Field Order Number 15, and the Freedman's Bureau Act, never materialized

(Foner, 2014). Efforts by freed black leaders to expand self-sufficient communities were largely thwarted (Blackmon, 2008; LaRoche, 2014), and the oppressive categories of "master" and "slave" were soon re-established in new, equally brutal forms of racial apartheid laws and extra-judicial violence. Per the National Association for the Advancement of Colored People (NAACP), between 1882 and 1968, there were over 3500 documented deaths by mob lynching of black people in the United States. It was only a century after the war's end, when black "followers" refused any longer to follow oppressive white "leadership," and birthed their own true leadership and followership in the Civil Rights Movement, that the legal structure of racial apartheid began to crumble (Morris, 1984).

Yet even to this day, echoes of the American apartheid system reverberate in the mass incarceration of African-American men and the overuse of lethal force toward them by law enforcement officers. African-Americans are incarcerated at five times the rate per capita as whites (Alexander, 2010). Police shootings of unarmed black men continue to make national headlines with distressing frequency. The reality of this is such that in my book advocating intelligent disobedience in the face of misuses of authority, I felt called upon to warn ethnic minorities, when confronted by armed law enforcement officers, to obey them scrupulously. Real or perceived injustices can be redressed later, in the safety of community support (Chaleff, 2015). In this racially charged climate, and in the absence of a historic truth and reconciliation process, how can intergenerational and interracial healing take place? One answer is emerging through the descendants of both enslavers and enslaved.

An uncomfortable truth emerging from the current commercially fueled social rage for DNA testing and ancestor mapping is that millions of "white" and "black" Americans (and assuredly this applies also in the Caribbean and South American cultures) share the same ancestors. The wicked wry humor that "integration began the first night of slavery" is more correctly and painfully named as the rape of black women by white slaveholders (Feinstein, 2019). It was ubiquitous and continuous for the 250 years the institution existed, with the resulting widespread mingling of genes. This makes "race" even more of a social construct than many argue it is, as even Caucasian-looking descendants are classified "black" if there is a fraction of African blood in their ancestry (Browne & Ferrante, 2001).

What do the Caucasian descendants of these moral outrages do with the knowledge when they find their own ancestors personally held scores or hundreds of slaves and fathered dozens of children they would not claim? What do the descendants of enslaved ancestors do with the knowledge of having hundreds of newly identifiable Caucasian cousins, many of whom have enjoyed the social and economic benefits of their race classification, while those of darker skin have not? There is justifiable bitterness, hostility, anger, and shame on both sides of this divide once denial is no longer an available strategy (Weinchek, 2006). Clearly, there is a great need, and a powerful opportunity, to begin addressing the consequences of this painful historic reality that continues to create distortions in our society, despite the visible progress that is too often used to deny the remaining debilitating disparities.

One effort at constructing a container for this new, volatile information is the creation of a not-for-profit group in the United States called Coming to the Table (CTTT). It was founded by the descendants of slaves and slaveholders personally wrestling with these issues (DeWolf & Morgan, 2012).

Coming To The Table takes its name from Martin Luther King Jr's stirring vision delivered in his immortal speech on the steps of the Lincoln Memorial in Washington, DC, in August 1963:

> I have a dream that one day on the red hills of Georgia, the sons of former slaves and the sons of former slaveholders will be able to sit together at the table of brotherhood.

We are required to update this quote to include the *daughters* of former slaves and slaveholders for obvious reasons. It may be less obvious why CTTT groups also update the language to read "[...] of former *enslaved people* and *enslavers*." This active syntax charges the language with the force that can be lost by reducing the acts of oppression to static nouns. The power of language is acknowledged and utilized to reframe our thinking and the consequences that flow from that thinking (Redding & Russell, 2012).

There are two key principles to the CTTT's approach. The first is that the effects of enslavement are intergenerational and even *epigenetic*. For those unfamiliar with this latter term, it is a newly validated branch of scientific research that focuses not on the DNA content of genes, but on the observation that, under varying conditions, genes are or are not expressed. The traits born of this process can be passed to descendants without the DNA itself being altered. It is now understood that trauma is transmitted not only culturally, but also biologically (Weinhold, 2006).

The second principle is that this trauma is experienced not solely by the target of the oppression but also by the perpetrator (Redding & Russell, 2012). In a different context, the contemporary US military recognizes the condition of "moral injury" as related to, but distinct from, "post-traumatic stress disorder." The National Center for PTSD defines moral injury as "perpetrating, failing to prevent, bearing witness to, or learning about acts that transgress deeply held moral beliefs and expectations." From this perspective, and through the tendency of culture to reinforce inequities derived from the earlier enslaver and enslaved roles, descendants of both parties are becoming aware of the need for a process of transformation, reconciliation, and methods for reducing the economic and social benefits gap that has accumulated over generations (Redding & Russell, 2012).

The four elements of the process as identified by CTTT include researching and understanding personal and collective history, creating connections across group divides, engaging in healing conversations and rituals, and taking action to mitigate and repair the continuing effects of the oppression (Redding & Russell, 2012). The group relies on facilitators to help those engaging in this work through a shared set of values designed to create both safety and truth-telling.

Those of us drawn to the study and practice of leadership and followership will detect clear notes of healthy leading and following in this construct. The parties come together for a mutual purpose – healing and transformation – and do so as much as possible with a shared set of values regarding the worth and dignity of each human being, their voice, and their reality. If transformation is to occur there must be authenticity. If authenticity is to occur, conditions of safety must be established. In its essence, this is well within the mainstream of contemporary leadership theory (Avolio, Gardner, & Walumbwa, 2005; Burns, 1979).

Yet, contemporary leadership theory is itself insufficient. Why? Too often the profile of the selected leaders and the style of leadership are based on cultural biases that operate without fully being raised to a conscious level where they can be reviewed, revised, managed, and themselves transformed. For example, as a society, we are increasingly and painfully aware of this tendency in terms of gender roles. There is a mere handful of female CEOs among the Fortune 500 companies in the United States. Books are being written, conferences held, and support groups formed to shift this stark imbalance and its adverse impact on high-level decision-making. While this imbalance is also observed in racial and ethnic terms, there seem far fewer efforts to transform it.

Several principles have emerged from recent social movements, and they are made conscious in groups such as CTTT that are seeking to create new and equitable power dynamics. For example, too often the dominant culture marginalizes certain groups, rendering them "invisible," and effectively does not hear their voices. Awareness and reduction of the tendency to marginalize historically disadvantaged groups needs to be a critical characteristic of contemporary leadership. Assumptions about power and inequity hidden in the structure of our language, and in the narratives and symbols of the dominant culture, are more likely to be revealed through the eyes and voices of those who have experienced and can name the code words and social mechanics holding those conditions in place. This facilitates creating newly shared realities about how to move forward together (Iwata, Lopez, & O'Mara, 2010).

Groups can use varying strategies to achieve this. In the CTTT movement, value is placed on shared leadership between black and white facilitators or chairs. In the corporate or non-profit worlds, boards of directors can elevate the importance of a candidate's proven interracial and interethnic awareness when selecting new leadership for their organization. Of course, boards that have only token minority representation are not fully equipped to do so. Here, the chicken clearly comes before the egg and board diversity must be given high priority.

How do followers fit into this picture? I argue that they have a critical role to play in both supporting leadership's efforts in this direction and bringing deficiencies in this regard to leadership's attention, much as they need to play that role toward other critical aspects of leadership initiatives and behavior (Chaleff, 2005; Kelley, 1993). Courage is required in doing this since leaders, except for those on the dangerous political fringe, do not see themselves as racist and may be quite resistive to the idea that their behavior is reinforcing racial inequities (Chaleff, 2009).

Because of this sincere, but unsubstantiated presumption of "racial blindness," well-timed, respectful, unflinchingly delivered feedback on how leaders or fellow board members or executives are nevertheless maintaining the existing power structure is needed where warranted. Leadership literature has become aware of *micro-messaging*, in which leaders inadvertently convey favoritism or disapproval in their voice, eyes, body language, word choice, and recognition of different individuals in the group (Young, 2007). Racial studies have identified how these same micro-messages can be experienced as *micro-aggression* by those who have been traumatized in a lifetime of being distrusted and disadvantaged by the wider culture (Sue, 2010).

The follower role will need to be played skillfully by those in the group from both the majority and the minority cultures that are represented. In the racial justice movement, a concept has emerged of *white allies*. White allies are those Caucasians who see the ways in which bias continues to operate in a group and use the advantage of being white to speak up on behalf of those who do not feel safe to speak, or whose attempts to speak are not sufficiently heard (Campt, 2018). Care must be taken in this role not to presume to speak *for* members of the minority groups but to speak from the responsibilities that a member of the majority group has to hold itself to new and higher levels of awareness. Even though a vibrant, well-educated professional class of African-Americans contributes at all levels of contemporary society in the United States, when social conditions permit candor, such as in the safety of a CTTT circle process, nearly all have personal and familial stories of the caution with which they must navigate the White power structure. The black underclass must be even more wary, as evidence of the harsh consequences of encounters with the dominant culture exists everywhere in their lives (Cose, 2002).

These dynamics are cogent whether our personal or familial history is that of the perpetrator, the victimized, or the bystander. None of these roles are any longer acceptable in the language and actions of leadership or followership. We must replace them with culturally aware, courageous, and accountable leading, following and group membership. There are models for doing this. It is our responsibility to identify, adapt, promulgate, and champion those that can work in our organization and community cultures and integrate them into the group's fabric.

Perhaps, the wisest words on the responsibilities of leaders and followers in contributing to this transformation were, unsurprisingly, penned by the astute and acclaimed observer, James McGregor Burns: "Transformational leadership occurs when one or more persons engage with others in such a way that leaders and followers *raise one another* to higher levels of motivation and morality."

The editors of this important book posed a difficult question to me: Where does forgiveness and reconciliation fit into this picture? I will pose some thoughts in response.

The truth and reconciliation process that was used to heal the wounds of violence, whether white on black or black on black, in South Africa, Rwanda or Sierra Leone, addressed contemporary violence in which the perpetrators required forgiveness from their victims and the families of their victims in order to be re-integrated into society. Accountability and forgiveness were central to the process.

In the American experience, with its culture of individual rather than collective responsibility, the physical violence of slavery was perpetrated by previous generations. That creates contemporary resistance to assuming collective historic guilt. This may be similar in other cultures where the great crimes of genocide occurred in past generations.

Yet, the harm from these past events lingers. Often, so do the advantages, or privileges, that passively accrue by being a member of the demographic that prevailed. An awareness of this must be developed for the beneficiaries of past crimes, and of current injustices, if they are to engage in communal healing.

That is not to say that forgiveness of self, others, and even ancestors is outside the scope of this process. For example, law enforcement officers who recognize they were prone to excessive force might seek community forgiveness. Individuals who stood by silently when witnessing painful discrimination may need to forgive themselves. A parent or professional role model may need to be forgiven for transmitting the racist assumptions of their generation.

The approach of CTTT was incubated in the Restorative Justice model. Restorative Justice (Zehr, 2014) asks: Who was harmed? What are the needs and responsibilities of all affected? How do we work together to address the needs and repair the harm? Personal forgiveness for transforming a historic and structural culture of racism may not always hold the centrality it does in the immediate aftermath of violent societal eruptions. It is still relevant.

Certainly, the United States is not an isolated example of a dominant culture severely disadvantaging minority cultures. Throughout the Southern Hemisphere, historic oppression occurred in the form of colonialism rather than slavery, with both direct and indirect ramifications in those regions today. It is difficult to lift up these issues for rational discussion in the affected cultures. Even socially responsible people benefit from being in the dominant group, though they may not have sought this or been fully aware of it. Therefore, to some degree, it is often the disadvantaged minority who first forces the issue into awareness. But, once brought into awareness, and the veil of denial ripped off, we all share responsibility for dealing with the consequences of the disparities.

There will be justifiable anger and fear. Processes need to be put in place for constructively and meaningfully channeling these in the direction of justice and reconciliation, regardless of these being only imperfectly achieved. Whether we are in a leader role or a follower role, in the dominant culture or the minority culture, we can initiate or add our voice to this conversation. Only then will we be able to transform and make more equitable the narratives and practices by which we lead, follow, live together, and govern.

ACKNOWLEDGMENTS

I wish to thank my colleagues at Coming to the Table: Jodi Geddes, the President; Tom DeWolf, the Executive Director; and Dr Judith James, the Co-facilitator of Northern Shenandoah Valley chapter.

REFERENCES

Alexander, M. (2010). *The new Jim Crow: Mass incarceration in the age of color blindness*. New York, NY: The New Press.

Avolio, B., Gardner, W. J., & Walumbwa, F. (2005). *Authentic leadership theory and practice: Origins, effects, and development*. Bingley: Emerald Publishing.

Blackmon, D. (2008). *Slavery by another name: The re-enslavement of Black Americans from the Civil War to WWII*. New York, NY: Doubleday.

Browne, P. Jr., & Ferrante, J. (2001). *The social construction of race and ethnicity in the United States* (2nd ed.). Upper Saddle River, NJ: Prentice Hall.

Burns, J. M. (1979). *Leadership*. New York, NY: Harper & Row.

Campt, D. W. (2018). *White Ally toolkit workbook: Using active listening, empathy, and personal story telling to promote racial equality*. Newton Center, MA: AM Publications.

Chaleff, I. (2005). *The courageous follower: Standing up to and for our leaders* (2nd ed.). San Francisco, CA: Berrett-Koehler.

Chaleff, I. (2009). *The courageous follower: Standing up to and for our leaders* (3rd ed.). San Francisco, CA: Berrett-Koehler.

Chaleff, I. (2015). *Intelligent disobedience: Doing right when what you're told to do is wrong.* Oakland, CA: Berrtett-Koehler.

Cose, E. (2002). *The envy of the world: On being a black man in America.* New York, NY: Washington Square Press.

DeWolf, T. N., & Morgan, S. L. (2012). *Gather at the table: The healing journey of a daughter of slavery and a son of the slave trade.* Boston, MA: Beacon Press.

Feinstein, R. A. (2019). *When rape was legal: The untold history of sexual violence during slavery.* New York, NY: Routledge.

Foner, E. (2014). *Reconstruction: America's unfinished revolution, 1863–1877* (updated ed.). New York, NY: Harper Perennial.

Iwata, K., Lopez, J., & O'Mara, J. (2010). Leading for diversity. In E. Beich (Ed.). *ASTD leadership handbook.* Alexandria, VA: ASTD Press.

Kelley, R. E. (1993). *The power of followership: How to create leaders people want to follow and followers who lead themselves.* New York, NY: Doubleday/Currency.

LaRoche, C. J. (2014). *Free black communities and the underground railroad.* Urbana, IL: University of Illinois Press.

Mandela, N. (1994). *Long walk to freedom.* New York, NY: Little, Brown and Company.

Morris, A. D. (1984). *The origins of the civil rights movement: Black communities organizing for change.* New York, NY: Free Press.

Redding, A. H., & Russell, P. (2012). *Revisiting the history of enslavement in the United States: A curriculum guide for engagement and transformation.* Harrisonburg, VA: Coming To The Table.

Sue, D. W. (2010, November 17). Microaggressions: More than just race. *Psychology today.* Retrieved from https://www.psychologytoday.com/us/blog/microaggressions-in-everyday-life/201011/microaggressions-more-just-race

Thomas, H. (1997). *The slave trade: The history of the atlantic slave trade, 1440–1870.* New York, NY: Simon and Schuster.

Tutu, D. M., & Tutu, M. A. (2014). *The book of forgiving: The fourfold path for healing ourselves and our world.* New York, NY: HarperCollins.

Weinchek, H. (2006). *The hairstons: An American family in black and white.* New York, NY: St. Martin's Press.

Weinhold, B. (2006, March). Epigenetics: The science of change. *Environmental Health Perspectives, 114*(3), A160–A167. doi:10.1289/ehp.114-a160

Wheatley, M. (1999). *Leadership and the new science.* San Francisco, CA: Berrett-Koehler.

Young, S. (2007). *Micromessaging: Why great leadership is beyond words.* Chicago, IL: McGraw-Hill.

Zehr, H. (2014). *The little book of restorative justice.* New York, NY: Good Books.

2

THE ROLE OF WORK WITH PSYCHOLOGICAL TRAUMATIZATION AND SELF-HELP IN PEACEBUILDING AND RECONCILIATION

Charles David Tauber and Sandra Marić

ABSTRACT

Psychological trauma has not been considered to be a primary factor in reconciliation, peacebuilding, and (re-)integration into society during and after conflict and with vulnerable groups. Frequently, it is seen by those in leadership "soft" and often has been characterized as "irrelevant" in comparison with such factors as politics and economics.

We believe that bottom-up work is equally important as top-down work, if not more so, in creating viable societies, particularly during and after conflict and with marginalized groups as refugees, people with mental health reactions, former prisoners, and other vulnerable groups. We have seen that people whom we call "peer supporters" under good supervision can function extremely well. In our experience, in many cases, "experts" do not understand the issues and cultural aspects vital to such groups and thus function less well than people with less formal education but who are within the communities concerned.

The CWWPP has developed a highly participatory method known as Pragmatic Empowerment Training (PET) to train and supervise such people.

We stress that these are long-term processes and that current expectations of donors and others for short-term solutions have been unrealistic. We see such work as preventing violence and encouraging integration.

Keywords: Psychological trauma; peacebuilding; transgenerational trauma transmission; secondary traumatization; self-help; peer support

INTRODUCTION

The study of trauma represents an area of the complex relationship among the emotional, cognitive, social, and biological forces. Psychological trauma has been seen as mental illness. Rather, we regard it as a natural reaction to events in the life of an individual, a family, a group of people (women, former soldiers, and minorities as examples), a place, or the world (climate change), given the background, personality, and other influences to which people have been exposed. Psychological work has been stigmatized. People are seen as "crazy" and "weak." We think that *not* to have such reactions after traumatic events would be pathological.

In the context of peacebuilding, work on trauma has been characterized as "irrelevant" and "peripheral" in comparison with politics and economics. Yet, psychological trauma has serious consequences for individuals and societies. In our view, *not* dealing with trauma is an error of the art of peacebuilding. We stress that such work is a crucial foundation upon which sustainable peace can be built.

Arguments that are made are that dealing with psychological trauma is expensive and that there is insufficient capacity to deal with it. We would argue that this is a vicious cycle, namely that the events causing the traumas – wars and violent conflicts – are at least partially caused by unprocessed traumas.

PRELUDE

The Coalition for Work with Psychological Trauma and Peace

The CWWPP and its methodology arose from work starting in 1988 with the joint Amnesty International-International Physicians for the Prevention of Nuclear War Medical Examination Group (MEG) and other groups working with asylum seekers and those assisting them in The Netherlands. These groups also provided medical and psychological assistance where other physicians and others would not.

Many of those assisting the asylum seekers had little education in working with people and were not obtaining psychological supervision. They asked for assistance. The methodology of Pragmatic Empowerment Training (PET), described later, was developed in response to these needs.

In the early 1990s, a working group was formed on the medical and psychological situations arising from the wars resulting from the breakup of the Federal Socialist Republic of Yugoslavia. The CWWPP was formed informally in 1994 from members of this working group and was officially registered as a *stichting* in The Netherlands in 1997. It is registered as a foreign organization in Croatia and Bosnia-Herzegovina and has formed a local organization in Croatia. It uses a fiscal agent in the United States.

The CWWPP carries out a number of activities:

- creating capacity through training local people;

- working directly with individuals and groups of traumatized people, not discriminating on the grounds of ethnicity, religion, age, sexual orientation, etc.; and

- advocacy for reconciliation and human rights.

Currently, the CWWPP also is working with "people on the move," aka migrants. The CWWPP works onsite and online.

PSYCHOLOGICAL TRAUMA AND ITS RELATIONSHIP WITH PEACEBUILDING

The field of trauma and peacebuilding is complex and has effects at a number of levels. Peacebuilding emerged in the 1980s as a way to prevent and respond to conflicts. One accepted definition of peace-building calls it a process that facilitates the establishment of durable peace and tries to prevent the recurrence of violence by addressing root causes and effects of conflict through reconciliation, institution building and political as well as economic transformation.[1] We strongly believe that practitioners working in conflict and post-conflict regions need to be familiar with the concepts of trauma.

Rather than post-traumatic stress *disorder* (PTSD), we use the phrase *traumatic reactions*. There are a number of reasons for this. We believe that these reactions are natural and *not* pathological. We would find it pathological if people did not have them. Second, these reactions are individual and plural for each level at which they occur. While aspects of them are common, the combination and the expression of them is unique to the specific individual, entity, and situation. Making these reactions pathological leads to stigmatization of the process, which we think is counter-productive.

One of the problems of dealing with traumatic reactions is that, in most societies, there is an overly medicalized system that should be more socially and culturally sensitive. The term psychosocial "attempts to express the recognition that there is always a close, ongoing circular interaction between an individual's psychological state and his or her social environment" (Agger, 2001). Such an approach is directly intertwined with peacebuilding work.

If a broader concept of healing is used, in which the individual is not treated as separate from his or her social context, then the shift from "victim" to "survivor" is as much a question of social justice as a question about any personal process the individual undertakes.

A DEFINITION

A common definition of a *traumatic situation* is one that threatens the physical or psychological status of a person or entity or those of someone or something related to the person or entity. An example would be an auto accident to a person or to someone close. It also could be the loss of jobs in the same sector. Also, it might be something that happened in the past to people of the same ethnic group or religion or gender. Thus, we all constantly are being exposed to traumatic situations.

The first framework for traumatic incidents was developed in the 1970s because of the long-term psychological effects of the Vietnam War on soldiers. In the mid-1980s, the International Society for Traumatic Stress Studies was established as one of the first formal initiatives to recognize trauma as a distinct multidisciplinary field of study that explores how trauma affects not only individuals but also communities.[2] Wars, natural disasters, climate change, forced migration, and their impact on individuals and communities have become an integral area of study.

LEVELS

Traumatic situations occur at various levels. At an individual level, this can be *intrapersonal*, that is, a shift in the situation within the person, or it can be an external situation. There also can be a traumatic situation at the family level. Further, traumatic situations can occur at the group level. A group here indicates people who have something in common. Additionally, traumas can occur at regional and national levels. An example of traumatic events at the global level is climate change. Thus, it is seen that traumatic situations not only occur individually but also collectively and must be dealt with accordingly at the micro- or macrolevels. This has strong implications for peacebuilding.

Vamik Volkan commented that trauma in individual victims may cause new social and political processes at a broader social level and may result in altered behavior being transmitted from one generation to another. Neglecting the effects of trauma in one generation may lead to future generations carrying the suffering of previous ones, which Volkan terms *transgenerational transmission* (1997). This type of transgenerational transmission can go on for hundreds, and some say thousands of years. Recent studies have indicated that there may be a genetic component. It is extremely important in peacebuilding, as it may lead to future conflicts, psychological and physical suffering, and impaired functioning at the group and individual levels. Thus, it is important to work with the original trauma as early as possible.

NARRATIVES

A *narrative* is the way that an entity describes a traumatic event and its consequences. Narratives incorporate traumas and other factors. There will be narratives at each level described earlier. Narratives have strong influences on processes at all levels and can be manipulated internally and externally. The reframing of narratives is an important aspect of therapy for the individual and the collective entity as well as being crucial in peacebuilding.

TYPES OF TRAUMATIC EVENTS

The classification of traumatic events is still under discussion:

- A "simple" or "Type I" traumatic event is defined as one that was short-lived, that was a single occurrence and that was relatively mild. All of those terms can be defined in various ways, and thus, situations are highly individual.

- A "complex" or "Type II" traumatic event has been defined as one that took place over a long period of time, primarily to an individual. Sexual abuse has been the "classical" example.

The typology of trauma becomes more complicated when dealing with long-term processes such as longer wars, discrimination of minorities, and so on. Each situation is unique and must be dealt with accordingly, and thus, there are no formulas for dealing with specific types of traumatic events.

This is in contrast to what frequently occurs in the medical community and in the realm of governments, inter-governmental organizations, and donors, who use such works as the Diagnostic and Statistical Manual of the American Psychiatric Association (DSM) or the International Classification of Disease (ICD). This leads to work with traumatic reactions by the use of formulas; that is, one size fits all. Frequently, the results that are the opposite of those desired.

THE COURSE OF TRAUMATIC REACTIONS OVER TIME

When a person undergoes a trauma, it takes a while for it to register in the person's psyche. This is the *latent period*. Its length depends on internal and external influences. What occurs then is a series of physiological, biochemical, and psychological reactions known as "fight or flight." This lasts for as long as the trauma is occurring. On the one hand, a person can function in a "superhuman" fashion in terms of physical and/or psychological strength. An alternative reaction is that the person freezes and cannot react adequately. When the trauma ends, there again is a latent period before it sinks in that the traumatic event is over. Strong physiological, biochemical, and psychological dips occur. This is a critical period. On the one hand, there is a relief, and on the other, there now is space for the reaction to the traumatic event to take place. Thus, the person or entity is extremely vulnerable during this period and can collapse. Recovery then takes place at a speed and in a manner that is dependent on the individual and the environment.

During long-term traumatic events, such as wars, poverty, and so on, there are other phenomena that may take place. The precise nature of the process is dependent on specific circumstances. People – and collective entities — develop coping mechanisms that may be adaptive or maladaptive, but that somehow release tension. These mechanisms frequently persist after the end of the traumatic events and can form barriers to development and peacebuilding.

THE CONSEQUENCES OF TRAUMATIC EVENTS AND OF NARRATIVES

General Consequences

There are a number of general consequences of almost every traumatic event:

- The first is the loss of trust in virtually everyone and everything in the vicinity of the traumatized entity. Frequently, such trust is difficult to regain. It frequently leads to societal consequences, that is, in institutions, organizations, countries, etc., and can lead to violence.

- A second consequence is the loss of predictability. This lack of predictability can create great anxiety of various sorts, both within a person and externally. It can, in turn, lead to an increased lack of trust, which creates another vicious cycle.

Psychological Consequences

Virtually every type of psychological consequence is possible. Reactions are very individual. Elizabeth Kübler-Ross and David Kessler (2007) defined what she called the stages of the processing of trauma, which we now know to be symptoms, to be denial, bargaining, anger, depression, and acceptance. We would add anxiety and dependence to these. Acceptance is usually partial and can vary with time, as can all of the phenomena given above.

Guilt, shame, and blame are almost inevitably involved in trauma. The person or entity will have guilt and shame for not having acted as she/he/it believes that it should have and may blame others for what happened.

There can be a number of other psychological phenomena associated with trauma. In general, a person finds his/her individual mechanisms of coping.

Horowitz (1976) and Kleber described a model with alternating phases that may ultimately lead to some resolution of the trauma. First, there is an "outcry" in which the person consciously recognizes that the trauma exists. Next, there are alternating phases of reliving the trauma and processing it. The reliving phase is what the name suggests, that is, that the trauma is very present within the person, and the expected phenomena would occur. Thus, a person can be aggressive, angry, dependent, etc. The alternating phase, that is, processing, is one of withdrawal. Such phases can alternate for many years. Also, there can be gaps in processing. Restarting the process may be triggered by external or internal events, such as anniversaries, changes in living conditions, and so on.

Physical Consequences

Virtually all people who have had traumatic experiences have physical consequences. These are most severe in people who use denial as a psychological mechanism. The psychological pressure must go somewhere and expresses itself through the body.

All systems of the body can be affected. Thus, people get circulatory system problems such as high blood pressure, heart attacks, and strokes. Other problems include those of digestive system such as stomach pain and ulcers, endocrine problems such as thyroid dysfunction and diabetes, joint problems, and immune problems, including cancer. Sexual problems in men and women are common.

Societal Consequences

Societal consequences of trauma are many and varied. Many people, whether or not they admit it, are highly dysfunctional in their work and family lives. The effects on children and the following generations already have been mentioned. Because of their parents', teachers', and other leaders' traumas, young people may be psychologically traumatized and thus show signs of various types of dysfunction.

Influences on Reactions to Trauma

There are many influences on how trauma is experienced and on the way people and entities interact after traumatic experiences. No two sets of reactions are identical. Personality is important. Also, education, in general, and about trauma has strong influences. Experience, again in general, and trauma and stress in particular are of great influence. Some people who have experienced trauma have developed positive coping mechanisms while the mechanisms of others are less so. An environment that is empathetic will encourage easier recovery. Some cultures stigmatize expression of issues, particularly among men.

PRAGMATIC EMPOWERMENT TRAINING

One major goal of PET is to substantially increase capacity with regard to psychology and peacebuilding in people without previous education in either. The curriculum includes an introduction to working with people, self-care, inter-personal and group communication, basic psychology and counseling with a focus on trauma, non-violent conflict transformation, civil society, integration, and human rights.

The methodology is participant-centered. The participants decide on precise topics. There is far more discussion and exercising than lecturing. Participants are seen to be experts on their own situations and thus add significantly to the process. In the CWWPP's practice, the facilitator asks the participants what has happened since the previous session. A topic for discussion is then chosen and all add to it. The facilitator keeps track of the curriculum so that all desired topics are covered.

This assists with other aims of the method. The first is psychological and professional supervision of the participants. Such supervision is required in many Western countries but is almost never practiced in other regions.

Another function of PET groups is therapy by another name. In many cultures, people obtaining therapy are considered to be "crazy," and the process is highly stigmatized. Our experience is that trust is built quickly in PET groups, and thus, work on personal issues can occur.

SELF-HELP GROUPS

In our experience, the line between PET and self-help groups is very thin. In self-help groups, people come together to deal with a common issue. Frequently, the members of the group know more than the "experts," as they can relate better to their peers, and thus, the interventions are more effective.

RELATIONSHIP TO PEACEBUILDING

The very fact of conflict implies trauma. It is crucial for mediators, arbitrators, facilitators, and others to deal with the traumas of each of the parties to the conflict individually and collectively. While, superficially, this may seem to be a longer and more complex process, we strongly believe that it leads to more long-lasting results. This frequently involves shuttle diplomacy. It also implies that people involved in peacebuilding processes need to be trained in the psychological processes involved with trauma. Also, because of secondary traumatization, they need to have regular psychological supervision.

The method of encouraging talking and increasing trust through PET groups, by its very nature, contributes to peacebuilding.

One example occurred in an area in the Balkans that had been through ethnic and religious conflict. The town was divided. People on both sides had undergone high levels of trauma, including torture, destruction of their homes, and so on. We worked on both sides separately in small groups, concentrating on the traumas. We were open about working on both sides. After about two years, people in one of the groups, spontaneously, asked to meet people from the other group. After checking, we arranged such a meeting. We mediated. While it was tense at first, the people later got together more frequently.

We have seen this pattern repeated a number of times. We also have seen a substantial number of people from larger and smaller local and international organizations working on peacebuilding ask for assistance with secondary traumatization. This has included field workers as well as lawyers and even a few military and administrators. They reported higher levels of functioning after the work with us. We don't know definitively whether this made a difference to the peacebuilding process, but we suspect so.

DIFFICULTIES

The difficulties of this approach already have been stated. First, they lie in the insensitivity of the peacebuilding community, although there are exceptions such as Adam Curle, John Paul Lederach, John Burton, and others. Many times, trauma is given only lip service. Not integrating trauma sensitive approaches in peace building, sometimes may be doing harm (Anderson, 1999).

A larger difficulty is the insensitivity of politicians at various levels, who call work with trauma "peripheral" or "irrelevant." Arguments that are made are that dealing with psychological trauma is expensive and that there is insufficient capacity to deal with it. Our answer to the first is that it is more expensive, in monetary and human terms, *not* to deal with the trauma. With regard to capacity, we agree that it is low. This was pointed out in a series of articles in *The Lancet* in 2007. In our view, the situation has not improved in the intervening years. We also would argue that this is a vicious cycle, namely that the events causing the traumas are, in turn, at least partially caused by the traumas.

Unfortunately, we have seen similar reactions by donors, and thus, it becomes very difficult for the very small number of organizations working in this area to obtain funding.

One further issue is that it is difficult to obtain quantifiable results. These are long-term processes and we cannot see measurable scales after short periods. Yet, years later, we hear from people whom we see intentionally and by chance that this kind of work has had profound influences on their lives and on the lives of those around them. This lack of strictly quantifiable results puts off donors and others.

CONCLUSIONS

Conflict and post-conflict environments have long-term negative psychological impacts. Attention must be devoted to the work on psychological trauma and its accompanying physical and societal consequences. This is essential if viable and positive peace is to be achieved. Practitioners working in post-conflict regions also are repeatedly exposed to severe trauma and have therefore become susceptible to its long-term consequences on health and emotional well-being. They need to be familiar with the basic concepts of trauma. They also need to deal with it within themselves.

We do not believe that, currently, there is a sufficient number of professionals to deal with the situation, nor can a sufficient number be trained within the foreseeable future. In post-conflict societies, there are strong stigmas against mental health. We thus see the best solution in well-trained and well-supervised "barefoot therapists/peacebuilders"/"peer supporters" who are constantly in the field. Much of the training and supervision can be done online.

We strongly believe that the healing of the wounds of trauma is a prerequisite to reconciliation and development and, as Professor Adam Curle puts it, a condition for peace. We believe that this is a component of the problem that, until now, has not been integrated into conflict resolution strategies. Genuine peacebuilding requires sustained personal, community, and political attempts to integrate the suffering of the past into the present.

ACKNOWLEDGMENTS

We would like to extensively thank our long-time US donor, who wishes to remain anonymous and who is one of the few people who understand the need for compassionate psychological assistance to war victims and migrants. We would like to thank the Hulpfonds of Dutch Yearly Meeting of the Society of Friends for their support over the years. We would like to thank the Swiss Trauma Therapy Foundation and the St Gallen Evangelical Church for their support.

NOTES

1. Johns Hopkins University, School for Advanced International Studies, Conflict Management Toolkit, www.sais-jhu.edu/cmtoolkit/approaches/peacebuilding/index.html.

2. Psychologists for Social Responsibility, Personal and Community Reconstruction, Resilience and Empowerment in Times of Ethnopolitical Conflict, Washington, D.C., 2002.

REFERENCES

Agger, I. (2001). Psychosocial assistance during ethnopolitical warfare in the former Yugoslavia. In D. Chriot & M. Seligman (Eds.), *Ethno-political warfare: Causes, consequences and a possible solution* (pp. 305–318). Washington, DC: American Psychological Association.

Anderson, M. (1999). *Do no harm: How aid can support peace—or war.* Boulder, CO: Lynne Rienner Publishers.

Horowitz, M. (1976). *Stress response syndromes.* New York, NY: Jason Aronson.

Kübler-Ross, E., & Kessler, D. (2007, June 5). On grief and grieving: Finding the meaning of grief through the five stages of loss. Scribner. Retrieved from https://www.bookdepository.com/On-Grief-Grieving-Finding-Meaning-Grief-Through-Five-Stages-Loss-Elisabeth-K%C3%BCbler-Ross/9781476775555. Accessed on November 27, 2016.

Volkan, V. (1997). *Bloodlines: From ethnic pride to ethnic terrorism.* New York, NY: Farrar, Straus and Giroux.

3

MERCY, JUSTICE, AND RECONCILIATION: POPE FRANCIS, INCLUSIVE LEADERSHIP, AND THE ROMAN CATHOLIC CHURCH

Douglas Cremer

ABSTRACT

Pope Francis has highlighted the important global crises regarding the plight of refugees, the victims of war, the consequences of poverty, and the impact of climate change. He has done this while the Catholic Church is undergoing a serious internal crisis related to the ongoing revelations of clerical sexual abuse and a divided, unaccountable leadership. In calling for increased activity for peace, reconciliation, and justice among the Church's members, Francis is offering to share leadership with followers of the Church in a revolutionary and inclusive way. Ira Chalaff's concept of courageous followership: assuming responsibility while also serving others, challenging leadership while also participating in transformation, and taking moral action while also speaking directly to the hierarchy, points to a way that members of the Church can constructively apply the call from Pope Francis to the lives of their local communities with an eye to making a global impact. The Church will not be able to follow the pope's call to external leadership on the inclusion of refugees and the restraint of disastrous climate change unless it is also able to reform its internal relationships and restore confidence in a leadership badly damaged by the clerical sex abuse crisis.

Keywords: Pope Francis; courageous followers; Catholic Church; sexual abuse; refugee crisis; climate change

Amidst all of the challenge and turmoil within the Roman Catholic Church, the first six years of Pope Francis' leadership have stood out for his consistent stand on merciful and compassionate leadership on major world issues, ranging from refugees and war to climate change and economic justice. In one of the first acts of his papacy, Pope Francis went to the small Italian island of Lampedusa, located south of Sicily, equidistant between Tunisia and Malta, and a major point for African and Middle Eastern refugees attempting to enter the European Union. Speaking to the people of Lampedusa, in many ways the epicenter of the refugee crisis, Pope Francis evoked the biblical story of the murder of Abel by his brother Cain and the divine question, "where is your brother?" and called on the world to take responsibility for the significant loss of life during the dangerous crossing of the Mediterranean Sea (Francis, 2013b). In doing so, on his first visit outside of the Vatican since becoming pope, he highlighted the needs of the powerless and issued a direct challenge to the powerful. He reiterated and emphasized this message in his significant letter on the environment, *Laudato Si'*, where he challenged the wealthy country of the world to take responsibility for the human costs of climate change on the world's poor (Francis, 2015).

He has also been challenged for his changing stance on the ongoing sexual abuse crisis and the need for greater accountability for the Church's bishops, more than 5000 men who make up the Church's local leadership. Pope Francis has reinvigorated hope and fervor among the Church's followers (as well as among many non-Catholics) through refocusing the Roman Catholic Church's perennial emphasis on peace and social justice on the idea of mercy (Francis, 2016b). Coming into the papacy at this moment of global crises, institutional conflict, and dynamic change, Francis sees the key to the reconciliation of so many contesting forces in the world and in the Church in the Christian interpretation of forgiveness, best viewed through his renaming of the parable of the prodigal son as the parable of the merciful father. In that well-known parable, a son who has squandered his inheritance reaches rock bottom and decides to return to this father, begging for forgiveness. Before the son arrives home, however, that father sees him coming in the distance and, before hearing a word of repentance from the son, orders a celebration to be started (Francis, 2014). Even the movement toward forgiveness, however hesitant or unspoken, is a call for mercy in Francis' interpretation. While discussing the divisive external topic of the reception of refugees into the European Union and the United States or the equally divisive internal topic of the reception of communion for those both divorced and remarried outside the Church, Francis' focus has been on the application of mercy, not for the wealthy and powerful who continue to dominate and abuse so many (and not leaving them out, either), but for those cast aside by the forces of war, economic competition, sectarian conflict, and climate change.

Francis' increased emphasis on mercy has had wide-ranging impact, from his famous "Who am I to judge?" question (quoted in Donadio, 2013), to his emphasis on pastoral care in "Amoris Laetitia" (Francis, 2016a), and to his calls to accept and care for the environment, refugees, and immigrants across the planet. While his predecessor, Benedict XVI, was mostly known for his teaching and his defense of timeless truths, Francis has ignited the imaginations of the Church's leaders and followers, as well as ignited his share of controversy along the way. Nevertheless, his renewal of the Church's commitment to acts of mercy, to be in the world, as Vatican II said, "to give witness to the truth, to rescue and not to sit in judgment, to serve and not to be served," (Paul VI, 1965) and to acts of humility and service, has given new meaning to efforts at peace and justice, focused on forgiveness and reconciliation, which in turn has led to new initiatives in local communities across the world. He has restored the idea of discipleship for all members of the Church, but especially for the leaders of the Church, who often need to be reminded that they are first and foremost followers of the teachings of Jesus of Nazareth. After five years, these changes in approach and emphasis are rippling through the Church in ways that will be difficult to reverse. Understanding what a world driven by mercy would look like for leaders seeking to create a more just and peaceful world is increasingly an important task.

As a global organization, the Roman Catholic Church under Pope Francis thus faces daunting external and internal challenges. These challenges come together in a particularly acute manner as the laity, the non-ordained members of the Church, develop new models of followership and leadership. Ordination to the clerical state has long been the "sine qua non" of leadership in the Church, but this has never been absolute. In an organization in which followers have been conditioned toward passivity and seeking leadership or influence on leadership without ordination has been resisted, those lay members of the Church who are concerned with peace and reconciliation, with forgiveness and mercy, with accountability and justice, have to discover and create new models of participation and responsibility. Keeping with the lived reality of followers in the Church, many can (and have begun to) adopt various interactive, independent, and shifting roles as followers, especially as they bring to bear their professional experience, academic expertise, and ministerial service on the crises inside and outside the Church (Howell & Méndez, 2008). This trend can already be seen in the increasing calls for lay leadership in developing strategies to support and admit refugees, resist rising nationalism and racism, and support restructuring economic and environmental practices, while simultaneously combating the sexual abuse crisis and creating lay review boards for bishops accused of covering up clerical sexual abuse and crimes.

THE ROMAN CATHOLIC CHURCH TODAY

There is a certain image of the Roman Catholic Church that is both widely common and well entrenched in the popular imagination. It is incredibly large, a global organization of 1.3 billion people, almost 20% of the world's population, equally divided between the western and eastern hemispheres. It is organized as a hierarchy, with a leadership comprising almost one half million ordained members of the clergy, recognized by their practice of celibacy (a promise to remain single and never to marry) and their common use of black clothing and a Roman collar, organized as bishops and priests in about 3000 geographical dioceses across the world. It exercises its power in an authoritative manner, where Church teachings and practices are understood as God-given and timeless, and the followers of the Church are directed through their clerical leaders, assisted by about 3.5 million non-ordained, or lay, catechists, teachers, missionaries and ministers (*Pontifical Yearbook*, 2017). Overall of this presides the Bishop of Rome, Jorge Bergolio of Argentina, currently known as Pope Francis, a benevolent father and leader.

This image of the Roman Catholic Church as a top-down organization, a unified pyramid of power, with a dominant all male and celibate clergy ruling over a passive and obedient laity, composed mainly by members of nuclear and extended families, is both true and misleading. It affects both the way those outside the church see it and the way many inside the Church view their own organization. Yet anyone who is familiar with any large, global organization recognizes that this image is also far from the lived reality of many within the Church and those who also come into contact with its leaders and members. The Roman Catholic Church is also an organization with competing centers of power, strong regional differences, and a wide spectrum of theological leanings and orientations. When viewed from the standpoint of the followers of the Church, the popular image of the Church is far from inclusive of the difference and diversity it contains.

Beginning with religious orders, such as the three most widely recognized orders of the Dominicans, the Franciscans, and the Jesuits, and hundreds of others, to various lay ecclesial movements, officially recognized organizations within the Church run by non-clerical leaders, and hundreds of lay-led centers, publications, institutes and universities, the Roman Catholic Church has many foci of leadership, some exercised by clergy and others exercised by those who are normally thought of exclusively as followers in the traditional image (Faggioli, 2016; Rapley, 2011). Like many large and complex organizations, who leads and who follows is a constantly shifting position dependent upon roles, structures, and relationships (Kellerman, 2008). These orders, movements, and other organizations do not fit cozily into the image of a strictly hierarchical church structure, with the pope over the bishops, the bishops over the priests, and all of them over the laity.

Moreover, these roles are often (and have regularly been) highly contested positions. Conflicts arise between religious orders, between lay movements and local bishops and, most openly, between different centers of non-clerical power in centers, publications, institutes, and universities. All of these smaller organizations within the Church often represent different theological and political commitments, including advocates of traditional Masses and prayers, challengers concerning issues of sexuality and gender identity, defenders of liberation theology, and activists for global peace, to name just a few (Faggioli, 2017; Hogan, 2015). These are not recent developments, although the lines of disagreement and contest may be; historically, even beginning in the early church, such divisions, and the need then for reconciliation and the promotion of unity, have been evident.

Finally, these disagreements and contests are further complicated by regional diversity. The bishops themselves are organized in smaller or larger national or regional Episcopal conferences, for example in Latin America, Germany, and the United States. The conferences represent their people, both clergy and lay, in Rome when necessary, and have tremendous influence on how church matters are handled in their respective areas (Francis, 2013a). The image of a Euro-centric church, dominated by a mostly Italian leadership as heirs of the old Roman Empires, has not been true since the

election of Karol Wojtyla of Poland as Pope John Paul II in 1978, his succes-
sion by Josef Ratzinger of Germany as Pope Benedict XVI in 2005 and, most
recently, Jorge Bergolio of Argentina as Francis in 2013, the first pope from
the Americas and from the southern half of the world.

As if this already and always existing complexity in the organizational
culture of the Roman Catholicism is not enough, the twenty-first century has
been a time of immense challenge and change. While it had been going on
for several decades, the eruption of the crisis surrounding clerical sexual
abuse of children and adolescents in Boston in 2002 began more than a
decade of turmoil in the Church (The Investigative Staff of "The Boston
Globe", 2002; Shupe, 1998). In increasing number throughout the United
States (Los Angeles, Orange, Portland, San Diego, and Tucson, among
others), and eventually including significant accusations, evidence, and settlements in Australia, Ireland, Chile, Canada, Austria, and Germany, the crisis
has culminated as of late 2018 with the release of the Pennsylvania grand
jury report of more than 1000 cases of sexual abuse, assault, and rape by
more than 300 clergy, mainly over several decades from the 1940s through
the 1980s, the trial of Cardinal George Pell in Australia, and the revelation
that Cardinal Theodore McCarrick, the former archbishop of Washington,
DC, had abused altar boys and pressured young seminarians into sexual
relationships for years (Smith, 2018). The last two incidents reach deep into
the leadership of the Church, bookending the disgrace of Cardinal Bernard
Law of Boston in 2002. The result has been a deep shaking of followers'
confidence in Church leadership, open questioning of clerical authority,
stressful considerations of even remaining a member of the Church given the
ongoing and seemingly never-ending revelations of abuse and crimes at the
highest levels of the Church leadership.

The question for members of the Church, then, is how to both lead and follow in this challenging time. There is, despite, appearances, an increasing lack
of clarity about defined roles, leading to both confusion and opportunity.
Organizations and publications such as the Lepanto Institute, *First Things*, and
the EWTN Global Catholic Network, among others, are calling for a return or
restoration of former, strictly hierarchical roles, imagining a time when the
clarity described in the initial paragraph above was actually the case. Others,
such as the Women's Ordination Conference, Call to Action, and Future
Church, are calling for redefining the clerical caste entirely, opening ordination
to the priesthood to married men and women. Between these options lie many

other possibilities for reform and the need for many people to assume a variety of intermediary positions within the Church is increasingly apparent. One model of this kind of intermediate role lies in the restored permanent diaconate, composed mainly of married men in their 40s and older, who ordained for the service of the Church. There are almost 20,000 permanent deacons in the United States and almost 50,000 worldwide who have occupations and careers independent of the Church and serve as ministers of the sacraments, preachers, and teachers, and often lead charitable ministries for the poor, the imprisoned, and the homeless (United States Conference of Catholic Bishops, 2005).

THE NEED FOR "COURAGEOUS FOLLOWERS"

Regardless of which particular roles are created, it appears the new models of followership and leadership are urgently necessary if the Church is to restore confidence in its internal leadership and its credibility to affect positive change for peace and security in the wider world. Of the various theories of such change, Ira Chaleff's construction of "the courageous follower" appears most promising and fitting for a church in such crisis (Chaleff, 2009). By developing the courage to assume responsibility as well as to serve, to challenge and to participate in transformation, and to take moral action and to speak to the hierarchy, members of the Church can find ways to exercise their authority, given to them as baptized Christians, as part of the priesthood of all believers and the people of God (Paul VI, 1964). This conception of the Church, as elaborated in Vatican II's constitution, balances individual participation and hierarchical leadership within the overall organization. It is a balance that has often been lacking and never fully integrated in the structure of the Church and the attitudes of its members, but it provides a much-deferred starting place for reform. Those accustomed to being only followers need to assume leadership as well, a transition that Francis has repeatedly called for in his words and actions.

The leaders within the Church, who will thus increasingly come from the lay followers, can follow the model laid down by Pope Francis himself, developing the grace to accept responsibility, admit error, ask forgiveness, call for the priority of the weak, the poor, the displaced, the sufferer of violence and discrimination. The work of peace and justice, carried out by lay organizations such as Catholic Charities, Caritas International, and

Catholic Relief Services, provides models of leadership coordinated with hierarchical authority that can begin to address reconciliation between clerical authority that has been abused lay leadership that must continue to emerge. Moreover, the paths laid out by Pope Francis and his emphasis on mercy also correspond well with Chaleff's dimensions of courageous followership, but without Chaleff's tendency to remain within a rather strict leader–follower binary. Francis, recognizing the multiplicity of the Church, its embrace of difference and global reach, has particularly called on the lay members of the Church, the followers, to serve while also assuming responsibility, to participate in as well as challenge transformation and to speak to the hierarchy in a manner that calls for and takes moral action.

Service has long been the role of followers in the Church, as one would expect, and often this has taken the form of passive and conformist activity (Kelley, 1992). Francis' Church of mercy, however, does not call for the sheep to remain sheep; in fact, he very early called on clerical leaders to take on the smell of the sheep, to be so close to those they care for pastorally that the views, concerns, work, and suffering of the lay followers become part of who they are at an intimate level (Francis, 2016b). This cannot happen without the sheep also being close to the pastors, honestly and openly sharing with them the responsibility for governing the local Church. As long as the image of the sheep and the shepherd has been used to encourage passivity, it has also served as a model of collaborative responsibility for the entire sheepfold (Francis, 2014). Service in the Church, and to the world, cannot be done solely at the direction of leadership; effective feedback, conflict resolution, and personal growth are difficult, if not impossible to achieve, without the ability to forgive, both oneself and others, and begin the path toward reconciliation.

In addition, the followers of the Church need to challenge the leadership effectively and consistently, not simply in a way where power remains solely in the hands of the clergy, but in a manner that fully participates in the transformation of the Church. Francis has continued to call for the Church to change, to realize the promises of the Second Vatican Council for a church more open to the world and lived internally more in the spirit of the council (Kasper, 2015). The laity in their own roles ought to model the kinds of attitudes and behavior they seek in their leaders. The call to dialogue, to keep open lines of honest communication and recognize the need for confronting failures, is a hallmark of Francis' efforts and is an essential element of a reforming church (Boff, 2014).

Lastly, none of this can happen without the willingness of the followers of the Church to take moral action and to speak clearly and strongly to the hierarchy. The laity has many levers of influence, from their financial and intellectual contributions to their labor and networks. They also have the power of organization and resistance, working in ways to change the behavior of the leadership and assume leadership roles themselves. Francis has emphasized the power of collegiality, not only among the bishops of the Church, but in the relationships between the clergy and the laity (McElwee & Wooden, 2018). Collective action, from leaders and followers alike, in fact, by followers who assume leadership roles when necessary to drive change and reform, and at multiple levels: local, national, regional, and global, is a core principle in a church driven by mercy.

THE COURAGE TO LEAD AS A FOLLOWER

The leadership of Pope Francis in the past six years has centered on openness, forgiveness, and collaboration. He has shown himself willing to listen to the followers of the Church, their cares, and concerns, in determining the direction of his leadership. The withholding of judgment, the willingness to listen, and the inclusion of others are all hallmarks of his efforts at reform, a change fully in the spirit of the Second Vatican Council. The compelling need for extended efforts in aid of the environment, refugees, migrants, and the victims of war, and the equally desperate need for transparency and reconciliation within the Church in the wake of the ongoing clerical sex abuse and leadership crises, will require an active and leading role for the members of the Roman Catholic Church, ordained and lay alike, united in an inclusive vision of collaborative and collegial leadership. Pope Francis' refocus on discipleship, on recovering the role of follower for the Church's leadership, on re-embracing the necessary humility and sacrifice, as well as his call for the followers to assume leadership roles to strengthen the Church, all under the aegis of a church of mercy, provides some hope for the success of his reforms in a time of institutional crisis and dynamic change.

If the followers, as emerging leaders within the Catholic Church, assume responsibility as they take on the willingness serve, they can heed Pope

Francis' call to engage the world in a compassionate and giving manner. If they rise to the challenge and participate in the transformation of the world and the Church, they will implement Pope Francis' call to mercy and care for the least powerful among us. If they take moral action and speak clearly to the hierarchy, they will change the organizational culture of a church in need of completing the opening to the world called for at Vatican II, beginning the healing of those who suffered from clerical sex abuse as well as a planet suffering from climate change. Any effective change in the way an organization tackles and succeeds in addressing external issues must be accompanied by a similar change in the way that organization addresses internal ones. Pope Francis has been very effective in drawing the world's attention to the major crises of the day and energizing the followers of the Church to advocate for the changes required. It remains to be seen if he can lead a similar transformation within the Church itself, and to do so, many more that have been used to simply following will have to learn to take the lead.

ACKNOWLEDGMENT

I would like to thank H. Eric Schockman and the editors of this book for their support and helpful suggestions.

REFERENCES

Boff, L. (2014). *Francis of Rome and Francis of Assisi: A new springtime for the church*. D. Livingstone (Trans.), Maryknoll, NY: Orbis.

Central Office of Church Statistics of the Secretariat of State (Ed.). (2017). Pontifical Yearbook 2017. Vatican City: Vatican Publishing.

Chaleff, I. (2009). *The courageous follower: Standing up to and for our leaders* (3rd ed.). San Francisco, CA: Berrett-Koehler Publications.

Donadio, R. (2013, July 29). On gay priests, Pope Francis asks, "Who Am I to Judge?" *The New York Times*.

Faggioli, M. (2016). *The rising laity. Ecclesial movements since Vatican II*. New York, NY: Paulist Press.

Faggioli, M. (2017). *Catholicism and citizenship: Political cultures of the church in the 21st century*. Collegeville, MN: Liturgical Press.

Francis. (2013a). *Evangelii Gaudium (The joy of the Gospel)*. Vatican City: Vatican Press.

Francis. (2013b). *Visit to Lampedusa*. Retrieved from http://w2.vatican.va/content/francesco/en/homilies/2013/documents/papa-francesco_20130708_omelia-lampedusa.pdf

Francis. (2014). *The church of mercy: A vision for the church*. Chicago, IL: Loyola Press.

Francis. (2015). *Praise be to you (Laudato Si'): On care for our common home*. San Francisco, CA: Ignatius Press.

Francis. (2016a). *Amoris Laetitia (The joy of love)*. Vatican City: Vatican Press.

Francis. (2016b). *The name of god is mercy: A conversation with Andrea Torinelli*. O. Trancy (Trans.), New York, NY: Random House.

Hogan, L. (2015). Conflicts within the Roman Catholic Church. In A. Thatcher (Ed.), *The Oxford handbook of theology, sexuality and gender*. Oxford: Oxford University Press.

Howell, J. P., & Méndez, M. J. (2008). Three perspectives on followership. In R. E. Riggio, I. Chaleff, & J. Lipmen-Blumen (Eds.), *The art of followership: How great followers create great leaders and organizations* (pp. 25–40). San Francisco, CA: Josey Bass.

The Investigative Staff of "The Boston Globe". (2002). *Betrayal: The crisis in the Catholic Church*. Boston, MA: Little, Brown and Co.

Kasper, W. (2015). *Pope Francis' revolution of tenderness and love*. W. Madges (Trans.), New York, NY: Paulist Press.

Kellerman, B. (2008). *Followership: How followers are creating change and changing leaders*. Boston, MA: Harvard Business School.

Kelley, R. (1992). *The power of followership*. New York, NY: Bantam Dell.

McElwee, J. J., & Wooden, C. (Eds). (2018). *A Pope Francis Lexicon*. Collegeville, MN: Liturgical Press.

Paul VI and the Second Vatican Council. (1964). *Lumen Gentium (The light of the nations)*. Vatican City: Vatican Press.

Paul VI and the Second Vatican Council. (1965). *Gaudium et Spes (Joy and hope)*. Vatican City: Vatican Press.

Rapley, E. (2011). *The lord as their portion: The story of the religious orders and how they shaped our world*. Grand Rapids, MI: Eerdmans Publishing.

Shupe, A. (Ed.). (1998). *Wolves in the fold: Religious leadership and abuses of power*. New Brunswick, NJ: Rutgers University Press.

Smith, P. (2018, July 26). Abuse accusations against priests, bishops and cardinals reach levels not seen in years. *Pittsburgh Post-Gazette*.

United States Conference of Catholic Bishops. (2005). *National directory for the formation, ministry, and life of permanent deacons in the United States*. Washington, DC: USCCB.

4

USES OF A HOLDING ENVIRONMENT AS CONTAINER FOR STEPPING UP AND STEPPING BACK IN THE CONTEXT OF TRUTH AND RECONCILIATION

Sarah Chace

ABSTRACT

This chapter explores the dual constructs of Winnicott's notion of holding environment and Altvatar et al.'s notion of "stepping up and stepping back" into leadership roles. The merging of the two constructs provides a double lens through which to analyze the Truth and Reconciliation Commission (TRC) process in post-apartheid South Africa in the mid-1990s. Reporting from that era provides first-hand recollections and transcripts of the process. In addition, the political moment of transition and healing via TRCs serves as an arena in which to consider the importance of a holding environment when undertaking social justice missions in which leadership and followership are ineluctably entwined. While the outcome of South Africa's TRCs is considered imperfect, I suggest that the establishment of similar such holding environments would further dialogue and efforts toward peace and reconciliation in the United States around issues of race.

Keywords: leadership; holding environment; Truth and Reconciliation; stepping up and stepping back; Followers; Winnicott

The term holding environment has been extant in the psychological literature for over half a century (Winnicott, 1960) and in the past 25 years has been introduced into the literature of leadership, loosely speaking, and adult development. This phrase, while used as short hand in the literature of psychoanalysis, has been widely and disparately defined in other strands of disciplinary literature (e.g., Heifetz, 1994; Heifetz, Grashow, & Linsky, 2009; Kahn, 2001; Kegan, 1982; Petriglieri & Petriglieri, 2010). For the purposes of this chapter, I am defining it as "a container that fosters growth."

In terms of the larger project of this book – i.e., peace, reconciliation, and social justice leadership in the twenty-first century, with a particular focus on the role of leaders and followers – the term is useful when considering such projects as the South African Truth and Reconciliation Commission (TRC) following the dissolution of apartheid in the early 1990s. The TRC was launched in 1995 (Rosenberg, 1996, p. 90) as South Africa underwent a painful transition from a brutal apartheid government of white supremacy to a democracy led by a racial majority of black Africans, whose first elected leader was Nobel Laureate Nelson Mandela. These commissions, which took the form of courts of reconciliation as opposed to justice in the normative sense, served as an intervention to heal a deeply wounded society. While there is some argument as to how much the "truth" was actually told in these settings in exchange for amnesty, the intervention was for the most part deemed effective (Abaunza, 2013; Gibson, 2006; Ignatieff, 1997) and has been adapted elsewhere (e.g., uses of the Gacaca courts following the Rwandan genocide in 1994). These sorts of commissions were also established in Latin America following the dissolution of dictatorships and years of "disappearances" (Ignatieff, 1997; Rosenberg, 1996, 1999). Yet the relative novelty of such interventions, commissions that call for amnesty in exchange for truth-telling, as opposed to the Nuremberg trials (Boraine, 2000; Rosenberg, 1999) invites further sensemaking (cf., Weick, 1993) in order to internalize and apply these sorts of interventions even more effectively. Exploring these episodes of reconciliation following the atrocities of systemic racism, whether in war or times of "peace,"[1] the term holding environment both assists us in our understanding and adds texture to our analysis of leadership and followership.

In terms of leadership and its numerous constructs, I employ the notion of holding environment in combination with the notion of leadership – in particular, of "leadership" as a fluid process of "stepping up and stepping back" (Altvatar et al., n.d.; Yorks et al., 2007). This image of stepping up and stepping back, which implicitly calls for a holding environment, speaks to the question of how to encourage people to access their innate power, as distinct from "empowering" them (Altvatar et al., n.d.). What follows is a brief treatment of three powerful ideas: That of the holding environment and that of "stepping up and stepping back" — both of which merge in the historical context of the TRC efforts in South Africa in the 1990s. The case of the South African TRC will be viewed through the lens of "stepping up and stepping back" within the confines of a purposefully conceived holding environment. It is here articulated as a holding environment conceived of and sanctioned by both the government of South Africa and the Episcopal Church of which Bishop Desmond Tutu was the head (Meredith, 1999).

The figure below illustrates this somewhat complex set of intersecting ideas:

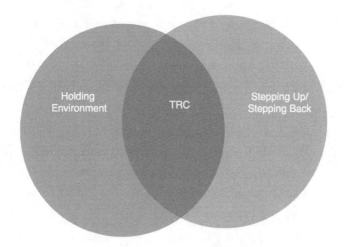

The Venn diagram above offers a visual depiction of how the constructs of holding environment and stepping up and stepping back overlap within the setting of the TRCs. Indeed, the notion of leadership and followership coming together in the action of stepping up and stepping back implies an environment that gives actors permission to engage in such fluidity. The TRC is an example of this fluidity taking place in a well-known political moment.

The chapter is organized as follows. First, I explore the definition of "holding environment," beginning with Winnicott. This section is followed by an examination of the leader—follower relationship as seen through the framework of Altvater et al.'s (n.d.) construct of the "stepping-up, stepping-back" model of leadership (Altvater et al., n.d.; Yorks et al., 2007). Finally, the chapter discusses the intersection of these two ideas in terms of real-world efforts made toward a lasting peace and reconciliation. Examples of leadership-as-fluid are drawn from reporting on the TRC transcripts and trials. In the discussion and conclusion, I point at suggested avenues of social justice in which these ideas might be useful if applied.

WHAT IS A HOLDING ENVIRONMENT?

Psychological Origins

As stated earlier, in general terms a holding environment may be defined as *a container that fosters growth*. The child psychologist D.W. Winnicott (1896–1971) has described the holding environment as a place of protection for an infant being held by a "good enough" mother (Rodman, 2003). Such holding minimizes anxiety in the infant, and this kind of primal anxiety, he asserts, arises as a fear of annihilation. "In this phase," Winnicott has written:

> Being and annihilation are the two alternatives. The holding
> environment therefore has as its main function the reduction to a
> minimum of impingements to which the infant must react with
> resultant annihilation of personal being. (Winnicott, 1960, p. 571)

In Winnicott's formulation, the ideal holding environment is comprised of boundaries, initially located in the family unit, that foster "empathic interpretation" and contain "tolerance and containment of aggression and sexuality" (Shapiro & Carr, 1991, pp. 35–36). For the purposes of this discussion, I am omitting discussions of sexuality and focusing on the larger purpose of containment and positive growth. It is, in addition, useful to think of this original definition in which anxiety is contained – anxiety over the "annihilation of personal being." When extrapolating the notion to such scenarios as South Africa's use of TRC's, it is not too extreme for us to consider the word *annihilation* as pertinent to the work of the commissions. Not only were perpetrators of crimes against humanity confessing to the literal annihilation of others, they were also confronting the annihilation of their own pretense at leadership, as many who made such confessions held positions of authority.

BUILDING ON WINNICOTT'S DEFINITION

Numerous scholars have used the term to suit their own purposes. Some allude to Winnicott directly; others omit any mention of him while freely using the term he invented. And while the theme of boundary and growth appears to be a commonality in the larger conversation surrounding holding environment – one which ventures beyond the psychological literature – specific definitions of the term vary. Heifetz (1994) refers to it as a form of power to keep attention on an issue (as, for example, the bully pulpit that the President of the United States commands). A decade and a half later, Heifetz et al. (2009), by contrast, refer to the holding environment as a "cohesive social system" (p. 305). Petriglieri and Petriglieri (2010) refer to certain institutions as "identity workspaces" comprising a holding environment:

> We suggest that individuals are likely to invest an institution with the function of an identity workspace when it provides a coherent set of reliable social defenses, sentient communities, and vital rites of passage. These three mutually reinforcing elements allow an institution to be experienced as a holding environment.
> (Petriglieri & Petriglieri, 2010, p. 44)

Kahn (2001) has explored the various uses of holding environments at work as well and acknowledges the varieties of success and failure in colleague and adult friend relationships as varieties of holding environment.

Across the literature, the notion of a holding environment as a container which fosters growth continues to fit as a working definition. Yet it is the example of Shapiro and Carr which most closely aligns with the ineluctable entwinement of the leader–follower relationship. Here I would substitute the terms *mother* and *parent* with the term *leader* and the term *child* with the term *follower*:

> Although it may appear that the mother provides the holding environment for the child, in fact there is mutuality in the arrangement. The loved child also has an affirming role within the

parent-child unit, which is the initial organization that manages the developmental task. The holding is created collaboratively.
(Shapiro & Carr, 1991, p. 77)

While it is obvious to any student of leadership that one whom a follower chooses to adhere to, emulate, or empower as leader is in a different position than a wholly dependent infant is upon its mother, still, the illustration of entwinement is pertinent to this discussion. The entwining of the parent and the child in mutually affirming positions echoes that of Hughes, Ginnett, and Curphy's (2014/2017) Interactional Framework, based on Hollander (1978), a figure depicting a Venn diagram that encompasses intersections of Leader, Follower, and Situation. Barnard (as cited in Wren, 1995), when speaking of authority, depicts another dimension of the mutuality of leader ("person of authority") and follower: "The decision as to whether an order has authority or not lies with the person to whom it is addressed, and does not reside in 'persons of authority' or those who issue orders" (as cited in Wren, 1995, p. 196). Here, the entwinement of leader and follower might better be characterized as entanglement.

The quote serves as a segué to the discussion of Truth and Reconciliation. During the TRC "trials" in which perpetrators confessed and acknowledged their crimes to victims and/or the family members of victims, a key determination in the granting of amnesty rested with whether or not the perpetrators had been carrying out orders from above or had been gratuitously sadistic or cruel. The question abides as to whether and why those who obeyed the orders issued by authorities who demanded killings of "the other" during apartheid needed to obey. Although it lies beyond the scope of this chapter to explore the nuances of authority/follower relationships among those who perpetrated crimes in the apartheid era, it is worth considering what kinds of non-nurturing (in Kahn's view, "failed") holding environments existed such that atrocities could be committed on the sides of both pro- and anti-apartheid forces.

STEPPING UP, STEPPING BACK

The exploration of leadership as a power dynamic that is intentionally fluid has been explored by Ospina and others (Altvater et al., n.d.; Yorks et al., 2007).

In a report on a foundation-supported leadership program issued under the auspices of the Wagner School of Public Service at New York University, practitioners and scholars collaborated in a cooperative inquiry (CI) that unpacked this dynamic. In an article by Yorks et al. (2007), a metaphor of "the Dance" is invoked to describe what it means to step up and step back: "How can we create the space/opportunities for individuals to recognize themselves as leaders and develop leadership?" was the driving question (Yorks et al., 2007, p. 489). In this exploration, in a given scenario ones who typically held authority over others could intentionally step back, while those who were typically deferential to such authority could step up or "cross over" (Altvater et al., n.d., p. 5) into roles of leadership, taking up their authority, often through narrative (Altvater et al., n.d.). This act of intentional crossing over has filled participants with a memorable sense of power:

> Once people claim a space by crossing over, they reframe the way
> they see themselves in the world. They have taken up their authority
> to influence others. Only in one person stepping back and another
> crossing over can the power dynamic truly shift in this way. In this
> relationship, the shift is irreversible. Once you have "crossed over,"
> you will never be the same. As [one participant] said, "they can't take
> my leadership away." (Altvater et al., n.d., p. 5)

Yorks et al. have described their CI project in which social justice was explored as a democratic process of leadership. As part of their methodology, subgroups were formed that prosecuted the question of how to articulate the "nature of effective progressive leadership" (p. 488). One subgroup explored the "dance" of leadership as a "fluidity of roles" in which different subjects stepped up into and stepped back from roles of leadership. The subgroup identifying itself as The Dance asked the questions "How can we create the space/opportunities for individuals to recognize themselves as leaders and develop leadership?" (p. 489). In the group's findings on social justice leadership, the notion of leadership as a collective enterprise, one that belongs to no one individual person for any given length of time but rather belongs to the community was conceived. This echoes Uhl-Bien, Marion, and McKelvey's (2007) definition of adaptive leadership as a function of emergence. "Leadership as a phenomenon exists in the space between and among people, not in the individuals themselves" (Yorks et al., p. 494). This vision of leadership as an action (in this context, the "action" of social justice) emphasizes fluidity:

> Effective social justice leadership, recognizing that capacity can
> only be developed by being enacted, facilitates fluid movement
> between roles for all people, from follower to leader, from teacher
> to learner, from expert to novice and back again. (Yorks, et al.
> p. 494)

This fluidity underscores the dance of stepping up and stepping back, as the subgroup in this cooperative inquiry on the theme of social justice describes it:

> The Dance goes on to describe this shift in the leadership
> relationship as a process of "stepping back and stepping up." This
> is something other than traditional notions of delegating. Rather
> there is a genuine shift in the relationship, in which someone steps
> back (whether they do it consciously or not) and someone steps up
> (in our conversations we've terms the latter *crossing over*). (Yorks
> et al., 2007, p. 494)

The popular best-selling novel *The Help* (Stockett, 2009) offers a vivid fictional illustration of a person in a position of dominance inviting members of an oppressed class to "step up" and give voice to their truth of black service in an abusive white-dominated society in the American South. The depiction of American apartheid society offers the reader a fictional view of the interior voices of black women living in Mississippi in the early 1960s. One such character, Minny, imagines what it would mean to tell the truth about her situation of being a maid. While sitting with her best friend Aibileen in a pew at their church, she considers Aibileen's invitation to be interviewed by a white woman named Skeeter about the experiences of being a "domestic":

> The Reverend laughs. He gets up and treads slowly to the pulpit.
> Everything goes still. I can't believe Aibileen wants to tell Miss
> Skeeter the truth.
>
> Truth.

It feels cool, like water washing over my sticky-hot body.
Cooling a heat that's been burning me up all my life. (Stockett,
2009, p. 151)

TRUTH AND RECONCILIATION

In the context of the TRC events that took place in South Africa, all who participated had the occasion to be leaders — including those perpetrators who stepped into the arena of truth-telling themselves. This inclusive definition may be considered more plausible in the framing of leadership as an action of stepping up and stepping back. Into the space provided by the holding environment of the commissions where truth-telling trumped all except what the commissioners judged as the most gratuitously sadistic of crimes, each perpetrator exercised leadership in a positive sense by having the courage to admit to his or her wrongdoing under apartheid. Similarly, each victim who spoke of the atrocities perpetrated upon him or her also became a leader as she or he gave voice to what had happened. On either end of the spectrum, both actors took up agency and were leading their society toward a state of reconciliation, however fragile. Those who occupied sanctioning positions of leadership in upholding this effort — e.g., Bishop Desmond Tutu — were in a sense stepping back from traditional roles of court authority in meting out justice and overseeing retribution in order to make space for the unique voices of leadership among the South African citizens.

The following dialogue is excerpted from Meredith's (1999) account of the TRC's emergence and work. In it, Mr Jacobs is a victim of torture, and Mr Benzien is a victim of what he is forced to admit. Each of them steps up and steps back into the holding environment of the TRC. The dialogue excerpted below begins with Peter Jacobs recollecting a specific episode of being tortured by Jeffrey Benzien, who is described by Meredith (1999) as "a former warrant officer still [at the time of the TRC] employed by the police in its air wing (p. 122)." According to this narrative, when Mr Benzien was active in interrogating suspects, he was known for his obliviousness to human suffering as he employed torture tactics to extract information from his victims:

> JACOBS: So you would undress me, tie my blue belt around my feet;
> throw me on the ground, put the handcuffs with the cloth over my

arm to prevent marks. You do that [give electric shocks] quite a few times. But at some point, I think it is about the fourth time, when I thought I am dying, you said, "Peter, I will take you to the verge of death as many times as I want to. But you are going to talk and if it means that you will die, that is OK." Do you remember that?

BENZIEN: I concede I may have said that, Sir.

JACOBS: I want you to tell me, *because this is important for me*. The truth commission [TRC] can [grant] amnesty, but this is important for me. *Did you say that?*

BENZIEN: Yes, *I did say that*. (Meredith, 1999, pp. 131–132, my emphasis)

In this small excerpt, what one must assume was the anguished poignancy of co-witnessing an episode of torture that exemplifies the motion of stepping up and stepping back into naming the truth of that which happened.

TRC AS HOLDING ENVIRONMENT

Under the auspices of both the government and the Church, South Africa's TRC became a holding environment of unparalleled intensity. Bishop Desmond Tutu, as the highest authority from the Church, referred to the ordeal of listening to the victims of apartheid bear witness as "'looking the beast in the eye'" (Meredith, 1999, p. 4). The metaphor is apt, as the holding environment of TRC was at times strong enough to contain the rage of the victim and/or his/her survivors as well as what must have been the acute anxiety of confessing, to the point of intimacy, by meeting someone's gaze. Reporting on the effects of the TRC, Ignatieff (1997) paints the following pictures of family members asking for an accounting. In one, the father of a young woman who was purported to have joined the guerilla branch of the African National Congress (ANC) was discovered to have been murdered years later after she disappeared. Here he confronts her killers, as the discovery of her murder was made under the auspices of TRC. Speaking of the father's rage, Ignatieff (1997) writes, "There was a time when [the father] wanted to take an axe to them. Now he wants to sit down with them and look them in the eye" (p. 88). In another episode, speaking of a widower's anguish Ignatieff also reported on "another hearing, [in which] a husband who had lost his wife asked the men who had killed her to look him in the eye and ask forgiveness. And they did" (p. 90). There are additional reports of how the act of perpetrators' stepping into the arena of "the truth" was paramount to the success of TRC. "If the policemen will reveal that last segment of *the truth*, [the victim's father] might have it in himself to forgive them" (Ignatieff, 1997, p. 88, my emphasis).

DISCUSSION AND CONCLUSION

More than 20 years following the termination of the TRC in South Africa, its outcomes are still uncertain. The corruption and internecine violence of the African National Congress in that country are now considered commonplace (Onishi & Gebrekidam, 2018). Certainly, there was not a universal approbation of its success (Meredith, 1999). Neither were they the same as the Nuremberg trials, which "used the concept of collective guilt" – for example, the execution of a Nazi newspaper editor "purely for speech crimes" (Rosenberg, 1999, p. 357). It is reasonable to consider as settled opinion, however, that the use of truth commissions is a more productive way for societies to move forward, however haltingly, from episodes of universal trauma. In a way, the TRC in South Africa provided a rough reflection of a therapist's office, where the sole purpose is unfettered speech, and progress occurs when genuinely honest utterances are received within a relatively "safe" environment. Although such commissions have taken place locally in the United States (see, for example, a US-adapted TRC that took place in North Carolina in 2004, which examined circumstances surrounding the death of five anti-KuKluxKlan demonstrators in 1979 [Greensboro Truth and Reconciliation Commission, 2006]), there has been no universal effort made in this direction to heal the original sin of slavery in this country. The race riots in Charlottesville, VA in August 2017 exposed a festering sore; in the current political moment in the United States, genuine dialogue is hard to come by among opposing political or ideological groups. Yet until this country takes it upon itself to "look the beast in the eye," it is reasonable to speculate that racism will continue to erupt in episodes of both micro- and macro-aggression. The boundaries of an intentional holding environment such as a sanctioned arena for truth-telling may be the only way out of this dilemma.

NOTE

1. The quote marks are an acknowledgement of the hollowness of this word in an apartheid society that sanctioned violence against its members.

ACKNOWLEDGMENTS

I would like to thank H. Eric Schockman for his insightful editing, as well as that of other reviewers for this volume of the Building Leadership Bridges series. The New York Society Library's holdings and office spaces served as wonderful sources of support. Thanks also to the Villa Ippocampi in Koutouloufari. My colleague Nathan Harter, as usual, pointed the way.

REFERENCES

Abaunza, M. M. (2013). *Ubuntu's potential for further development in the South African Education System.* Unpublished Master's thesis. Georgetown University, Washington, DC.

Altvatar, D., Godsoe, B., James, L., Miller, B., Ospina, S., Samuels, T. … Valdez, M. (n.d.). *A dance that creates equals.* New York, NY: New York University, Robert F. Wagner School, Graduate School of Public Service.

Boraine, A. (2000). *A country unmasked: Inside South Africa's Truth and Reconciliation Commission.* Oxford: Oxford University Press.

Gibson, J. L. (2006). The contributions of truth to reconciliation: Lessons from South Africa. *Journal of Conflict Resolution, 50*(3), 409–432.

Greensboro Truth and Reconciliation Commission. (2006). Retrieved from http://www.greensborotrc.org

Heifetz, R. A. (1994). *Leadership without easy answers.* Cambridge, MA: Harvard University Press.

Heifetz, R., Grashow, A., & Linsky, M. (2009). *The practice of adaptive leadership.* Boston, MA: Harvard Business Press.

Hollander, E. P. (1978). *Leadership dynamics: A practical guide to effective relationships*. New York, NY: Free Press.

Hughes, R. L., Ginnett, R. C., & Curphy, G. J. (2014/2017). What do we mean by leadership? In B. Redekop (custom Ed.), *Theories and perspectives on leadership* (pp. 50–83). New York, NY: McGraw-Hill.

Ignatieff, M. (1997, November 10). Digging up the dead. *New Yorker*, pp. 84–93.

Kahn, W. A. (2001). Holding environments at work. *The Journal of Applied Behavioral Science, 37*(3), 260–279.

Kegan, R. (1982). *The evolving self: Problem and process in human development*. Cambridge, MA: Harvard University Press.

Meredith, M. (1999). *Coming to terms: South Africa's search for the truth*. New York, NY: Public Affairs.

Onishi, N., & Gebrekidam, S. (2018, September 30). Hit men and power: South Africa's leaders are killing one another. *New York Times*, p. A1.

Petriglieri, G., & Petriglieri, J. L. (2010). Identity workspaces: The case of business schools. *Academy of Management Learning & Education, 9*(1), 44–60.

Rodman, F. R. (2003). *Winnicott: His life and work*. Boston, MA: Da Capo Press.

Rosenberg, T. (1996, November 18). Recovering from apartheid. *New Yorker*, pp. 86–95.

Rosenberg, T. (1999). Afterward: Confronting the painful past. In M. Meredith (Eds.), *Coming to terms: South Africa's search for the truth* (pp. 327–370). New York, NY: Public Affairs.

Shapiro, E. R., & Carr, A. W. (1991). *Lost in familiar places: Creating new connections between the individual and society*. New Haven, CT: Yale University Press.

Stockett, K. (2009). *The help*. New York, NY: Berkley Books.

Uhl-Bien, M., Marion, R., & McKelvey, B. (2007). Complexity leadership: Shifting leadership from the industrial age to the knowledge era. *Leadership Quarterly, 18*, 298–318.

Weick, K. (1993). The collapse of sensemaking in organizations: The Mann Gulch disaster. *Administrative Science Quarterly, 38*(4), 628–652.

Winnicott, D. W. (1960). The theory of the parent-infant relationship. *International Journal of Psycho-Analysis, 41,* 585–595.

Wren, J. T. (1995). *The leader's companion.* New York, NY: Free Press.

Yorks, L., Aprill, A., James, L., Rees, A. M., Amparo, H., & Ospina, S. (2007). The tapestry of leadership: Lessons from six cooperative-inquiry groups of social justice leaders. In P. Reason & H. Bradbury (Eds.), *The SAGE handbook of action research: Participative inquiry and practice* (pp. 487–496). Thousand Oaks, CA: SAGE.

PART II

COMMUNITY BUILDING: TO MAKE, BUILD, AND MAINTAIN PEACE

H. Eric Schockman, Vanessa Alexandra Hernández Soto and Aldo Boitano de Moras

Being a social leader and carrying out community work is a high-risk activity, especially in societies with vast social inequities, fragile democracies, marked clientelism, corruption, and violence as a mechanism of social control to preserve power by elites allied with hegemonic power and at times with crime.

In this section, we will explore how community work can be an enduringly transformative force contributing to a virtuous circle: making, building, and maintaining peace. We will explore the importance of leadership and followership for community building.

With esteemed contributors from many different disciplines, each of the ensuing chapters explores from different perspectives critical aspects of this crucial virtuous circle. This section includes four regionally diverse case studies of community building to identify how leadership and followership can better contribute to building and sustaining peace. From essential reflections on the youth role and perspectives on reconciliation in the aftermath of the genocide against the Tutsi, to the always necessary and robust voice and leadership of women in reconstruction of the social fabric in Uganda and Sri Lanka to an institutional work of leadership and followers of young

African students committed and prepared to promote social and peacebuilding social justice.

Returning to the three enumerated concepts of the virtuous circle, to make peace, we mean by the understanding all those minimum agreements and conditions necessary between governments and states, civil society, and groups raised in arms (or already disarmed) to end an armed confrontation and its disastrous consequences. By building peace, we mean a broad process of social and political transformation aimed at overcoming the conditions of exclusion and inequality, consolidating the presence and capacities of the State, the civil society, and the community, promoting participation and openness democratic, all this in order to overcome in the process the structural causes and consequences that perpetuate cycles of violence. Finally, to maintain peace, we understand those long-term cultural transformations that promote and ensure non-violent processing of social conflicts.

This section of the book focuses on how through community building we can face the cracking of the social fabric and the possibilities of collective action; the rupture of the economic tissue and its translation into a structure of inequality, of social and territorial exclusion; and finally, the political exclusion that has impeded a change in the elites and a future in sustainable peace.

As the Ingabire and Richters' chapter highlights, there have been increasing calls to understand further and to stop underestimating the role that youth as followers and leaders can play in achieving reconciliation by breaking the cycle of inherited family trauma and hatred. Genuine reconciliation and sustainable peace are long-term processes in which the younger generations have a crucial role to play. This chapter underscores the importance of engaging young people in community building, conflict prevention, and reconciliation efforts. Furthermore, the power of knowledge and peace education plays in our communities to build a peaceful youth driven by ethical values and mutual respect.

Young people account for over half of the world's population. It is estimated that 600 hundred million youth live in fragile and conflict-affected societies; despite their efforts for sustaining community-led peace processes yet, they continue to be marginalized, undervalued, and unrecognized by the world leadership.

After decades of the inaction of decision-makers in the face of the climate crisis, young people across the globe are showing leadership for climate action, aiming to drive world leaders into work to get us moving toward a more just, sustainable, and prosperous future. "Fridays for Future" is a vivid example of youth leading change with a long-term transformation agenda. The school strikes sparked by Greta Thunberg, a 16-year-old Swedish student who began with a solo protest, have been rapidly gaining momentum with over 2,000 demonstrations in over a hundred countries asking the business community to listen to young people and keep their interests and their future at the heart of climate action.

As evidenced throughout the chapters of these books, young people are often the primary actors in grassroots community building work. Empowered young people can play a critical role in preventing conflicts and ensuring sustainable peace. They often act as bridges, playing a pivotal role in connecting parts of the societal fabric. Young people in conflict and post-conflict communities are crucial agents in building peace and positive social change. They need to be recognized as a critical bridge to formal peace processes; they should have a role in shaping peace processes. Their leadership should be amplified, and their concerns should be listened and considered. To face today's global challenges, world leaders should commit to empowering young people as current and future leaders.

The last two chapters of this section explore the role of social enterprise and economic empowerment in building sustainable peace by giving women agency and power in their communities using as case studies in Sri Lanka and Uganda. Female leadership must confront a myriad of issues, such as male chauvinism, the lack of guaranteed fundamental rights such as food, drinking water, and electrification. These and many other elements are traversed when reading the life stories of these women. We find in them a hopeful saga, a story that allows us to conclude that one of the keys to peace lies in the possibility of fostering new leadership as a basis for social action. The following chapters argue that the key issue keeping women out of leadership positions and drastically underrepresented in the formal peace process it is not lack of capacity nor leadership skills but lack of access to influential positions due to economic exploitation and marginalization. If women are surviving in the margins, how can we expect them to fully participate in society and further contribute to sustainable peace? In this context, Lisa Liberatore compels us to challenge the pervasive "rescue narrative" in peace processes taking place in the developing world. Organizations from the developed world approach peacebuilding as a project that often disenfranchises and disempowers the people they are trying to help. The author further argues that when women are economically empowered rather than becoming dependent on the help of outsiders their communities are closer to reaching gender equality and achieving positive peace.

One of the biggest challenges of today's world leadership is to build inclusive and peaceful communities. We need common community-led efforts to solve global problems. The following chapters prove that we can use leadership to divide or to rise together, building communities rooted in peace, justice, and dignity. The chapters herein invite us to reflect on the vital importance of the promoting and strengthening leadership and followership at grassroots and community level in the reconstruction of the social fabric in societies affected by war or other kinds of violence, as necessary conditions to build a more just society.

5

SECOND-GENERATION PERSPECTIVES ON RECONCILIATION AFTER GENOCIDE: A CASE STUDY OF RWANDA

Chantal Marie Ingabire and Annemiek Richters

ABSTRACT

This study was conducted in the Western Province of Rwanda to explore to what extent youth aged between 18 and 22 years participate in reconciliation processes and what the factors enabling and hindering reconciliation are that, from the perspective of youth, policies and practices should take into account. Six focus group discussions and 20 individual interviews were conducted in 2017. Respondents recognized the range of efforts undertaken by the government following the 1994 genocide against the Tutsi to promote unity and reconciliation. The "family" was identified as an additional key setting to discuss reconciliation in a free and open manner. However, it was observed that some parents tend to shy away from such discussions due to the heaviness of their past genocide-related experiences in addition to the changing family lifestyles and obligations that limit the time allocated to dialogue. Youth suggest specific interventions targeting the microlevel including, in particular, the family to maximize efforts made at macrolevel regarding reconciliation. Programs that promote parents' healing and provide them with specific skills for effective communication may be deployed to ensure a smooth transition from the painful past. Additionally, since genuine reconciliation is a long-term process, youth have a key role to play in it. Hence, they as

*followers should be provided with tools to increase their critical think-
ing and challenge family and peer narratives if needed.*

Keywords: Youth; instrumental reconciliation; socio-emotional
reconciliation; intergenerational; genocide; Rwanda

INTRODUCTION

The 1994 genocide against the Tutsi in Rwanda is generally considered as
the worst tragedy of the 1990s and the most intense genocide since World
War II (Dorn & Matloff, 2000). Approximately one million people were
killed within a period of 100 days (MINALOC, 2004). Coming to terms
with this past was and still is, like for any post-conflict society, a major challenge. The Rwandan government set up a range of mechanisms to deal with
the consequences of the horrific, mostly intimate violence and the high number of genocide-related crimes. A major one was the initiation in 1999 of the
National Unity and Reconciliation Commission (NURC). Its mandate is to
prepare and coordinate programs that aim at promoting national unity and
reconciliation, educate the population in areas of peacebuilding, eradicate
divisionism, carry out research, and avail publications on the promotion of
peace, unity, and reconciliation (NURC, 2007).

The study presented in this chapter aimed to explore how youth in
Rwanda understand reconciliation, to identify factors youth see as promoting and hindering reconciliation at family and community level and to formulate from the perspective of youth recommendations for policy and
practice in the field of reconciliation.

For the framing of this study, we adopt the needs-based model of reconciliation as presented by Shnabel and Nadler (2008). This model distin-
guishes between instrumental and socio-emotional reconciliation (SER),
which are mutually interdependent. SER refers to the process of seeking to
remove the emotional and identity-related barriers to overcome a conflict
through the successful completion of an apology—forgiveness cycle.
Instrumental reconciliation (IR) is a prerequisite of SER. IR refers to the process of securing a basic level of trust between conflicting parties which
enables the achievement of superordinate goals that are important for each
party and IR. It is based on the premise that ongoing cooperation between

adversaries will result in a reconciled future. In the literature, one often finds a similar distinction made between respectively thin and thick reconciliation, in Rwanda termed *kubana* (coexistence,) which is a matter of necessity, and *ubwiyunge* (reconnection), which is a matter of the heart and a state of feeling in a social relation (cf. e.g., Ingelaere, 2016).

METHODOLOGY

The study used a qualitative exploratory approach and was conducted between August and September 2017, in Rubavu District, the Western province of Rwanda. The sample included young adults born after the 1994 genocide (18–22 years old) with different sociohistorical backgrounds, that is, being born in a family with at least one parent who is a genocide survivor, genocide perpetrator, bystander, or new returnee (Rwandans who fled the country during previous political conflicts between 1959 and 1994 and subsequently returned). Study participants were identified through civil society organizations and government initiatives working in the field of peacebuilding (unity and reconciliation clubs in schools), supplemented by youth out of school and thus not taking part in any such organization or initiative. Six focus group discussions (46 participants) and 20 individual interviews were conducted. All discussions and interviews were taped, transcribed verbatim, translated into English and subjected to a thematic analysis using a qualitative data analysis computer program Nvivo. Rwanda National Ethics Committee granted approval prior to data collection (No.111/RNEC/2017).

FINDINGS

We first present what youth understand by reconciliation in general terms, to be followed by youth's perceptions of what they are exposed to in terms of parental reconciliation messages, attitudes and behavior and subsequently youth's assessments of the discourse of reconciliation in youth groups and reconciliation practices by the members of these groups. Lastly, youth's views on how to overcome the reconciliation challenges they face in real life and their recommendations for policy and practice are put forward.

YOUTH'S UNDERSTANDING OF RECONCILIATION

Respondents highlighted that following the 1994 genocide, there was a need for the government to establish mechanisms that would promote social reconstruction, including, in particular, unity and reconciliation between genocide perpetrators, survivors and bystanders and the prevention of putting in practice prevailing feelings of revenge. The government discourse is a discourse on "unity and reconciliation," which explains that while discussing reconciliation the two are usually presented together. According to some respondents, unity meant living together as one without any division, while reconciliation mainly implied processes of transcending conflicts through peaceful relationships among former antagonists. Genuine reconciliation is perceived by most as a long-term process that requires Rwandans to look back and understand factors that led to divisionism, conflicts, and genocide so as to inform the country's future. This process requires getting pro-reconciliation messages from parents, schools, peers, clubs and/or communities as prerequisite to positive attitudes and good interpersonal behaviors.

Respondents shared elements of both instrumental and socio-economic reconciliation as constituting overall reconciliation. What could be interpreted as instrumental reconciliation encompassed the inclusion and participation of Rwandans in various country programs, freedom of Rwandans to work in every part of the country irrespective of one's origin, and school enrollment and performance evaluation that are merit-based as opposed to a history of segregation that has severely marked the country in the past. What could be interpreted as SER is manifested by a change in psychological orientation toward the "other," which according to respondents is characterized by forgiveness on the side of some genocide survivors, remorse and asking apology on the side of some perpetrators, reduction of mistrust in communities through living together and interethnic marriages.

PARENTAL RECONCILIATION MESSAGES, ATTITUDES, AND BEHAVIORS

Youth's understanding of the meaning of reconciliation mainly comes from their exposure to discourses on reconciliation in the public sphere. In the family setting, topics related to reconciliation were found to be rarely discussed while the family is being considered as the most trusted source of information for youth. In so far as discussions do take place, they are triggered by events such as those organized during the annual 1994 genocide commemoration period. Some youth reported sometimes receiving messages contra reconciliation in the family setting, parental narratives being shaped by parents' sociohistorical backgrounds. This divergence from public discourses on reconciliation is perceived as hindering interpersonal relationships among youth. Some respondents judged it difficult for survivor parents to forget and to unite with the out-group while perpetrator parents may still value their genocidal actions as justified. Others emphasized that some parents with a different sociohistorical background tend to be united, especially in communal activities, and share everything within their neighborhood, while their feelings about the past and how one should behave do not always match their usual behavior in community settings. One example given concerned intermarriage. Getting married to someone from a different ethnic background can be a shock to the respective families, possibly leading to a lack of family support to the couple and disruption of a couple's relationship. This was identified as an indicator of reconciliation not yet fully achieved, especially at parental level.

> You may be loving each other but if parents are not happy, they
> will not support your marriage nor visit you afterwards. When you
> get problems, they can't give you any help, saying that you have
> disobeyed them. Unity in our families is still questionable, especially
> related to intermarriage.

Other respondents reported that there are parents who are willing to engage their descendants in discussions related to reconciliation, tending to focus on the negative consequences of the genocide and emphasizing the importance of the prevention of future atrocities and the promotion of peace.

Some of the perceived reasons why parents do sparsely engage their descendants in reconciliation-related discussions included the lack of recognition of the need of youth to learn about the past, limited time allocated to family dialogue, incapacity of parents to engage in a constructive dialogue, and parents being affected by genocide-related trauma and/or ideology.

> Our families feel that we are not concerned with issues of unity and
> reconciliation. They feel that it concerns mature people who
> witnessed the genocide. We only learn them in schools and in

Itorero; but as youth, we do not always get a chance of discussing the subject in detail.

Established in 2007, the Itorero program is a home-grown initiative that helps to instill positive values in Rwandans, especially youth, give back to their communities, promote patriotism, community cohesion, and social responsibility and volunteerism.

YOUTH GROUPS AS A SOURCE OF RECONCILIATION MESSAGES AND RELATED PRACTICES

A sizeable number of respondents underlined the role played by youth as members of various groups, mainly found in school settings, in promoting unity and reconciliation through participation in activities aiming at wider social changes. These groups contribute to fostering social cohesion, promoting cultural values, learning and discussing about the country's history including the genocide, releasing youth from their emotional burden as a result of their past parental histories, the development of a sense of empathy, and the participation in outreach activities outside of school settings.

According to some respondents, discussions on reconciliation in the context of peer groups were, however, sometimes ambiguous. On the one hand, they were found often open and free, irrespective of differences in sociohistorical backgrounds of its members and understanding of the course of historical events. On the other hand, some of the respondents' peers still expressed fear and mistrust and were perceived as less likely to share their emotions, ideas, and problems in a group setting. Additional challenges to school-based reconciliation included negative reconciliation-related messages provided by parents which partly explain the adherence to genocide ideology among some peers who express divisionism in the absence of critical thinking.

I know a boy who used to tell us at school that if he dares marrying a girl from the other ethnic background, his parents would kill her or he himself could kill her the first night. Though we took it as a joke, it may be real.

Logistical challenges in relation to the lack of trainings and educational materials limiting the self-confidence and knowledge regarding reconciliation among the members of the groups were also noted.

> Most of the time we get information only when we have been
> visited by people from various government organs or other NGOs.
> This is not always enough as trainings for us to be able to teach
> others.

While youth groups for reconciliation are found as key to promote the process of reconciliation, they were mainly found in school settings and not as
much at grassroots level (sector and cell level) according to respondents out
of school, which prevents them to benefit from reconciliation messages.

PROPOSED RECOMMENDATIONS FOR POLICY AND PRACTICE

Respondents urged their fellow youth to be role models for those who still
have negative ideas on unity and reconciliation by getting engaged in positive
actions and working together while supporting those in need. They also suggested that youth need to increase their level of critical thinking to be able to
challenge both their peers and their families when deemed appropriate.

To promote positive intergenerational dialogues, respondents advocated
for specific programs that can assist parents when it comes to knowing how
and when to share what kind of information about the past, as many parents
were found struggling with this, fearing to cause trauma to their descendants. The promotion of unity and reconciliation among parents should further draw from community dialogues, for instance as part of parents'
evening programs – a weekly meeting held at village level in which adults
meet to discuss daily issues – to introduce positive values needed to reconstruct the country. Strengthening the social cohesion (i.e., among neighbors)
through these various community initiatives was also found relevant to foster interpersonal reconciliation at the community level.

> When parents have misunderstandings with neighbors, even their
> descendants will not be able to live in good terms with others.
> Hence, promoting unity in families and communities, will also
> promote unity among youth.

The establishment of unity and reconciliation groups across all schools and
community settings and equipping them with relevant knowledge and skills
in the field of unity, reconciliation, and peacebuilding was perceived as
highly needed. Initiatives targeting youth out of school settings can be done

through involvement of youth working in different committees at local level which can in turn engage their fellows. Special attention to youth tailored-approaches, such as films, music, drama, and sports, was proposed to be implemented through youth centers available in each administrative sector. Few respondents also suggested the reduction of youth unemployment as equally important to prevent enrollment in negative behaviors.

> When youth are not working, they become idle and may get involved in discussions that hinder reconciliation. They can also engage in drugs abuse which may hamper public safety.

While the government has put in place a number of social protection policies and programs for equal and equitable development for all Rwandans and strengthening their reconciliation, few respondents advocated for their proper implementation to ensure that those in need feel more considered. Lastly, few accounts suggested carrying out an evaluation of what has worked effectively when it comes to reconciliation programs among youth to inform future strategies.

DISCUSSION

The current study identified the meaning Rwandan young adults attribute to reconciliation, in particular, reconciliation among peers, the factors they perceive as promoting or impeding reconciliation and their recommendations for policy and practice.

A main finding is that some respondents drew attention to the discrepancy between what is being publicly promoted (i.e., forgiveness, apologies, unity, and reconciliation) and what they see happening in families and communities. They see more of instrumental than of SER. The same observation was made by survivors who were children or adolescents during the 1994 genocide by Rieder (2014). However, these respondents differed from ours in terms of age category; all of them were born before the genocide and thus grew up with memories of their own genocide experiences.

Our respondents (born after the 1994 genocide) might not be regarded as an important category to target with reconciliation messages and programs, as they are not direct victims or individually responsible for any genocide-related crime. However, our findings suggest that their social relations with peers of the out-group are shaped by what their parents transmit to them in terms of their genocide-related experiences and subsequent attitudes and behavior toward the out-group. Münyas (2008) found the same in post-genocide Cambodia, arguing that youth depend on the knowledge transmitted in their environments through for instance family narratives, teachings in schools, and a culture shaped by the past genocide for developing their understandings of the past.

The contradiction between public and parental narratives on reconciliation as observed by youth in our study might be attributed to parental intention. However, it may also be explained by the inability of parents to engage in reconciliation-related discussions. According to McEvoy-Levy (2006), to curb discourses and values that sustain divisions and are pregnant with future conflict, it is essential to know what kind of information youth have ingested and how they reproduce or transform it. Kosic and Livi (2012) similarly argue with reference to the post-conflict situation in Croatia that the more youth are exposed to constructive family communication as opposed to aggressive and avoiding communication, the more they feel confident and competent to engage in positive social relationships which increase their propensity to reconciliation with the out-group.

The promotion of pro-reconciliation narratives at a family level can go hand in hand with youth education as a powerful tool to attain interpersonal reconciliation (Mukashema & Mullet, 2013; Vonhm, 2015). The scale-up of reconciliation groups in school and community settings with proper training of its members and availability of didactical materials was also recommended. The groups are deemed to provide safe spaces in which youth may express their thoughts and feelings, heal from psychological wounds, induce them to empathize with others, and explore their contribution to how best to deal with the past by for instance finding narratives that give meaning to life and ongoing relationships (Münyas, 2008).

The need of using tailored interventions, namely drama and sports, while promoting reconciliation among youth was another suggestion made. A sport program was established in the aftermath of the 1994 genocide targeting social change in Rwanda and the UK as well as a study exploring the reconciliation processes through sports in South Africa corroborate with this finding (Football for Hope, Peace and Unity, 2017; Höglund & Sundberg, 2008, p. 806). Höglund and Sundberg (2008) argue that reconciliation should be understood beyond the conventional definition which focuses on truth-seeking, forgiveness, and justice between perpetrators and victims and rather focus on a restructuration of a larger set of relations through integration of separate categories of individuals. The authors demonstrated that participation in sports activities serves to increase social cohesion by breaking down stereotypes, transforming negative attitudes about "the others," empowering communities in the creation of a homogenous and less conflict-prone society while enabling individual development of the self.

The importance of youth employment toward achieving reconstruction and reconciliation among youth was also emphasized. The youth in Rwanda today represent 67% of the population with a 21% unemployment rate (National Institute of Statistics of Rwanda, 2017). There is an imperative need to ensure that their sense of innovation, dynamism, confidence, and enthusiasm is channeled toward sustainable development to reduce divisions between in- and out-groups, prevent reoccurrence of crises, and minimize the risks of youth growing up as susceptible to being used as perpetrators of conflicts and civil disorders (Ikemenjima, 2008; Kosic & Tauber, 2012).

Our study partly differs from the studies by McClean Hilker (2009) and Power (2013) on Rwanda, which suggest that the Rwandan national identity is pasted over the silenced ethnic ones, posing a threat to the reconciliation process among first and second generations and increasing potential risks for a recurrence of violence to be equally extensive as the previous genocidal one. Youth in our study did not necessarily find it important to focus on ethnic backgrounds as a basis of peacebuilding rather advocated for tailored interventions that fit youth's needs according to their age category to ease their understanding of the past, the current, and the future. The difference in findings might however be related with the age categories of respondents involved in the three studies – our study targeting only youth born after 1994.

While our study has provided preliminary answers to the understanding of reconciliation among Rwandan youth, findings should be interpreted while keeping in mind that we do not claim representation of Rwandan youth across the country due to the small sample used.

CONCLUSION

There is a need to understand and not to underestimate that reconciliation does not concern only mature people nor only those who witnessed the genocide, were direct victims or individually responsible for any genocide-related crime, but that youth as followers can play an important role in achieving reconciliation by breaking the cycle of inherited family trauma and hatred. Genuine reconciliation is a long-term process in which the younger generation has a key role to play.

Given what we know today about intergenerational trauma, initiatives addressing youth mental health should be mainstreamed, as well as activities and policies that contribute to positive intergenerational dialogue relevant to foster community reconciliation. Another vital aspect of policies and practices should focus on enabling youth as followers with the tools to increase their level of critical thinking, enabling them to challenge both their peers and their families when deemed appropriate, which Chaleff (2015) refers to as intelligent disobedience. Helping youth to transcend familial narratives, divisionism and preventing violence, empowering them while providing opportunities for them to lead (to transform themselves to self-empowered leaders), and nurturing them as peace-builders, as change-makers will bolster the foundations for sustainable development and for durable peace.

ACKNOWLEDGMENTS

Authors acknowledge the respondents in this study and the research assistants Nicolas Habarugira and Jeanine Nyinawabega. Community-based Sociotherapy Rwanda supported the authors throughout the study period and during the dissemination of findings. The African Peacebuilding Network of the Social Science Research Council provided financial support for the study and Vanessa Hernández provided editorial assistance.

REFERENCES

Chaleff, I. (2015). *Intelligent disobedience: Doing right when what you're told to do is wrong.* Oakland, CA: Berrett-Koehler Publishers.

Dorn, W., & Matloff, J. (2000). Preventing the bloodbath: Could the UN have predicted and prevented the Rwandan genocide? *The Journal of*

Conflict Studies, *20*(1). Retrieved from https://journals.lib.unb.ca/index.php/JCS/article/view/4333

Football for Hope, Peace and Unity. (2017). Retrieved from http://fhpuenterprise.org/about/

Hilker, M. L. (2009). Everyday ethnicities: Identity and reconciliation among Rwandan youth. *Journal of Genocide Research*, *11*(1), 81–100. doi:10.1080/14623520802703640

Höglund, K., & Sundberg, R. (2008). Reconciliation through sports? The case of South Africa. *Third World Quarterly*, *29*(4), 805–818. doi:10.1080/01436590802052920

Ikemenjima, D. M. (2008). Youth development, reintegration, reconciliation and rehabilitation in post-conflict West Africa: A framework for Sierra Leone, Liberia and Cote d'Ivoire. *International NGO Journal*, *3*(9), 146–151.

Ingelaere, B. (2016). *Inside Rwanda's gacaca courts: Seeking justice after genocide*. Madison, WI: The University of Wisconsin Press.

Kosic, A., & Livi, S. (2012). A study of perceived parental communication and propensity towards reconciliation among youth in Vukovar (Croatia). *Journal on Ethnopolitics and Minority Issues in Europe*, *11*(4), 51–80.

McEvoy-Levy, S. (2006). *Troublemakers or peacemakers? Youth and post-accord peace building*. Notre Dame: University of Notre Dame.

MINALOC Ministère de l' Administration Locale, du Development Communautaire et des Affaires Sociales. (2004). *Denombrement des victims du genocide*. Kigali. Retrieved from https://www.kgm.rw/wp-content/uploads/2017/04/denombrement_des_victimes_du_genocide_perpetre_contre_les_tutsi_avril_2004.pdf

Mukashema, I., & Mullet, E. (2013). Unconditional forgiveness, reconciliation sentiment, and mental health among victims of genocide in Rwanda. *Social Indicators Research Journal*, *113*(1), 121–132. doi:10.1007/s11205-012-0085-x

Münyas, B. (2008). Genocide in the minds of Cambodian youth: Transmitting (hi)stories of genocide to second and third generations in

Cambodia. *Journal of Genocide Research*, *10*(3), 413–439. doi:10.1080/14623520802305768

National Institute of Statistics of Rwanda. (2017). *Labour force survey 2017*. Kigali. Retrieved from http://www.miniyouth.gov.rw/fileadmin/MINIYOUTH_Policies__Laws_and_Regulations/LEBOUR_FORCE_SURVEY_REPORT_FEB_2017.pdf

National Unity and Reconciliation Commission. (2007). *The national policy on unity and reconciliation*. Kigali: The Government of Rwanda.

Power, H. (2013). Unresolved identity conflicts as a barrier to reconciliation in Rwanda. *International Public Policy Review*, *7*(2), 1–10.

Rieder, H. (2014). Growing up after conflict: Intergroup behavior and attitudes toward local justice and reconciliation among Rwandan descendants of genocide survivors and former prisoners. In H. Rieder (Ed.,), *Legacies of the 1994 Rwandan genocide: Organized violence, family violence, mental health and post-conflict related attitudes examined among families of genocide survivors and former prisoners* (PhD thesis, pp. 57–86). Konstanzer Online-Publikations-System (KOPS). Retrieved from http://nbn-resolving.de/urn:nbn:de:bsz:352-0-266133

Shnabel, N., & Nadler, A. (2008). Instrumental and socio-emotional paths to intergroup reconciliation and the need-based model of socio-emotional reconciliation. In A. Nadler, T. Malloy, & J. D. Fisher (Eds.), *Social psychology of intergroup reconciliation* (pp. 37–55). New York, NY: Oxford University Press.

Vonhm, M. E. (2015). *The role of education to build peace and reconciliation in post conflict settings*. Retrieved from https://www.beyondintractability.org/library/role-education-build-peace-and-reconciliation-post-conflict-settings

6

RESEARCH LEADER–FOLLOWER DEVELOPMENT FOR PEACEBUILDING AND SOCIAL JUSTICE: THE AFRICA YOUNG GRADUATE SCHOLARS DEVELOPMENT PROGRAM

Sylvester B. Maphosa and Alphonse Keasley

ABSTRACT

Leadership development is an essential yet complex process that manifests over a long period of time. Owusu et al. assert that in African researchers' graduate programs, the learners receive theory, research methods and grant writing instruction without significant attention to leadership development. So, how do researchers, academics, administrators, and think-tanks plan and carry out leadership–followership development within organizational and transitional justice fields? The research capacity building of young African scholars in the knowledge production community has the potential to lead to the development and articulation of norms and values that will seek to address fundamental issues of transformation, direct, structural, and cultural violence, and assist in addressing a wide range of problems associated with violence of social injustice. We draw lessons from the Africa Young Graduate Scholars (AYGS) 2017 conference and writing retreat, which drew 22 young scholars (with 10 females and 12 males) who had completed original research and five facilitators (two females and three males) from universities in Botswana, Cameroon, Democratic Republic of Congo

(DRC), Kenya, South Africa, Swaziland, and Zimbabwe for developing research leader–follower insights.

Building research leadership–followership capacity in knowledge production communities in the context of conflict prevention is crucial for establishing sustainable peace. It is recommended that: (1) the AYGS be replicated on other parts of the continent and throughout the diaspora; (2) publications from emerging leaders and followers in the research/knowledge production community begin to increase; and (3) establishment and expansion of leadership development programs for research leaders and followers in African graduate programs.

Keywords: AYGS; AISA; HSRC; research capacity building; knowledge systems; social justice; Ubuntu philosophy

INTRODUCTION

It is becoming increasingly recognized that our collective ability to tackle complex social problems will require the creation of supportive institutional environments and development of competent cadres of research leaders and followers (Bashour, 2013; Evans, 2012; Jones, Bailey, & Lyytikäinen, 2007; Marjanovic, Hanlin, Diepeveen, & Chataway, 2012; Owusu, Kalipeni, Awortwi, & Kiiru, 2017), involved in managing and pushing research and knowledge productivity to leverage social justice across all levels of society. The development of new, adaptive, and innovative institutional arrangements that can "[…] produce educated and skilled citizens from all backgrounds and persuasions [make] the best possible contribution to reconciliation and social justice" (du Toit, 2016, p. 56). Herein, African institutions including universities, research institutes and think-tanks, government and non-government organizations have an important role to play in advancing a robust and thoughtful research leadership–followership culture including well-placed practices and procedures in knowledge production. Yet, building research capacity is a complex process and manifests over a long and deliberate innovative period of time. So, how do researchers, academics, administrators, and think-tanks plan and carry out building research leadership–followership capacity that advances more peaceful, inclusive societies?

In this chapter, we report on a case study of innovative institutional support and collaboration on development of competent young African scholars engaged in becoming leaders and followers in knowledge production, the Africa Young Graduate Scholars (AYGS) platform and writing retreat, of the Africa Institute of South Africa (AISA), in the Human Sciences Research Council (HSRC), Pretoria, South Africa, that contribute on promoting social justice and peacebuilding.

We outline the formal knowledge system embedded in AYGS process acknowledging shared responsibility for learning across the knowledge system. Our goal — in response to the International Leadership Association (ILA) Building Leadership Bridges (BLB) Series book *Peace, Reconciliation and Social Justice Leadership in the 21st Century: The Role of Leaders and Followers* — is to deepen the understanding of how the approaches and methods that constitute building research capacity, namely (a) capacity building and development of research leaders and (b) capacity building for researchers could be integrated in a more systematic and comprehensive way. This is crucial to yield dividends in the formulation of well-informed development policies and help ensure their implementation (EDCTP Forum, 2011) in the search for solutions to the region's development challenges (Owusu et al., 2017). Hence, the call to action and continuation of this work as an agent of positive change and peacebuilding breaking the barriers for peaceful relationships and improve the people's lives.

We define peacebuilding in this chapter to denote a range of measures targeted to reduce the risk of lapsing or relapsing into conflict by strengthening national capacities at all levels for conflict management and laying the foundations for sustainable peace and development. Peacebuilding strategies must be coherent and tailored to the specific needs of the country concerned, based on national ownership, and should comprise a carefully prioritized, sequenced, and therefore a relatively narrow set of activities aimed at achieving the above objectives. Building research leadership—followership capacity in knowledge production community in the context of conflict prevention is crucial to establish a sustainable peace.

CONCEPTUAL FRAMING

For the purposes of this study, a knowledge system is defined as a network of actors connected by social relationships, either formal or informal, who dynamically combine knowing, doing, and learning to bring about specific actions for sustainable peaceful and equitable relationships/development. This definition places the relationships between individuals, society and institutions, and their capacities to generate and respond to new knowledge under analysis, for example, the Truth and Reconciliation (TRC) of South Africa of 1994 to present, and current consultations on land reform and expropriation without compensation. Most knowledge systems are by-products of attempts to achieve more tangible goals, such as access for all socioeconomic groups to quality public services in education, health, jobs, and housing; gender equality; youth governance; ethnic and racial discrimination; and environmental regulations. Yet, the actual achievement of those goals depends in part on the ways in which knowledge is generated, shared, and used in decision-making. In knowledge systems analysis, it is the performance of the whole system, the collective ability to generate, mobilize and apply high-quality knowledge that is of concern. As such, this study is concerned not with the AYGS per se, but with the broader knowledge system that underpins actions to promote social justice and peaceful societies.

Two key fundamentals provide the foundation for this examination of building research leadership—followership capacity in the knowledge production community: (1) the South African contextual environment that supports social justice, and (2) a recent unique research article that calls for developing strong research leaders and followers in the African knowledge production community. These elements combine well to underscore requisite research leadership—followership capacity building for the twenty-first-century thought leaders and practitioners in contexts of fragility and post-conflict reconstruction.

Many governments in Africa encourage their universities, research institutes and think-tanks, government and non-government organizations to respond to the increasing numbers of violent conflicts, the job market and the changing nature of the global economy, which has increasingly become knowledge based (Karbo, 2013). Knowledge is recognized as both a resource and a source of power in both local and global relations. In some sense, each society (and each class within a society) is expected to produce its own institutions and its own intellectuals. Thus, the research capacity building of young African scholars in the knowledge production community has the potential to lead to the development and articulation of norms and values that will seek to address fundamental issues of transformation, direct, structural and cultural violence, and assist in addressing a wide range of problems associated with violence of social injustice. As Karbo affirms, developing peacebuilding capacities through research and knowledge production will be a logical and integral part of processes that seek to address problems and threats of violence in society (Karbo, 2013).

SOCIAL JUSTICE IN SOUTH AFRICA

The social justice tradition, couched in the language of transformation, has been identified by most social scientists as possessing the greatest potential societal advancement (Starr, 1999, p. 22). The transformation agenda is broad, in that it advances social justice beyond redistribution to recognition and absolute freedom. This is embodied in Young's (2000) theory of justice as freedom from the five faces of oppression, namely exploitation, marginalization, violence, powerlessness, and cultural imperialism (Young, 2000, p. 35). Each of the five faces of oppression represents a form of injustice that may be experienced in society. Justice as freedom from the five faces of oppression envisages a knowledge-based society in which socioeconomic justice is achieved through knowledge and technology to identify constraints and to plan and manage – redistribution of the resources of society, humane treatment of all, equal recognition of the worth of all members of society, empowerment and celebration of diversity (Gewirtz, 1998, p. 477; Young, 2000, p. 48) – development effectively, efficiently, and sustainably (The African Capacity Building Foundation, 2004). It involves both the development of human resources, institutions, and society, and a supportive policy environment (The African Capacity Building Foundation, 2004). It is the process by which individuals, groups, organizations, and societies develop their abilities individually and collectively, to identify their problems and constraints on development, set development objectives, formulate policies and programs, and perform functions and objectives (The African Capacity Building Foundation, 2004). Every society has inherent capacities that are compatible with its own functions and objectives. Young's (2000) broad conceptualization of social justice is constructive because it improves on a more restrictive liberal and conventional conceptualization of social justice. In addition to its broad agenda, it also encompasses the notion of collective human agency, indicating that human emancipation is closely intertwined with individual and community/collective liberation, as embodied in the Ubuntu philosophy.

Conceptually, Ubuntu philosophy stands for humaneness, which is built on the foundations of a relational worldview embedded in most African cultures. This is reflected in both the philosophy of non-violent conflict and the idea of social transformation, which tap on moral and creative human potential to resolve conflicts and bring about positive change in a just manner in recognition of human interrelatedness and connections. There is greater realization that the focus of any meaningful resolution of conflict and peacebuilding should not be about the mere settlement of disputes. Rather, it should embrace ways through informed strategies by knowledge production and means by which the parties can be brought to live together and cooperate in the future to avoid recourse to conflict and war. It is important that bridges are built across social divides to ensure that conflict (or recourse to it) does not arise and that violent conflict can no longer be an option; societies must change for the better.

Taking cognizance of the importance of reconciliation, forgiveness, and transformation for the advancement of society, South Africa, over the last 24 years, spearheaded strategies and plans of action, informed by, and interacting with, various pieces of legislation such as the Promotion of National Unity and Reconciliation Act (34 of 1995), and policies in an integrated manner. The most influential of these are discussed below.

The Constitution of the Republic of South Africa, 1993 (Act 200 of 1993), provides a historic bridge between the past of a deeply divided society characterized by strife, conflict, untold suffering and injustice, and a future founded on the recognition of human rights, democracy, and peaceful coexistence for all South Africans, irrespective of the color, race, class, belief, or sex, affirming the values of human dignity, equality, and freedom. Importantly, the Constitution states underscore a need for understanding but not for vengeance, a need for reparation but not for retaliation and a need for Ubuntu but not for victimization. Thus, in 1994, the TRC was established to promote national unity and reconciliation in a spirit of understanding which transcends the conflicts and divisions of the past.

The Reconstruction and Development Program (RDP) in 1995 sought to promote a more equal society through reconstruction and development as well as strengthening democracy for all South Africans. As was first articulated in the original 1994 RDP document the ANC government sought to mobilize whole society and country's resources toward eradication of apartheid and the building of a democratic, non-racial and non-sexist future by creating a strong, dynamic, and balanced economy; develop human resource capacity of all South Africans; ensure that no one suffers racial or gender discrimination in hiring, promotion or training situations; develop a prosperous, balanced regional economy in Southern Africa; and democratize the state and society. In short, this policy was aimed to address and redress the inherited gross inequalities of apartheid, socially, economically, and spatially.

A plethora of policy documents focusing on transforming and reconstructing higher education exist. For instance, the National Education Policy Investigation (NEPI) in the 1990s, a policy initiative informed by a progressive philosophy of education and reform, evident in principles of democracy, non-sexism, non-racism, and a unitary system (Department of Education, 1995). The NEPI-framework could be seen as an attempt to democratize education policy formulation, because its researchers comprised a wide range of people, including political leaders and academic practitioners (Chetty, Chisholm, Mkwanazi, Motala, & Tickly, 1993), who participated in a collective, inclusive process to formulate policy options, taking into account the diversity and multicultural stakeholders of the education enterprise. Other efforts include the "Size and Shape" document: Towards a New Higher Education Landscape — Meeting the Equity, Quality and Social Imperatives of South Africa in the 21st Century (June 2000), the National Plan for Higher Education (NPHE) (February 2001) and the New Academic Plan for Programs and Qualifications in Higher Education (January 2002). Common recurring themes raised in these documents are framed in the language of democracy, transformation, human rights, and progressive critical academic culture (White Paper, 1995, pp. 11–12, "Size and Shape" document, 2000, pp. 24–28). The enhancement of the culture of democracy is closely linked to the promotion of social justice, particularly as the country is an emerging democracy (Truth and Reconciliation Commission, 1998).

NEED FOR AFRICAN RESEARCH LEADERS AND FOLLOWERS

In an exploration of the development of research leaders. Owusu, Kalipeni, Awortwi, and Kiiru (2017) conducted a study specifically on African scholars with sponsored research projects. The scholars were particularly interested in the type of leadership preparation that emerging research leaders were receiving for working with teams of African researchers. After examining the type of training that most researchers receive in graduate education, namely theory, research methods and granting writing, the authors of the study questioned the absence of direct leadership development.

The study was conducted in three phases: (1) a desk study; (2) focus groups with research leaders and associated team members who were attending a conference; and (3) an online survey of research leaders and their associated team members who had conducted studies in Africa. For the online survey, 119 (out of 464 invited) research leaders responded and 37 (out of 183) team members responded.

In their quest to understand how to nurture emerging African research leaders and to increase productivity from current African research leaders, the authors reported three significant findings. Based on the comparison between what research leaders identified to be the top five competencies and attributes as needing improvement, there was a significant gap between research leaders and research team members. In particular, research leaders reported on getting research results into policy, embracing publicity and/or visibility, heightening one's international recognition as an authority on the subject, one's accomplishments and successes, and "maverick" individuality. Research team members responded by knowing and interacting with research users, delivering outputs on time, writing winning proposals and receiving grants, getting research results into practice. This difference suggested that there is a gap in the leadership development between African research leaders and African research team members that could benefit from further study and more importantly leadership development considerations.

Another finding was related to the hindrances for African women research leads. Though this finding was mostly anecdotal, the authors found that the reports were consistent with their desk study and focus group participants' comments. The noted causes included cultural and historical influences, the absence of educational opportunities for African women, patriarchal systems in some African countries, and family expectations and needs.

The last key finding concerned the type of leadership style that research team members called for in research leads. Most notably, relationship/people-oriented, task-oriented, and democratic/participative leadership styles were most important to the respondents. The authors stated:

> In line with evidence from other research in the literature, the respondents [research team members] seem to be screaming out their desire for Ubuntu but suggest that it might be far from inherent or prevalent.

They continue with open-ended comments from research leaders about the way that Ubuntu informs their leadership styles. In all, their research findings regarding leadership style highlight the several positive experiences that African research leaders and African research team members have in engaging in research, especially the collective involvement with colleagues from other disciplines.

This extensive analysis of the Owusu research is presented here because it reflects ideas that are inherent in the long-running AYGS conference, that is, the need for capacity building of young scholars for knowledge production and the need for leadership development within the knowledge production community. Further, the finding on Ubuntu links peace and reconciliation elements in an unexpected and uniquely African way: that is, research team leaders and research team members "scream" for cooperation, compassion, trust, respect, and dignity. These are all operational elements of Ubuntu that have historically led South Africans in their transition to the Republic that it is today and that thought leaders of tomorrow can carry forth, if introduced to them as a part of their leadership/followership development.

THE AFRICAN YOUNG GRADUATE SCHOLARS: RESPONDING TO THE SOCIAL JUSTICE AGENDA

To illustrate the complexity and multiplicity of social justice, this section looks at one way in which intellectuals and academics have responded to or interpreted the call for greater equality and social justice in society through collaboration and knowledge production. Social justice knows no national and cultural boundaries (Atweh, 2009). Hence, the social justice implications of regional collaborations can and should not be overlooked. However, not all action towards achieving equity, no matter how well intentioned it is, is sufficient to achieve social justice (Atweh, 2009).

The vision of AISA is premised on "development through knowledge" and informs knowledge development and applied and comparative research that focuses on the development challenges and opportunities facing the African continent. The guiding principles of this work align with and draw from the Constitution and National Development Plan of South Africa which highlights a capable state as an essential precondition for South Africa's development and recognizes the importance of solid research for evidence-based decision-making in planning, policy, and practice. These aspirations align with Sustainable Development Goals 4, 10, and 16 on quality education, reduced inequalities, and peace, justice and strong institutions, respectively. As well as the broad goals of the African Union (AU) Agenda 2063 of a prosperous and peaceful Africa driven by its peoples anchored on the principles of unity, dignity, diversity, equality, and prosperity for all are included. Thus, AISA collaborates with other research institutions, actors, and key stakeholders on the continent and the diaspora and makes a significant contribution to addressing the many dimensions of the study of Africa in Africa and reversing the continent's global marginality in terms of knowledge production. For instance, the governance, peace, and security unit in AISA under the leadership of Sylvester Bongani Maphosa has long been invested in peacebuilding and peace education evidenced by several publications – such as *Building Peace from Within: An Examination of Community-based Peacebuilding and Transitions in Africa* (2013); and, *Peace Education in Fragile African Contexts: What's going to make a Difference?* (2016) – including seminars, Fulbright fellowship, and international affiliations.

The AYGS conference is an annual event organized by AISA since 2006. The main purpose of AYGS is to provide space for strengthening research and knowledge capacity among young scholars in historically disadvantaged institutions in South Africa. However, this platform has evolved and now connects with all universities in South Africa and in Africa. It is organized annually around topical themes and creates a platform of community for young scholars and "[built] founded on inclusive and interactive relationships and networks that create spaces for collective action and foster concern for systemic engagement" (JPD, 2012). The 11th AYGS 2017 gathering was organized in partnership with the University of Fort Hare (UFH) and themed "Re-imagining leadership, youth and gender for sustainable development" in Africa.

The complexity of facilitating capacity development raises a series of questions on why and how to do it. Case study research has shown that factors shaping and developing capacity can include political, cultural, economic, social, and historical influences; the dynamics of the organizational and institutional system in which an intervention is being made; the strategy underlying the intervention, including the entry point, scale of resources and change process; and the nature of the demand and supply for capacity (Karbo, 2013). Karbo further avers that supporting and undertaking capacity development requires, therefore, a broader systems perspective; it asks for interventions that go beyond a more narrow strategy focusing essentially on knowledge transfer and skills development (Karbo, 2013).

The methodical sequence leading to 11th AYGS in March 2017 involved conceptualizing a conference on "re-imagining leadership, youth and gender for sustainable development" in Africa. AISA is supported by a Government of South Africa Parliamentary grant from tax payers' contribution to create a better South Africa and contribute to a better Africa and a better world through research and knowledge development. We released the Call for Abstracts in early August 2016 through HSRC and AISA outlets including via local newspapers and networks in Africa. A total of 101 abstracts were submitted by September 2016, and from which 30 promising abstracts were selected and invited to submit full papers for the conference. The selection of abstracts was made through a double-blind peer review process.

In March 2017, during the second-day conference, 30 presentations were delivered based on the research the young scholars had completed covering a range of study areas and issues including (1) capacity building for social change; (2) gender and culture; (3) youth, women and inclusion; (4) climate change and adaptation strategies; and (5) community coping. The institutions represented at the conference by presentations included the HSRC; UFH; University of Venda (Univen); University of the Free State (UFS); University of South Africa (UNISA); Stellenbosch University; University of Western Cape (UWC); North West University – Mafikeng Campus (NWU); University of Limpopo (UL); United Nations Development Programme (UNDP), South Africa; University of Colorado Boulder, United States; the German and Finish embassies in South Africa; University of Botswana (Institute of Development Management); Kenyatta University, Kenya; Pan African University – Institute of Governance, Yaoundé, Cameroon; Catholic University of Bukavu, Democratic Republic of Congo (DRC); National

University of Science and Technology (NUST) – Institute of Development Studies, Zimbabwe; and Zimbabwe Human Rights NGO Forum.

The contact and interaction generated critical dialogue on current African realities and the future of the continent. A two-part keynote address was presented by Lindiwe Dhlamini, a research associate of the United Nations Development Program (UNDP) on Leveraging the 2016 Africa Human Development Report on "Accelerating Gender Equality and Women's Empowerment in Africa", and Alphonse Keasley, the Associate Vice Chancellor, University of Colorado Boulder on "Self-Leadership, Authentic Leadership and African Personhood." Feedback during proceedings formed an important element of the conference and helped identify 22 promising chapters that were considered for publication and hence invited to a follow-up writing retreat in November 2017.

The eventual forum drew 22 students and young researchers, 10 females and 12 males, all in their mid-20, and had completed original research; plus five facilitators (two females and three males) representing universities, non-government organizations (NGOs), and think-tank hosts. The 22 participants came from universities in South Africa, Botswana, Cameroon, DRC, Kenya, Swaziland, and Zimbabwe. The writing retreat emphasized the inclusion of universal sustainable development goals Agenda 2030, and the AU Agenda 2063 in reimagining leadership, youth, gender, and sustainable development.

There were four central issues that emerged. First is the importance of collaboration, among the selected participants and mentors/facilitators as well as during the conference and writing retreat process. Second, preparation for the conference and writing retreat involved not only work on writing but also the mentors' encouragement of positive collegial relationships between the mentors and the participants throughout the contact and space of interaction. This meant identifying a cohort of participants committed to the conference and retreat and coordinating preparatory work in advance of the conference and retreat, motivating the participants to overcome any insecurities. The mixture of diverse intellectual perspectives yet familiarity with basics of research and knowledge development fostered vibrant intellectual exchange. Thus, after the conference, participants not only learned to collaborate as they prepared for the writing workshop, but also learned from each other and taught each other given variation in research areas and issues. Third, the AYGS 2017 forum encouraged the building of collegial relationships and leadership capacities among the participants during the conference, before and after the retreat. Fourth, follow-up on the conference and writing retreat is crucial and entail, for example, the formation of a virtual (electronic) writing group and the publication of a related set of chapters in a special issue of a refereed journal.

Thus, the AYGS 2017 conference held in March and the follow-up writing retreat held in November opened up to a hands-on approach in which participants actually participated, took responsibility for their work, engaged in small-group discussions, and met one on one and collectively with mentors engaged on finer points of revising their drafts. As some participants met one on one with mentors, others devoted time to revising their drafts. By the time the conference and retreat ended, the platform offered students and young academics time to critically engage with colleagues in small groups and over tea and meals also providing invaluable feedback. The contact and interaction allowed participants to conceive of and practice writing and revision as an iterative process. This iterative nature of the AYGS 2017 and retreat equipped the participants to move their manuscripts forward and take immediate responsibility for their own writing and goal achievement. The platform created the opportunity to reflect on the recommendations, revised, and sought immediate and further guidance and mentoring. Further, this iterative process exposing students and young academics to decolonial thinking, the politics of knowledge generation as well as power, identity and epistemological issues also allowed as an effective way, the participants to edit, reflect, and refine within an intense and relatively short period of time. With these features, the AYGS 2017 forum as designed and implemented led many participants to report feeling empowered to continue working after the official retreat ended, indicating an improvement in motivation and self-efficacy.

When viewed via the research by Owusu et al., the AYGS 2017 addressed many of the concerns identified in their study. First, the AYGS participants in both sessions demonstrated a strong interest in knowledge production and the willingness to brave the scrutiny of their work in a public forum. Indeed, such commitment to scholarly engagement is key to the research endeavor in that a researcher desires to share the depths of their thinking and their facility with research thinking and methodological tools; thus, the participants were ideal candidates for followership. As followers, they were committed to the vision of the AYGS and willing to advance its objectives through their scholarly work.

Next, the AYGS, in the spirit of the South African founding documents, included individuals from various backgrounds, particularly those who had been historically marginalized. Notably, an equal number of women were part of the cohort during both the initial session and the follow-up session. Moreover, a key part of the theme of the conference was related to gender. In all, women followers were not tokenized as members of 2017 AYGS conference, thus providing the opportunity for future women leaders in the knowledge production arena.

Finally, the true spirit of Ubuntu was evidenced by the 2017 AYGS leaders, including the sponsoring AISA, the university faculty, and the keynote speakers. The expression of trust, respect, compassion, and dignity – all Ubuntu qualities – was present in abundance. At no point during either conference was there an absence of the desire to participate, in spite of the strenuous nature of deep thought and concentration to craft worthwhile written expression. The atmosphere promoted a conducive development of future knowledge production leaders and followers who could be future advocates of peace, reconciliation, and social justice.

CONCLUSION

This discussion, while acknowledging the diverse mechanisms and capacities to do peacebuilding effectively, offer a multistage, inclusive, participatory, consultative, and collaborative design for research and knowledge development as infrastructures for peace modalities that enhance leadership competency and self-efficacy (Bass & Bass, 2008; Jirsa, 2004; Palanski, 2012; Senge, 1990). It also provides space encouraging gender equity and fostering peer-to-peer mentoring. The innovative AYGS 2017 and writing retreat deliberately focused on reimagining leadership and thus equipped the participants to take responsibility for their writing, moving their manuscripts forward, and achieving their goals as leaders in knowledge development and/or research productivity and dissemination.

The following are the recommendations:

- Replication of AYGS on other parts of the continent and diaspora.

- Publications from emerging leaders.

- Establishment and expansion of leadership development programs for research leaders and followers in Africa.

ACKNOWLEDGMENTS

Sylvester Bongani Maphosa: I acknowledge generous support from the HSRC, AISA and the government of South Africa in funding the AYGS forum and collaboration with the following institutions that made this AYGS 2017 case study: the UFH, Univen, Free State University, UNISA, University of Stellenbosch, UWC, NWU – Mafikeng, UL, the UNDP, plus the German and Finish embassies (all in South Africa); University of Colorado Boulder (USA); University of Botswana; Kenyatta University (Kenya); Pan African University (Yaoundé, Cameroon); Catholic University of Bukavu (DRC); NUST (Bulawayo, Zimbabwe), and the Zimbabwe Human Rights NGO Forum (Harare, Zimbabwe). Above all, we thank the ILA and the BLB book series in championing the cause of "the vision of a future where all life can thrive."

Alphonse Keasley, Jr: To my colleague and collaborator, Sylvester Bongani Maphosa, your commitment to all of our joint scholarly endeavors has been a tremendously satisfying contribution to my professional life. To the Office, Diversity and Community Engagement team at the University of Colorado Boulder (CU-B), I am most appreciative of your faith in my scholarly work in South Africa.

REFERENCES

Atweh, B. (2009). What is this thing called social justice and what does it have to do with us in the context of globalisation? In P. Ernest, B. Greer, & B. Sriraman (Eds.), *Critical issues in mathematics education*. Charlotte, NC: Information Age Publishing (IAP).

Bashour, M. N. (2013). *Scant funding for research facilities hurting Africa*. Retrieved from www.scidev.net. Accessed on 10 July 2018.

Bass, B. M., & Bass, R. (2008). *The handbook of leadership: Theory, research, and managerial applications* (4th ed.). New York, NY: Free Press.

Chetty, D., Chisholm, L., Mkwanazi, Z., Motala, S., & Tickly, L. (1993). Competing strategies: The ERS and NEPI Options. *Indicator South Africa, 10*, 49–64.

Department of Education. (1995). *White paper on education and training.* Notice 196 of 1995. Cape Town: Government Printer.

du Toit, F. (2016). Teaching the past as if people mattered: History education as peace education in post-apartheid South Africa. In S. B. Maphosa & A. Keasley (Eds.), *Peace education in fragile African contexts: What's going to make a difference?* Pretoria: AISA Publications.

EDCTP Forum. (2011, October 9–12). *Developing scientific research capacity in sub-Saharan Africa: Sixth EDCTP forum strengthening research partnerships for better health and sustainable development.* EDCTP Forum, Addis Ababa. Retrieved from http://www.edctpforum.org/wp-contentcontent/uploads/sixth_edctp_forum_abstract_book.pdf. Accessed on 10 July 2018.

Evans, L. (2012). Leadership for researcher development: What research leaders need to know and understand. *Educational Management Administration Leadership*, 40, 423–435.

Gewirtz, S. (1998). Conceptualizing social justice in education: Mapping the territory. *Journal of Education Policy*, 13(4), 469–484.

Jirsa, J. (2004). Forgiveness and revenge: Where is justice. In A. Cashin, & J. Jirsa (Eds.), *In thinking together. Proceedings of the IWM junior fellows conference, Winter 2003. IWM Junior Visiting Fellows Conferences* (pp. 1–28). Retrieved from http://www.iwm.at/wpcontent/uploads/jc-16-05.pdf. Accessed on 2 July 2018.

JPD Editors. (2012). The evolving landscape of infrastructures for peace. *Journal of Peacebuilding and Development*, 7(3), 1–7.

Jones, N., Bailey, M., & Lyytikäinen, M. (2007). *Research capacity strengthening in Africa trends, gaps and opportunities. A scoping study commissioned by DFID on behalf of IFORD.* Retrieved from http://www.odi.org/sites/odi.org.uk/files/odi-ssets/publications-opinionfiles/2774.pdf. Accessed on 6 August 2018.

Karbo, T. (2013). Capacity building for sustainable peacebuilding. In S. B. Maphosa & A. Keasley (Eds.), *Building peace from within: An examination of community-based peacebuilding and transitions in Africa.* Pretoria: AISA Publications.

Maphosa, S. B., & Keasley, A. (2013). *Building peace from within: An examination of community-based peacebuilding and transitions in Africa.* Pretoria: AISA Publications.

Maphosa, S. B., & Keasley, A. (2016). *Peace education in fragile African contexts: What's going to make a difference?* Pretoria: AISA Publications.

Marjanovic, S., Hanlin, R., Diepeveen, S., & Chataway, J. (2012). *Research capacity building in Africa: Networks, institutions and local ownership.* Working Paper No. 106. ESRC Innogen Centre. Retrieved from http://www. rand.org/pubs/external_publications/EP20121302.html. Accessed on 6 August 2018.

Owusu, F., Kalipeni, E., Awortwi, N., & Kiiru, J. M. M. (2017). Building research capacity for African institutions: Confronting the research leadership gap and lessons from African research leaders. *International Journal of Leadership in Education, 20*(2), 220–245.

Palanski, M. E. (2012). Forgiveness and reconciliation in the workplace: A multi-level perspective and research agenda. *Journal of Business Ethics, 109,* 275–287. doi:10.1007/s10551-011-1125-1.

Senge, P. M. (1990). *The fifth discipline: The art and practice of the learning organization.* New York, NY: Doubleday.

Starr, K. (1999). *What is social justice? Curriculum perspective.* Newsletter edition, September, pp. 11–23.

The Africa Capacity Building Foundation. (2004). *Reconstruction and capacity building in post conflict countries in Africa: A summary of lessons of experience from Mozambique, Rwanda, Sierra Leone and Uganda.* Occasional Paper No. 3. ACBF, Harare.

Truth and Reconciliation Commission. (1998). *Truth and Reconciliation Commission of South Africa Report* (Vol. 1–5), Cape Town: TRC.

Young, I. (2000). Five faces of oppression. In M. Adams, W. Blumenfeld, C. Casterieda, & H. Hackman (Eds.), *Readings for diversity and social justice.* New York, NY: Routledge.

7

WOMEN CAN MAKE A DIFFERENCE IN ECONOMIC MARGINALIZATION AND WOMEN'S RIGHT TO EQUALITY IN POST-CONFLICT CONTEXT OF SRI LANKA: REVIVAL OF CHALLENGES AND A PERSPECTIVE BEYOND THE UNRSC 1325

Ziyana Mohamed Nazeemudeen

ABSTRACT

The United Nations Security Council Resolution 1325 (2000) requires that women's experiences, needs, and perspectives are incorporated into the political, legal, and social decisions in order to achieve transitional justice. In a post-conflict society, peace, and security should be understood in a wider context of justice encompassing accountability process and mechanisms, reparations for victims and upholding the principle of equality in all spheres of lives. Thus, the objective of the UNSCR 1325 is to increase women's participation in decision-making in the peace process to address the wider context of women's situation in post-conflict society and committing to protect women's socioeconomic rights. It is obvious that women's mere presence in decision-making process is insufficient in restoring stability in post-conflict society. Women's participation will only be meaningful if they are empowered to be active rather than passive participants. Hence, it is argued that women's leadership could only be built, if they are given adequate representation in decision-making process and institutions. Women's participation in decision-making and women's economic empowerment has a symbiotic impact on each other. When women are not stable economically and unable to freely make social choices and take responsibilities, they will not have the courage to compete in an election. Thus, this brief study argues that the economic marginalization (overt and covert discrimination) exposes women to multiple discrimination in post-conflict society in Sri Lanka. Hence, countries like Sri Lanka need to address the existing gap in this sphere of women empowerment and leadership. It concludes that the realization of women's rights to equality in post-conflict Sri Lanka may be a slow process, but the Sri Lankan experiences provide a good case study on how to face the different challenges in post-conflict context.

Keywords: Women's right to equality; women's participation; post-conflict; Sri Lanka; UNSCR 1325; leaders and followers

INTRODUCTION

Sri Lanka suffered about three decades of internal armed conflict which came to an end in 2009. This prolonged period of violent conflict had widespread and monumental adverse impact on livelihood, rights, and liberties on innocent, defenseless, and vulnerable people such as children, women, the aged and disabled. Women are, undoubtedly, affected the most by the fallouts from the conflict and post-conflict upshots. They are, inadvertently, doubly burdened as victimized survivors of the conflict as well as careers of devastated victims, during the conflict and post-conflict eras. As a result, women's participation in decision-making and taking leadership roles in society is curtailed, and they were disempowered by vulnerabilities to take informed decisions as sensible followers.

Leadership is conceptualized within the definitional ambit of the following four thematic factors: position, person, result, and process (Keith, 2010). Of these factors, women's propensities and potentials to be leaders in social, political, and economic spheres in the society are narrowly measured on the 'person' factor. Such measurement directs the spotlight on stereotypical considerations rather than on factual issues such as physiological attributes related to personal traits and bodily appearance. These physiological prejudices are further conflated with concerns about women's low intellectual capacities within the broader perceptual context of "fitness for purpose." In practice, matters that have direct implications for the rights of women are dominated by men; hence, the decisional outcomes remain skewed toward perpetuating male dominance in leadership. This social exclusion of women based on 'person' factor automatically precludes them from the remaining three factors: position, result, and process. It is equally true in post-conflict situation. Moreover, exclusion of women in social, political, and economic spheres disempower them, and they will become prey to the social menace, bribery, and corruption. If women are given equal rights, they will be empowered as sensible followers. Sensible followers are persons who have knowledge of their rights and responsibilities and empowered in taking informed decisions without compromising their rights or following leaders blindly. In this context, ensuring women's right to equality in civil, political, and economic spheres is fundamental to empowering them both as leaders and as sensible followers.

STATE LEGAL OBLIGATION TO ENSURE RIGHT TO EQUALITY IN POST-CONFLICT

Rule of law is not confined to mere procedural aspects but includes substantive aspects, guided by rights-based approach. Finnis argues that practical reasonableness (Finnis, 2011, pp. 103−126) requires that any law or administrative action in providing basic goods (Finnis, 2011, pp. 85−90) should not have an arbitrary preference among persons, which means there should not be discrimination (Finnis, 2011, p. 106). However, occasionally some practices in the society which, although not founded on any discriminatory motives, may have discriminatory effects (Jenkins v. Kingsgate (Clothing Productions) Ltd European Court Reports (1981) 911, n.d.). Hence, even though law per se is not discriminatory, challenges in different structures in society may place women in a disadvantaged position. It is argued that there is a "third world difference" in the monolithic notion of patriarchy or male dominance (Mohanty, 2003; Thiruchandran, 1997). Thus, when considering Sri Lankan women, there should be an understanding as to the life experiences of women in the third world. In this regard, even though law ensures the equality before the law *in jure* and if there is no congruence between what written statutes declare and how officials enforce those statutes, the rule of law is compromised. Hence, ensuring the right to equality in both *in jure* and *de facto* realms is important to address both direct and indirect discrimination.

The Vienna Declaration and Programme of Action recognized that human rights are universal, indivisible, interdependent, and interrelated (VDPA, 1993, section 5). Apparently, the neglect of economic, social, and cultural rights has often proved to be a root cause of many conflicts (Malmstrom, O' Flaherty, & Gisvold, 1998, p. 157), and it hinders the justice in post-conflict or *jus post bellum* (Iverson, 2014). Therefore, it "[...] lessens the ability or willingness of victims and witness to participate in the formal process of post-conflict justice" (Chinkin, n.d., p. 1). The United Nations Declaration of Human Rights (UDHR, 1948) as well as the Convention on the Elimination of All Forms of Discrimination against Women (CEDAW, 1979), one of the first UN Conventions that incorporated both civil and economic rights, recognize that ensuring economic rights without any discrimination is the foundation for protecting human dignity. Moreover, CEDAW's General Recommendation No. 28 (General Recommendation 28 (CEDAW), 2010) further clarifies the state obligation toward non-discrimination and requires states to eliminate both sex-based and gender-based discrimination. Essentially, gendered socioeconomic inequalities make women more vulnerable in conflict and post-conflict situations, exclude them from participating in decision-making, and reinforce a culture of impunity for violence against women (True, 2013, p. 4). Thus, any reconciliation, development plan should be sensitive to the existing gap in the society and should be mainstreaming women's needs so as to ensure higher participation of women in all levels.

One of the first United Nations Security Council Resolutions (UNSCR) mainstreaming women's experiences of conflict and post-conflict was the UNSCR 1325 on "Women, Peace and Security" adopted in 2000 (UNSCR 1325, 2000). It has been argued that the "recognition that peace is inextricably linked with gender equality and women's leadership was a radical step" (UN Women, 2015, p. 5, Forward by Phumzile Mlambo-Ngcuka). The UNSCR 1325 is founded on four pillars: it demands women's *participation* in decision-making at all levels, *prevention* and *protection* of women and girls from gender-based violence and provide *relief and recovery* mechanisms for recognizing the humanitarian nature of refugee camps and settlements whilst ensuring that women's experiences, needs, and perspectives are incorporated into the political, legal, and social decisions in order to achieve transitional justice. Following this resolution, there are a number of resolutions adopted by the Security Council, in its quest to strengthen the main idea grounding this resolution, namely 1820 (2008), 1888 (2009), 1889 (2009), 1960 (2010), 2106 (2013), and 2242 (2015). Among them are the UNSCR 1889 (2009) and 2122 (2000). The UNSCR 1889 (2009) stresses the need to support socioeconomic rights in post-conflict societies.

In a post-conflict society, peace and security should be understood in a wider context of justice encompassing accountability process and mechanisms, reparations for victims and upholding the principle of equality in all spheres of lives. Thus, the objective of the UNSCR 1325 is to increase women's participation in decision-making in the peace process should be extended to address the wider context of women's situation in post-conflict society and committing to protect women's socioeconomic rights. This brief study argues that in Sri Lanka, the existing economic marginalization (overt and covert discrimination) of social exclusion exposes women to multiple discrimination. Hence, ensuring women's participation in decision-making both as leaders and as followers in both private and public spheres is hindered. Thus, upholding the equality of women in post-conflict is the biggest challenge in making women as leaders and/or as sensible followers.

SRI LANKAN EXPERIENCE

In Sri Lanka, after unsuccessful peace agreements (Sørbø, Goodhand, Klem, Nissen, & Selbervik, 2011), the conflict between the Liberation Tigers of Tamil Eelam (LTTE) officially ended on the May 19, 2009. Aftermath of the conflict, Sri Lanka is seeking avenues to establish sustainable peace. Equality is the foundation to a sustainable peace and equitable society. Principally, Sri Lankan law protects the right to equality through different laws and policies. The 1978 Constitution of Sri Lanka recognizes that all persons are equal before the law and are entitled to the equal protection of the law (The Constitution of Sri Lanka, 1978, article 12 (1)). At the same time, Article 12 (4) justifies incorporating special provisions or actions for the advancement of women and children. The Women's Charter adopted in 1993 by the government of Sri Lanka aims at eliminating discrimination against women recognizing a number of gender specific political and civil and economic rights which require special protection (Women's Charter, 1993, see respectively, part 1, sections 2 and 10). Moreover, the Women's Manifesto 2010 which has been formulated in the aftermath of the conflict identifies some critical areas of concern that women face in Sri Lanka anchored to the assurance of women obtaining peace, security, and economic development (Gomez, 2012, p. 10). A National Committee on Women was established through the Women's Charter, but the functionality of this committee was questioned as it did not give needed authority to this committee. Now, the National Action Plan for the Protection and Promotion of Human Rights 2017–021 recommends establishing a National Commission on women as one of the objectives to reach the goal of guaranteeing women's rights. Moreover, this plan includes activities to be carried out in order to provide a gender-sensitive transitional justice process (*National Action Plan for the Protection and Promotion of Human Rights 2017–2021 (Sri Lanka)*, 2017, pp. 54–56. See Goals 19, 20, 21 and 22).

In the aftermath of the conflict, the President of Sri Lanka issued a proclamation appointing a commission to reflect on the conflict phase and the sufferings the country had gone through as a whole and to assure an era of peace, harmony, and prosperity. The report of this Commission of Inquiry on Lessons Learnt and Reconciliation (Report of the LLRC, 2011) recognizes the importance of the UNRSC 1325 in post-conflict development and reconciliation efforts and its implementation. However, the Panel of Experts appointed by the Secretary General of the United Nations to advise him on the implementation and the promised Sri Lankan commitment to post-conflict accountability process claimed that "the LLRC is deeply flawed, does not meet international standards for an effective accountability mechanism" (Darusman, Ratner, & Sooka, 2011, p. v). This report recognizes a need for an accountability process based on national assessments, which involved broad citizen participation, needs and aspirations, consistent with international standards (Darusman et al., 2011, p. iv). In 2015, Sri Lanka cosponsored the United Nations Human Rights Council resolution on promoting reconciliation, accountability, and human rights in Sri Lanka, and it encouraged the Government of Sri Lanka (GOSL) to expedite measures for the accountability process, including to return land to its rightful civilian owners and to promptly restore normality to civilian life (Resolution A/HRC/RES/30/1, 2015, para. 10). A 90-member presidential task force was appointed by the president through a directive of May 7, 2009 for resettlement, development, and security in the Northern Province. It is mandated to prepare strategic plans, programs, and projects to resettle internally displaced persons, rehabilitate, and develop economic and social infrastructure of the Northern Province. Recently, the Prime Minister of Sri Lanka established a consultation task force (CTF) to seek the views and comments of the public on the proposed reconciliation mechanism in 2016, and this report was published in 2017 (CTF Report, 2016, p. vii). The report of the CTF also recommends assurance of women's economic, social, and political rights through law and practice. Furthermore, it recommends ensuring women's representation in key decision-making positions in all mechanisms as well as in everyday operational positions. Lastly, it urges that the government schematize measures to enable affected women to access and engage with the proposed mechanisms on reconciliation (CTF Report, 2016, p. 131, para 1.31 (c.d)).

All these measures can be implemented only if the reality of women's suffering is understood, as "for women and girls, the impacts of war are compounded by pre-existing gender inequalities and discrimination" (UN Women, 2015, p. 68). As such, in a post-conflict society, social, economic, and political exclusions constraint women's capabilities in providing leadership to a war-torn society, as women face economic hardships (True, 2013, p. 3).

The total estimated population of Sri Lanka is 20.66 million (Household Income and Expenditure Survey, Final Report, 2016, n.d., p. 71, Table A1). There are about 5.437 million households, and among them about 1.404 million households, which 25.8%, are headed by females (Household Income and Expenditure Survey, Final Report, 2016). Moreover, the female-headed households in the Northern and Eastern provinces are estimated to be 178,000 (Household Income and Expenditure Survey, Final Report, 2016). Even though a higher number of women-headed households exist in other provinces, women in war-torn areas live in extreme poverty due to various laws and customs which deprive women from equal enjoyment of economic rights. LLRC Report observes that women who have taken responsibilities as head of households face numerous challenges due to their position as uneducated, illiterate, and unskilled widows (LLRC Report, 2011, p. 184, para. 5.107). Due to the armed conflict, female-headed households in low-income families usually are victims of gender-based violence. The significant change in the sex ratio in the war-affected areas (Silva, 2012, p. 34) and decline in male population changed the compositions and role of the members of family. Thus, women are burdened with the double role as the caretakers of children, elders, and victims of war and as breadwinners in a threatening social context (CTF Report, 2016, p. 103, para. 1.31). The rate at which women-headed households proliferated as did exponentially the number of unemployed young girls worrying about their inability to raise a dowry, and footing their housing and utility bills make women feel highly insecure and more vulnerable. Such vulnerabilities expose these women to other social injustices like bribery and corruption. Consequently, women as followers are disempowered to take informed decisions in enjoying their rights and end up in the trap of bribery and corruption (Transparency International Sir Lanka, 2014; Lindberg & Herath, 2014). This situation exacerbates the conventional patriarchal system and socioeconomic marginalization and discrimination against women. Given this context, it is very doubtful whether women will make informed decisions in their private as well as public lives, which impact the process of empowering women as both leaders and sensible followers. The LLRC recommends that these women should be looked at not only as recipients but also as participants in the development and reconciliation process. One of the positive measures that has been taken by the GOSL is the adoption of the national policy on women-headed households. However, the issue remains outstanding as to the narrow definition of what constitutes a woman-headed household. Sometimes, families may have female breadwinner but for administrative purposes, the male who does not provide basic needs for the household remains as the head of household. In these situations, women who are actually breadwinners may inadvertently suffer exclusion from getting benefitted from engendered welfare interventions (Concluding observations Sri Lanka (CEDAW/C/LKA/CO/8) 8 March, 2017, n.d., para. 36 (a)).

In post-conflict situations, the preference for employing men is widespread (True, 2013, p. 3). As result, women's right to decent employment — employment in an ambience of freedom, equity, human security, and dignity — is always violated. The LLRC Report also observes that there are delays in providing livelihood support programs for women (LLRC Report, 2011, p. 182, para. 5.104). The majority of women (54%) are employed in informal sector (Department of Census and Statistics, Ministry of National Policies and Economic Affairs, 2016, p. 34). It has been reported that most uneducated woman are engaged in under-skilled and underpaid work in the informal sector and their wages nearly amount to 50% of the wages paid in comparison with those of male workers (Silva, 2012, p. 45). According to the labor force survey, women's contribution to the economy is less than half that of men (Department of Census and Statistics, Ministry of National Policies and Economic Affairs, 2016, p. 9, Table 3.4). This estimation does not take into account their contribution in the maintenance of household and domestic work. Since there are no adequate laws placed in restructuring the informal sector, women face numerous problems and become more vulnerable due to prevailing social attitudes and prejudices (Silva, 2012, p. 44) and are often compelled to succumb to the menace of human trafficking and other dehumanizing practices. This results in forced labor and sexual exploitation.

Chant argues that there should be a move from "feminization of poverty" toward a "feminization of responsibility and obligation." In that case, due consideration must be given to gender differences in inputs to household livelihoods as well as their outcomes for women's lives (Chant, 2006, p. 206). One of the responses that Sri Lankan government has taken is to suggest introducing a social security scheme for the informal sector, but this lofty aspiration has yet to come into fruition. Moreover, Sri Lanka has not ratified the ILO Convention on Domestic Workers (No. 189) 2011. Thus, considering full contributions of women to the economy is relevant in recognizing the need to empower them as change agent in a post-conflict society. Therefore, amending labor laws specially regularizing the informal sector and adhering to international equal opportunity in work, health, and safety standards on domestic workers is an absolute necessity.

Another concern is the numerous encumbrances that usurp the right of women to access and own productive land. Land grabbing by the state for development projects and military camps is a main issue that frustrate women's ability to access land in this post-conflict setting. Deprivation of land rights invariably violates women right to housing, livelihood, and security. Many women being the single heads of households are subjugated to males within their families, when it comes to inheritance and this creates numerous problems for such women in their quest to prove ownership or defend their entitlements of the land. For instance, one of the special laws in Sri Lanka which apply to the war-affected Northern Province of Sri Lanka, *Thesawalamai* Law (Jaffna Matrimonial Rights and Inheritance Ordinance no. 1 of, 1911, see sections 3, 6, and 8), requires a married woman to obtain husband's written consent to dispose her property. Inability to do so in the absence of their husband's death certificate and non-recognition by government officials of women's changed status makes women more vulnerable and exposes them to multiple forms of discrimination (Gomez, 2012, p. 10). Furthermore, the Land Development Ordinance (Land Development Ordinance No. 19 of, 1935, n.d.), which gives preference to male heir over a female, also discriminates against a woman's right to own property. The LLRC observes that land rights of women and their right to secured livelihood is an important aspect and notes that due to restrictions, livelihood activities are severely damaged during the conflict (LLRC Report, 2011, p. 182, para. 5.104). A bill to amend the Land Development Ordinance and to recognize equal rights to land was proposed and yet to see the progress of that initiative (Sri Lanka: Eighth Periodic Report of State Parties submitted to the CEDAW Committee, 2015, para. 21). The CTF report also highlights the development issues including land grabbing faced by people in the war-affected areas and recommends the establishment of the National Land Commission (CTF Report, 2016, p. 103, para 1.25). There are many post-war experiences faced by different third world countries that had greater achievements. Especially, in Rwanda, some female scale landholders and entrepreneurs have gained newly found rights to land (True, 2013, p. 1). This example indicates how a post-conflict situation could be used as a turning point to improve women's lives.

Postwar obligations require "the peace it establishes must be clear improvement over what exists" (Carter, 2013). Specially, it imposes a duty to the victor for the restoration, mainly through political and economic reconstruction (Bass, 2004). In this context, *reparation* should be compensatory and should not be delivered vindictively (Bass, 2004, p. 409). Post-conflict violations of socioeconomic rights exacerbate by earlier violations creating a double injustice for victims. It has particular resonance for women who are frequently victims of gender-based specific harms in conflict and for whom guarantee of economic and social rights is especially important (Chinkin, n.d., p. 4). Recently, GOSL passed two significant acts establishing an office on missing persons (Office on Missing Persons Establishment, Administration and Discharge of Functions, Act, No. 14 of, 2016) and an Office for Reparations (Office for Reperations Act, No. 34 of, 2018). These two transitional justice mechanisms would help to seek the truth and provide reparations for victims in order to restore the sustainable peace in Sri Lankan society.

Women's leadership could only be built, if they are given adequate representation in decision-making process and institutions. The Sri Lankan Constitution does not allow judicial review of laws that existed prior to the enactment of the Constitution; hence, Article 16(1) has been an impediment to eliminate existing discriminatory provisions in all personal laws, for example, *Kandyan*, *Thesawalamai*, and *Muslim Law*. Thus, women's capabilities and rights to free choice of participation in decision-making are limited by the current laws and constitute the social exclusion.

Women's participation in decision-making and their economic empowerment have a symbiotic impact on each other. When women are not stable economically and unable to freely make social choices and take responsibilities, they will not have the courage to compete in an election; hence, countries like Sri Lanka need to address the existing gap in this sphere of women empowerment and leadership. In the aftermath of the conflict, apart from the Presidential Task Force, there were special committees at the district level, established to address special issues of the respective districts (Gomez, 2012, p. 16). Moreover, Women's Rural Development Societies (WRDSs) have been formed in the District Secretariats around the country. Gomes observes that these are state-initiated and the most common form of mobilization of women. However, she argues that WRDSs should be ramped up to identify, design, implement, and monitor projects (Gomez, 2012, p. 16). Another progressive step that has been taken to empower women is the appointment of Women Development Officers (WDOs). The main objective of this is to empower women to combat domestic violence and any form of gender-based violence. Moreover, the Women's Ministry has initiated a project in North and East provinces to empower widows and women heads of households. This project includes revolving credit schemes and training for self-employment, betel cultivation, and cattle rearing for dairy products (Gomez, 2012, p. 20). The CEDAW Committee also urges Sri Lanka to include women in the country's post-conflict, reconstruction, and peacebuilding efforts. Particularly, it stresses the need for the state party to include provisions for economic and social rights in post-conflict reconstruction. It also recommends the implementation of the CTF (CTF Report, 2016), a recommendation in line with resolution 1325 (Concluding observations Sri Lanka (CEDAW/C/LKA/CO/8) 8 March, 2017, n.d., para. 17 (a)).

Participation of women in the formulation of government policies ought to increase to a level that corresponds to an increase in the number of women holding positions in public and administrative offices in Sri Lanka. However, political representation still remains low and women accounted for only five percent in the legislature and even lower in the executive branch as cabinet ministers. There are many countries which have introduced quota systems to promote women's representation in politics, especially through post-conflict peace operations (Bush, 2011, p. 104). Sri Lanka has introduced a quota for women in local government bodies. The Local Authorities Elections Ordinance (Chapter 262) was amended by the Local Authorities Election Act No. 22 of 2012 to include 25 percent quota for women in local government bodies. Moreover, there is a proposal to amend the Provincial Councils Elections Act, No. 2 of 1988 to introduce a guaranteed minimum quota of 30 percent for women in political parties' nomination papers for each province. The CEDAW committee recognizes these developments and recommends the introduction of the same at the national level (Concluding observations Sri Lanka (CEDAW/C/LKA/CO/8) 8 March, 2017, n.d., para. 29(a)). The CEDAW committee in its concluding observations on the eight periodic reports of Sri Lanka also expresses concerns about the limited participation of women in the Constitution reform process (Concluding observations Sri Lanka (CEDAW/C/LKA/CO/8) 8 March, 2017, n.d., para. 8). Even though Sri Lanka has secured the rank of 76th in the "Human Development Index" under High Human Development countries, it still ranks positioned 80th under the "Gender Inequality Index" (GII) (United Nations Development Programme, 2018). Therefore, a clear challenge remains in upholding the right to equality of women in Sri Lanka.

SUMMARY AND CONCLUSION

In the summary, it should be understood that women's mere presence in decision-making process is insufficient in restoring their stability in post-conflict society. Women's participation will only be meaningful if they are empowered to be active rather than passive participants. Essentially, protection of women's economic rights is important in order to ensure women's right to equality in post-conflict restorative process. Moreover, the state has legal obligations to protect women from economic marginalization and exploitation. The GOSL should realize that post-conflict peacebuilding processes brings opportunities for the advancement of women's rights and gender equality. To redistribute public goods and opportunities in order to achieve optimality and fairer social justice, the GOSL should reconstruct its laws and policies in order to facilitate the right to equality *in jure*. Furthermore, in partnership with the private sector, the GOSL should initiate practical measures to trigger a change in attitudes toward women who are impacted during conflict and post-conflict times. As a matter of priority, incorporating a gender-sensitive approach in all transitional justice mechanism is essential for sustainable peace in a post-conflict situation (Saavedra & Saroor, 2017).

The Government of Sri Lanka has recognized the prevailing gender disparities and the importance of mainstreaming women in its development agenda (United Nations Development Programme, 1995, p. 114). There are many programs established and planned to be established by the GOSL, and women are viewed as pioneers of development ((Mahinda Chintana, 2010, p. 186), Sri Lanka's National Action Plan for the Protection and Promotion of Human Rights 2017–2021, 2017). The realization of women's rights to equality in post-conflict Sri Lanka may be a slow process, but the Sri Lankan experiences provide a good case study on how it faced the different challenges in post-conflict context.

ACKNOWLEDGMENTS

I am grateful to Professor H. Eric Schockman and the other anonymous reviewer for their invaluable feedback on this article, and Hakeem Adamu Tahiru for his constructive comments on an earlier version of this text.

REFERENCES

Bass, G. J. (2004). Jus post bellum. *Philosophy & Public Affairs*, 38(4), 384–412. Retrieved from https://www.princeton.edu/~gjbass/docs/juspost.pdf

Bush, S. S. (2011). International politics and the spread of quotas for women in legislatures. *International Organization*, 65(1), 103–137.

Carter, J. (2013, March 9). Just war – Or Just a war. *The New York Times*. Retrieved from https://www.nytimes.com/2003/03/09/opinion/just-war-or-a-just-war.html

Chant, S. (2006). Re-thinking the "Feminization of Poverty" in relation to aggregate gender indices. *Journal of Human Development*, 7(2), 201–220.

Chinkin, C. (n.d.). *The protection of economic, social and cultural rights post-conflict*. Retrieved from https://www.ohchr.org/Documents/Issues/Women/WRGS/Paper_Protection_ESCR.pdf

Concluding observations of the Committee on the Elimination of Discrimination against Women_Sri Lanka (CEDAW/C/LKA/CO/8). 4 March 2017.

Convention on the Elimination of All Forms of Discrimination against Women (CEDAW). *Adopted and opened for signature, ratification and accession by General Assembly resolution 34/180 of 18 December 1979, entry into force 3 September 1981.* (1979).

CTF Report. (2016). Final report of the consultation task force on reconciliation mechanisms: Executive summary and recommendations. Retrieved from http://war-victims-map.org/consultation-task-force-on-reconciliation-mechanisms-final-report-executive-summary-and-recommendations/

Darusman, M., Ratner, S., & Sooka, Y. (2011). *Report of the Secretary-General's Panel of Experts on Accountability in Sri Lanka*. United Nations. Retrieved from https://www.un.org/News/dh/infocus/Sri_Lanka/POE_Report_Full.pdf

Department of Census and Statistics, Ministry of National Policies and Economic Affairs. (2016). *Sri Lanka Labour Force Survey, 2016* (Annual Report). Ministry of National Policies and Economic Affairs, Colombo.

Finnis, J. (2011). *Natural Law and Natural Rights* (2nd ed.). Oxford: Oxford University Press.

General Recommendation 28 (CEDAW). (2010). General Recommendation No. 28 on the core obligations of states parties under article 2 of the convention on the elimination of all forms of discrimination against women, CEDAW/C/GC/28, (16 December 2010). Retrieved from https://www.refworld.org/docid/4d467ea72.html

Gomez, S. (2012). *Women in times of transition, 1325 in Sri Lanka.* FOKUS.

Household Income and Expenditure Survey, Final Report. (2016). Ministry of National Policies and Economic Affairs, Sri Lanka. Retrieved from http://www.statistics.gov.lk/HIES/HIES2016/HIES2016_FinalReport.pdf

Iverson, J. (2014, May 6). Jus post bellum Symposium: Contrasting transitional justice and jus post bellum. *Opinio Juris.* Retrieved from http://opiniojuris.org/2014/05/06/jus-post-bellum-symposium-contrasting-transitional-justice-jus-post-bellum/. Accessed on September 16, 2018.

Jaffna Matrimonial Rights and Inheritance Ordinance no. 1 of 1911 of Sri Lanka.

Jenkins v. Kingsgate (Clothing Productions) Ltd, European Court Reports (1981) 911.

Keith, G. (2010). *Leadership: a very short introduction* (Vol. 237). Oxford: Oxford University Press.

Land Development Ordinance No. 19 of 1935 of Sri Lanka.

Lindberg, J., & Herath, D. (2014). Land and grievances in post-conflict Sri Lanka: Exploring the role of corruption complaints. *Third World Quarterly, 35*(5), 888–904.

Malmstrom, S. (1998). The relevance of international human rights law for the development of economic, social and cultural policy in Bosnia and Herzegovina. In M. O'Flaherty & G. Gisvold (Eds.), *Post-war protection of human rights in Bosnia and Herzegovina* (pp. 157–171). The Hague: Martinus Nijhoff.

Office for Reparations Act No. 34 of 2018 of Sri Lanka.

Office on Missing Persons (Establishment, Administration and Discharge of Functions) Act No. 14. (2016).

Report of the LLRC. (2011). The Commission of Inquiry on Lessons Learnt and Reconciliation appointed by the President of Sri Lanka. (2011). *Report of the Commission of Inquiry on Lessons Learnt and Reconciliation.* Retrieved from https://reliefweb.int/report/sri-lanka/report-commission-inquiry-lessons-learnt-and-reconciliation

Saavedra, R., & Saroor, S. (2017). *A gendered approach to transitional justice in Sri Lanka (women's perspectives and international best practices).* The South Asian Centre for Legal Studies. Retrieved from http://sacls.org/resources/publications/reports/a-gendered-approach-to-transitional-justice-in-sri-lanka-women-s-perspectives-and-international-best-practices

Silva, K. T. (2012). Changes in sex ratio and their possible effects on vulnerability and psychosocial stress in civilian populations in Northeast Sri Lanka. In D. Herath & K. T. Silva (Eds.), *Healing the wounds: Rebuilding Sri Lanka after the war* (pp. 33–57). Colombo: ICES.

Sørbø, G., Goodhand, J., Klem, B., Nissen, A. E., & Selbervik, H. (2011). Pawns of peace evaluation of Norwegian peace efforts in Sri Lanka, 1997–2009. *Report 5/2011 – Evaluation.* Norwegian Agency for Development Cooperation (NORAD). Retrieved from https://www.oecd.org/countries/srilanka/49035074.pdf

Sri Lanka, The Emerging Wonder of Asia, Mahinda Chintana, Vision for the Future, The Development Policy Framework, Government of Sri Lanka (The Department of National Planning, 2010. (2010). Retrieved from https://www.adb.org/sites/default/files/linked-documents/cps-sri-2012-2016-oth-01.pdf

Sri Lanka: Eighth Periodic Report of State Parties submitted to the CEDAW Committee, CEDAW/C/LKA/8. (2015). Retrieved from https://www.refworld.org/type,STATEPARTIESREP,LKA,56e7c3c84,0.html

Sri Lanka's National Action Plan for the Protection and Promotion of Human Rights 2017–2021. (2017). Retrieved from http://www.pmoffice.gov.lk/download/press/D00000000063_EN.pdf

The Constitution of the Democratic Socialist Republic of Sri Lanka (1978).

Thiruchandran, S. (1997). *Ideology, caste, class and gender.* New Delhi: Vikas Publishing House.

True, J. (2013). *Women, peace and security in post-conflict and peace building contexts (NOREF, March 2013).* Policy Brief. Norwegian Peacebuilding Resource Centre (NOREF). Retrieved from https://www.peacewomen.org/system/files/global_study_submissions/Jacqui%20True_NOREF%20policy%20brief.pdf

UN Women. (2015). *Preventing conflict transforming justice securing the peace: A global study on the implementation of United Nations Security Council Resolution 1325*. Retrieved from https://www.peacewomen.org/sites/default/files/UNW-GLOBAL-STUDY-1325-2015%20(1).pdf

United Nations Development Programme. (1995). *Human Development Report 1995*. Retrieved from http://hdr.undp.org/sites/default/files/reports/256/hdr_1995_en_complete_nostats.pdf

United Nations, Human Rights Council. (2015). *Resolution adopted by the Human Rights Council: 'Promoting reconciliation, accountability and human rights in Sri Lanka' [A/HRC/RES/30/1]*. Retrieved from https://reliefweb.int/report/sri-lanka/report-commission-inquiry-lessons-learnt-and-reconciliation

United Nations Development Programme. (2018). *Human Development Indices and Indicators 2018 – Statistical Update*. Retrieved from http://hdr.undp.org/sites/default/files/2018_human_development_statistical_update.pdf

United Nations Security Council Resolution 1325 on Women, Peace and Security adopted by the Security Council at its 4213th meeting, on 31 October 2000, S/RES/1325 (2000).

Universal Declaration of Human Rights (UDHR), adopted by the United Nations General Assembly on 10 December 1948.

Vienna Declaration and Programme of Action, adopted by the World Conference on Human Rights in Vienna on 25th June 1993.

Women's Charter (Sri Lanka) 1993.

8

ECONOMICALLY EMPOWERING WOMEN AS SUSTAINABLE CONFLICT RESOLUTION: A CASE STUDY ON BUILDING PEACE IN UGANDA THROUGH SOCIAL ENTERPRISE

Lisa Liberatore Maracine

ABSTRACT

The gendered consequences of war are often not fully realized, as women tend to carry the heavier burdens in post-conflict situations, yet at the same time can be left out of the formal peace process. Women can be part of the peace process informally through economic empowerment and sustainability. As most post-conflict situations are occurring in the developing world, one of the major issues in the peace process is the notion of a rescue narrative. Organizations from the developed world approach peacebuilding as a project that often disenfranchises and disempowers the people they are trying to help. Therefore, women must be empowered to contribute to their economic situations rather than becoming dependent on the help of outsiders. This amplifies the role of the follower by giving her the tools to be part of the solution and become self-sustainable.

This chapter argues for the role of social enterprise in building sustainable peace by giving women agency and power in their communities. It will look at these phenomena through the lens of a non-governmental organization, 31 Bits, that offers a valuable case study in the post-conflict Northern Uganda town of Gulu where they employ 100 plus women in a five-year program that equips them to become fully self-sustainable through the creation of jewelry hand-made from recycled paper. Their holistic approach moves beyond the nonprofit model of charity and survival for giving their beneficiaries the chance to thrive. In this way, it is not relief or rescue work but rather informal sustainable peace development. When women are economically empowered, their communities are closer to reaching gender equality and achieving positive peace.

Keywords: Gender; development; peacebuilding; sustainability; social enterprise; Uganda

INTRODUCTION

The gendered consequences of war are often not fully understood as women are forced to bear the heavier burdens in post-conflict situations, yet at the same time are left out of the formal peace process. According to the United Nations (2018), gender equality and sustainable development go hand in hand. Women are necessary actors, alongside men, in building positive peace not merely in the absence of war. Specifically, this chapter argues women can be part of the peace process through economic empowerment and self-sustainability, as it becomes a launching pad to greater gender equality. Economic empowerment gives women a greater voice and presence in their communities and families, in that it is "fundamental to the realization of human security" (Porter, 2007, p. 35). This concept of positive peace is more inclusive of women, Porter (2007) argues, which by definition "means more than the absence of violence, but includes all the processes that facilitate social justice and gender equality" (p. 29). Post-conflict situations are ideal times to ensure that women's rights are paramount. When women are economically empowered, there is greater peace and development in a community (Porter, 2013). This chapter will establish the linkages between peacebuilding, leadership, followership, gender equality, and social enterprise. It will first provide a foundational context regarding women's economic empowerment within peace and development work.

WOMEN AND PEACE

It is important to recognize the tension that exists between women and peace. As Sjoberg (2010) notes, "Feminists have argued that a more peaceful world is possible only where women realize their full potential in an environment of equal opportunities" (p. 169). She goes on to explore the notion that associating women with peace primarily casts them as victims and builds upon "the gendered assumption that men make war, women make peace" (Sjoberg, 2010, p. 154). Yet, it is undeniable that women bring experience and perspective to peace that is unique from men. Porter (2007) alternatively argues, "Women, like men, are victims of and actors in armed conflict. However, there are more women who are involved actively in building peace than in destroying lives" (p. 15). The reason for this can be tied to cultural norms and notions of femininity that do not allow room for conflict as Caprioli (2000) found in her research, "Women's relative pacifism may be a result of women [...] valuing community and connectedness over autonomy and individuation" (p. 53). Even still the ensuing tension between associating women with peace exists as Cohn (2012) notes, "This kind of feminization of peace, in turn, reinforces the masculinity of war", which can be harmful to the culture of a society (p. 175). It does not invalidate the invaluable role of women in peacebuilding but is significant to understand when addressing the topic.

As most post-conflict situations are occurring in the developing world, one of the major issues in the peace process is the notion of a rescue narrative. Well-meaning governments and organizations from the developed world approach peacebuilding as a project that often disenfranchises and disempowers the people they are trying to help. The handout model of most relief work is needed in some circumstances but is not sustainable long term to address poverty and conflict. Beneria (2001) confirms, "Poverty eradication programs must emphasize the need to generate decent jobs without which these programs will continue to be ineffective" (p. 49). Therefore, women must be empowered to contribute to their economic situations rather than becoming dependent on the help of outsiders. It has been demonstrated that women's economic sustainability is a crucial component of rebuilding society in post-conflict situations (United Nations, 2018). Which is why:

> Women's equal access to and control over economic and financial resources is critical for the achievement of gender equality and

empowerment of women and for equitable and sustainable
economic growth and development. (United Nations, 2018, p. v)

One way women can achieve greater economic empowerment is through
fair-trade artisan-based partnerships that create opportunities to sell their
craft on a larger scale. Minney (2011) affirms:

Fair Trade is a strategy for poverty alleviation, economic
empowerment and sustainable development. Its purpose is to create
opportunities for producers who have been economically
disadvantaged or marginalized by the conventional trading system.
(p. 145)

Economic sustainability among women leads to greater opportunities for
leadership and peace development.

A sense of empowerment and self-sustainability for women is central in
contributing to greater gender equality in post-conflict situations. Research
has shown, "Women workers feel empowered by having their own jobs and
are able to wrest greater control over their lives from their families" (Deo,
2006, p. 111). Women are given more decision-making power in their
households as a result of their economic empowerment. This creates a positive effect not only in family life but also in the community as a whole as
"women have to be involved in family decisions that affect their lives, those
of their children and the management of family income" (Fonjong, 2001,
p. 231). Razavi (2001) found in a study, "The ability to earn a wage, had
made a difference in how women were perceived and treated, as well as their
feelings of self-worth" (p. 36). It is significant to note this need for economically empowering women because of the unique benefit it brings to their
families and communities. Deo (2006) writes, "The money from women's
jobs is more likely to be put toward the basic needs of households than
money paid to men" (p. 110). Additionally, Richards and Gelleny (2007)
note, "Compared to men, women tend to save more of their earnings"
(p. 859), which could be contributed to outside factors due to Diaspora ten-
dencies leaving their homes to find work in other places. In contrast to men,
women have a greater economic impact on future generations in their family
lines. The United Nations (2018) reports:

Studies over an extended period have built up a robust body of
evidence to show that women's access to resources, including

education, paid work, credit, land, technology and other productive assets, have a far stronger impact on child survival, welfare and education than similar resources in men's hands. (p. 7)

A holistic understanding to sustainable conflict resolution then must include an economic component. One approach is employing the concept of social enterprise to build social capital.

SOCIAL ENTERPRISE AND DEVELOPMENT

Social enterprises are on the rise, yet can fail to remain sustainable long term due to lack of data and research over time. Social enterprise is defined as a business model or an organizational model where social networks are utilized at the very core and are motivated by social transformation to build social capital (Roberts, 2010). It is as Thompson and Doherty (2006) write, "Social enterprises – defined simply – are organizations seeking business solutions to social problems" (p. 362). Yet even more specifically Di, Haugh, and Tracey (2010) found:

Social enterprises seek to attain a particular social objective or set of objectives through the sale of products and/or services, and in doing so aim to achieve financial sustainability independent of government and other donors. (p. 682)

Social enterprise is built upon the foundation of community by connecting people in ways they were not able to connect prior. Social enterprises especially aim to add value through their work (Di et al., 2010). Qualitative and quantitative studies on social enterprise development have aided in building a research foundation for further work (Khienf & Dahles, 2015; Urban, 2015). There is a theme within the literature that addresses the concern for long-term sustainability with social enterprise. Khienf and Dahles (2015) note:

Research findings provide the empirical evidence for the much cited claim that the "need to build a sustainable organization" among NGOs has led to the adoption of "entrepreneurial and business-like strategies that are aimed at achieving greater financial stability." (p. 234)

It creates a natural parallel for development work especially in creating a framework for building peace through the economic empowerment of women.

Social enterprise creates a space for an amplified role of followers in collaborative and transformational leadership, which is ideal for women in development and peacebuilding. Burns (1978) writes of transformational leadership, "The genius of leadership lies in the manner in which leaders see and act on their own and their followers' values and motivations" (p. 19). In this way, it parallels with the concept of social enterprise by focusing on the role of both leaders and followers in collaboration toward end values, which include equality (Burns, 1978). Lyon and Humbert (2012) found in their study, "Social enterprises appear to provide a more egalitarian environment for women's involvement in governance" as a pathway to greater leadership opportunities for women (p. 841). There is growing research that indicates social enterprise is a better indicator of development work and long-term sustainability for women in leading them and the communities they inhabit out of poverty (Fotheringham & Saunders, 2014; Nicolás, & Rubio, 2016). Datta and Gailey (2012) affirm, "Social entrepreneurship ventures combine financial success with social value creation, offering a new way of thinking for all sectors of society" (p. 583). By giving women an opportunity for economic empowerment and self-sustainability through social enterprise, they become an integral part of creating social value. As Roberts (2010) notes, reconciliation in post-conflict situations "requires the regeneration of social capital to rebuild community relations" (p. 7). It can also create a foundation for positive peace to thrive. Yoosuf and Premaratne (2017) found in their case study, "Since poverty and economic marginalization are a major cause of conflict, creating better economic conditions [...] contributes to mitigating the causes of conflict" (p. 45). Social enterprise as an economic development model offers a viable solution for sustainable conflict resolution and the empowerment of women in their roles as both followers and leaders throughout the peacebuilding process.

31 BITS AS A CASE STUDY

31 Bits is an exceptional example of social enterprise that brings a fresh perspective to peace and development work. The organization started when the founder:

> traveled to Uganda in the summer of 2007 to volunteer. She began
> working with women at an after-school program and quickly

learned about the hardships they faced after years of conflict in the region. (Rosen, 2015)

The women in this community already knew how to create beautiful jewelry but found it difficult to sell in their communities, so she took the jewelry back home to the United States and quickly realized she had a market. Maleko (2007) writes of this phenomenon, "The experience shared [...] was that, while opportunities for increased trade were clearly articulated, women could not easily take advantage of the potential benefits because of challenges and constraints they face" – they needed a bridge (p. 22). The women *31 Bits* employees are considered entrepreneurs and specialists in their crafts. They are never referred to as victims, as Mohanty (2003) warns against, which can be a challenge with Western organizations as "humanitarian assistance often works to define women, girls, and gender relations in a [displaced] camp in homogenous ways as vulnerable and as victims" (Cohn, 2012, p. 90). It is important to define the role of followers in a way that sets them up for long-term success. *31 Bits* aims to bring economic stability to over 100 women artisans in Gulu, Northern Uganda. The organization provides the women it employs with life skills programs that enable them to envision a successful future and prevent them from depending solely on the organization itself.

In this way, it is not relief or rescue work but rather sustainable development and peacebuilding. They purchase the handcrafts directly from the beneficiaries at fair-trade prices. To maintain transparency with their beneficiaries, they negotiate a fair price for each piece, factoring the complexity, materials, and time involved in the making. They purchase a set amount of product from each beneficiary each month, so they know exactly how much they will be earning. This monthly wage enables them to provide housing, food, and healthcare for themselves and their families, and even gives them a chance to save for future business endeavors. They also provide training programs leading up to graduation to teach them to save and set aside for their future businesses. As Rosen (2015) goes on to say, *31 Bits'* "programs provide participants the skills they need to support their families and communities, allowing the company 'to empower women to be self-sufficient.'" The programs include finance training, community group development, AIDS and health education, vocational training, and English and literacy lessons. They write:

> We purchase jewelry from each woman on a monthly basis, providing them with an immediate, consistent, and fair income. Each piece of jewelry is handmade using 100% recycled paper and other local materials […] We are committed to working with each woman until she has graduated from our program and attained a sustainable means of income within her own community. (*31 Bits*)

Each fashion season *31 Bits* launches a new collection complete with new colors, designs, and concepts, thus validating its status as a fashion forward trend-setting company. They partner on a wholesale basis with hundreds of retailers across the United States. Their mission statement is "*Using fashion and design to empower women to rise above poverty*," and they have been doing this effectively in Northern Uganda for 10 years, beginning shortly after the peace formal process started.

BUILDING PEACE IN UGANDA THROUGH WOMEN-LED BUSINESS

The formal peace process in Northern Uganda began in 2006. Nabukeera-Musoke (2009) writes of the role of women in the process by, "Responding to the absence of women in the peace process, non-governmental and community-based organizations collaborated to form the Uganda women's Coalition for Peace (UWCP)" (p. 122). They were successful in part at mobilizing women and enabling them to find their voices in the peace process. These women contribute to the formal peace process because of economic sustainability programs that allow them to find their own sense of peace and security in their families and communities. Organizations and businesses such as *31 Bits* play a part in the informal peace process by empowering women to have agency and power in their communities. An International Alert (2010) report conducted in Uganda found:

> In contrast with the pre-war period, a high number of woman-headed households are now found in the two districts and, even in marriages, women are often the primary source of family income. In this sense, they are at the forefront of the region's economic recovery. (p. 4)

It goes on to report "women have taken on an expanded level of responsibility in household management, including decision-making, as their economic influence has grown" (p. 26). When women are economically empowered their societies are better able to reach gender equality and achieve positive peace. As Ahikire, Madand, and Ampaire (2012) write of Uganda, "The findings show a very high involvement of women in family decision-making, showing a high level of empowerment" (p. 7). This plays a major role in peacebuilding and development in this post-conflict situation. It lays a foundation for women-led business in peace and development work to be scaled throughout Uganda and also to become applicable in other post-conflict situations.

Similar to associating women solely with peace, feminist theorists argue the type of work conducted by *31 Bits* within the artisan-based industry can potentially reinforce prewar gender roles (hence not advancing gender equality) since the craft trade is almost exclusively female in its membership and audience (Kolmar & Bartkowski, 2009).

> This argument is based more on a handout model rather than an economic sustainability model. Hutchens (2010) contends, "As development scholars suggest, development initiatives that encourage women to make traditional crafts ... buttress gendered responsibilities by reinforcing the idea of women as keepers of tradition, who are illiterate, unemployed, confined to the private sphere and bear full domestic responsibilities" (p. 455).

Additionally, the role of fashion as a feminine industry may potentially keep women out of the masculine areas of society, such as the formal peace process in post-conflict situations. The main counterargument in response to this rationale points back to the economic sustainability programs that organizations like *31 Bits* seek to create for the women involved. Historically Mategeko (2011) found, "Women have socially been excluded from development worldwide and more so in developing countries like Uganda" (p. 818). This is due to their lack of presence and power in their communities. As seen in the case study, many of these women use the money they earn to create their own small businesses, begin agriculture initiatives, build apartment buildings, and pursue other traditionally non-feminine interests in society.

Organizations and businesses led by women in Uganda act as a launching pad and enable them to become stakeholders in their families and communities. As Porter (2007) writes, "women's peacebuilding activities revolve around processes that contribute to the healing of relationships and meeting everyday needs" (p. 33). These women may have otherwise been forced "to return to their 'normal place' in the community" but organizations like *31 Bits* allow them to "rethink and reshape gender stereotypes and hierarchies" (Sjoberg, 2010, p. 162). By bringing in an income, women are forging new roles in their society and have greater opportunity to let their voices be heard and contribute to overall development and peace. This contributes to peace-building as Porter (2007) writes, "Peace has to be grounded in the immediacy of fulfilling ordinary daily needs" (p. 118). Giving women jobs, enabling them to create businesses by working with their skill sets and providing necessary training help them to rebuild the economies of post-conflict situations. Culturally, many women in rural areas where poverty is most prevalent are skilled in hand artistry passed down through generations. Minney (2011) writes of this occurrence, "Hand skills mean the most economically marginalized people in rural areas can earn a decent living without leaving their families to migrate to cities in search of work" (p. 128). Organizations and businesses within this industry have the capacity to succeed in greater ways as they partner with women to amplify the work they have already been doing and providing a new outlet for exchange.

THE ROLE OF LEADERS AND FOLLOWERS

In conclusion, positive peace requires the active economic empowerment of women in a post-conflict society. It gives women greater negotiating power in prewar hierarchal relationships further undermining prewar norms and paves the way for reaching greater gender parity. Economic empowerment through social enterprise contributes to the peace process in an informal manner through building social capital, as women become stabilizers in their homes and communities. This can be achieved through what is known as traditional women's work, such as the craft trade, because it acts as a launching pad to gender equality and sustainable conflict resolution. Organizations that hope to contribute to the peace process through economic empowerment are most valuable when they allow women to reach self-sustainability and do not rely on using handouts as a relief method. *31 Bits* in Northern Uganda is an excellent example of an organization that understands the tension between women and peace but also realizes the potential that economically empowering women creates for sustainable peace. There are many others who are doing the same throughout Uganda, such as Krochet Kids, Sseko Designs, Akola Project, Noonday Collection, and Artisan Global. The approach of these companies and non-governmental organizations gives women the opportunity to thrive in their role as followers in the process of becoming leaders in their communities through their economic empowerment. It shows the scalability of a social enterprise model throughout a region and offers future implications for research in similar post-conflict situations globally.

Transformational leadership seeks to bring social change and agency to followers, which can be seen throughout this chapter as economic empowerment. It is empowerment from a collaborative approach as Porter (2013) writes,

> Empowerment responds to difference, thrives on security, mobilizes insecure communities to deal with conflict and is transformative in creating practical changes, including women's participation in decision-making across all levels of social, political, religious. (p. 10)

This leadership approach amplifies the role of the follower. In his foundational work on this concept, Bass (1990) writes of transformational leadership occurring:

> when leaders broaden and elevate the interests of their employees [followers], when they generate awareness and acceptance of the purpose and mission of the group [...] to look beyond their own self-interest for the good of the group. (p. 21)

By enabling women to have access to resources to be financially self-sustainable as identified throughout this chapter, they are given transformative agency in peacebuilding as followers. The research and fieldwork of the United Nations (2018) in this area has shown when women are economically empowered, it changes the course of a society.

ACKNOWLEDGMENTS

This chapter is dedicated to the courageous women entrepreneurs around the world, particularly the women of *31 Bits*. A special thank you to my husband, David, and my incredible family for championing me every step of the way.

REFERENCES

31 Bits. About us. Retrieved from http://31bits.com/about/.

Ahikire, J., Madand, A., & Ampaire, C. (2012). *Post-war economic opportunities in Northern Uganda: Implications for women's empowerment and political participation* (pp. 1–45). International Alert. Retrieved from https://www.international-alert.org/sites/default/files/publications/201209WomenEconOppsUganda-EN.pdf

Bass, B. M. (1990). From transactional to transformational leadership: Learning to share the vision. *Organizational Dynamics, 18*(3), 19–31.

Beneria, L. (2001). Shifting the risk: New employment patterns, informalization, and women's work. *International Journal of Politics, Culture and Society, 15*(1), 27–53.

Burns, J. M. (1978). *Leadership*. New York, NY: Harper & Row.

Caprioli, M. (2000). Gendered conflict. *Journal of Peace Research, 37*(1), 51–68.

Changing Fortunes: Women's Economic Opportunities in Post-War Northern Uganda. (2010). *Investing in Peace, 3*. International Alert. 1–52. Retrieved from https://www.international-alert.org/sites/default/files/publications/201009ChangingFortunesWomensEconomicOpp.pdf

Cohn, C. (2012). *Women & wars*. Cambridge: Polity Press.

Datta, P. B., & Gailey, R. (2012). Empowering women through social entrepreneurship: Case study of a women's cooperative in India. *Entrepreneurship Theory and Practice, 36*(3), 569–587.

Deo, N. (2006). Is globalization our friend? Women's allies in the developing world. *Current History, 105*(689), 105–111.

Di, D. M. L., Haugh, H., & Tracey, P. (2010). Social bricolage: Theorizing social value creation in social enterprises. *Entrepreneurship Theory and Practice, 34*(4), 681–703.

Fonjong, L. (2001). Fostering women's participation in development through non-governmental efforts in Cameroon. *The Geographical Journal, 167*(3), 223–234.

Fotheringham, S., & Saunders, C. (2014). Social enterprise as poverty reducing strategy for women. *Social Enterprise Journal, 10*(3), 176–199.

Hutchens, A. (2010). Empowering women through fair trade? Lessons from Asia. *Third World Quarterly, 31*(3), 449–467.

Khienf, S., & Dahles, H. (2015). Commercialization in the non-profit sector: The emergence of social enterprise in Cambodia. *Journal of Social Entrepreneurship, 6*(2), 218–243.

Kolmar, W., & Bartkowski, F. (2009). *Feminist theory: A reader* (3rd ed.) New York, NY: McGraw-Hill Education.

Lyon, F., & Humbert, A. L. (2012). Gender balance in the governance of social enterprise. *Local Economy: The Journal of the Local Economy Policy Unit, 27*(8), 831–845.

Maleko, J. (2007). *Mainstreaming gender into trade and development strategies: The case of East Africa*. United Nations Conference on Trade and Development. Retrieved from https://unctad.org/

Mategeko, B. (2011). The effect of social exclusion of women from development in Uganda. *Educational Research, 2*(2), 818–823.

Minney, S. (2011). *Naked fashion*. London: People Tree.

Mohanty, C. T. (2003). *Feminism without borders: Decolonizing theory, practicing solidarity*. Durham, NC: Duke University Press.

Nabukeera-Musoke, H. (2009). *Transitional justice and gender in Uganda: Making peace, failing women during the peace negotiation process*. PeaceWomen.

Nicolás, C., & Rubio, A. (2016). Social enterprise: Gender gap and economic development. *European Journal of Management and Business Economics, 25*(2), 56–62.

Porter, E. (2007). *Peacebuilding: Women in international perspective*. London: Routledge.

Porter, E. (2013). Rethinking women's empowerment. *Journal of Peacebuilding & Development, 8*(1), 1–14.

Razavi, S. (2001). Globalization, employment and women's empowerment. *United Nations Division for the Advancement of Women (DAW)*.

Richards, D. L., & Gelleny, R. (2007). Women's status and economic globalization. *International Studies Quarterly, 51*(4), 855–876.

Roberts, N. (2010). Entrepreneurship in peace operations. *Journal of Civil Society, 6*(1), 1–21.

Rosen, A. (2015). Show your love with a gift that gives. *CNN.* Retrieved from https://www.cnn.com/2013/02/13/world/iyw-social-entreprenuers/index.html

Sjoberg, L. (Ed.) (2010). *Gender and international security.* New York, NY: Routledge.

Thompson, J., & Doherty, B. (2006). The diverse world of social enterprise. *International Journal of Social Economics, 33,* 361–375.

United Nations Women. (2018). World Survey on the Role of Women in Development 2014: Gender Equality and Sustainable Development (pp. 1–129). *United Nations Entity for Gender Equality and the Empowerment of Women.*

Urban, B. (2015). Evaluation of social enterprise outcomes and self-efficacy. *International Journal of Social Economics, 42*(2), 163–178.

Yoosuf, A., & Premaratne, S. P. (2017). Building sustainable peace through business linkages among micro-entrepreneurs: Case studies of micro-enterprises in the north of Sri Lanka. *Journal of Peacebuilding and Development, 12*(1), 34–48.

THE GENEVA LEADERSHIP ALLIANCE: LEARNING TO LEAD (AND FOLLOW) IN PEACEBUILDING AND SOCIAL JUSTICE

Patrick Sweet

The Geneva Leadership Alliance has engaged 1,280 participants from over 114 countries. Our client/participant/beneficiary list stretches from NATO, to UN Agencies, to private firms, to foundations, and to small NGO directors from rural field outposts.

In September 2015 the Center for Creative Leadership and the Geneva Centre for Security Policy launched an Alliance for Advancing Leadership in Peace and Security, now known as The Geneva Leadership Alliance. GCSP has its roots in a training program designed on the initiative of the Swiss Confederation to strengthen national expertise in the field of disarmament in the midst of the Cold War, and it evolved into the Swiss contribution to the NATO Partnership for Peace program prioritizing education and policy research in areas of peace and security over military engagement. Today GCSP's Foundation Council consists of 52 member states. Combining expertise, practices, and collective intelligence of the GCSP and Center for Creative Leadership communities, the Geneva Leadership Alliance is developing individual leaders as well as building collective capacity to lead across national governmental agencies, NGOs, and intergovernmental agencies (like UN/EU agencies), in humanitarian and other endeavors.

The Geneva Leadership Alliance grows from the recognition inside and outside of the international peace and security community that:

- The forces and dynamics impacting peace and security today are far broader than traditionally addressed and include migration, resource scarcity, access to energy, health care, pandemics, corruption, as well as economic development, social entrepreneurship, pervasive technological innovation in weaponry, communication, macro- and microfinance, cyber security, ubiquitous (social) media, information access, and not the least, social justices, etc.

- The stakeholders and leading International Organizations (IOs) required to collaborate to advance peace and security in this broader context face ever-widening and more tightly interwoven complex flows of actors, actions, resources, and social innovation, all of which are undergoing increasingly rapid and unpredictable change and *disruption*. The Geneva Leadership Alliance mission humbly exists to learn and adapt as well as facilitate capacity building and training in effective leadership in this context.

WHAT HAS IMPACTED US IN THE LAST THREE YEARS?

Where many see diversity, we see common challenges facing us all. Repeating our time's mantra is that we all are experiencing a state of increasing pace of change, disruption, and frequency of volatile events. This International Leadership Association volume is written largely because of this state of our common humanity.

Against a volatile contextual backdrop is contrasted the following *common self-evident humanity* which is often overlooked (especially in leadership development initiatives). Leadership development efforts (we see) tend to overfocus on individual leader-centered competencies, values, and behaviors to the neglect of common, collective practices required to address tensions between groups, tribes, regimes. Most recently, there is growing recognition of diversity (often compensating for traditional, core- or unicultural dominance). Herein lies the paradox of commonality that emerges from diversity that we struggle to address and find essential.

Self-evident and often overlooked commonalities *paradoxically* emerging from diversity are as follows:

- *Under existential threat, people surprisingly aspire to similar core values.* The human hierarchy of needs and values, from survival to self-actualization, are of course impacted by individual and community existential threat. When family, security, stability, community bonding, justice, equity, religious freedom, etc., become aspirational due to existential threat, we also know *these common human values* also provide *the core* of community re-building, reconciliation, and rejuvenation, even though the expressions of these common values may look different across cultures, clans, communities, and tribes. These core elements are common denominators across all values studies where differentiation of cultural importance is emphasized rather than recognizing commonality, (e.g. Inglehart-Welzels World Values survey waves 1-6, http://www.worldvaluessurvey.org/ WVSContents.jsp). People and communities under stress lose sight of these; yet, bringing them back into focus provides social cohesion to reconstruct shared humanity.

- *Desire for self- and interpersonal respect is universal.* Everyone, in every collective, generation, tribe, or culture values respect — we just define and express it in different ways.

- *Trust is essential.* By and large, trust is valued at every level.

- *Polarization is powerful.* The destructive power of polarization is easily negatively leveraged under stress, while leveraging polarity as a positive *collaborative tactic* is virtually absent.

- *Leadership's ontology is mainly person-centered.* Leading as a set of learned "practices" is rarely separated from the concept of leader. Leaders are often seen as special and a scarce resource. Collective capability to lead is intuitively understood, but rarely developed.

- *Integrity is desired to be a pre-requisite for power.* Corruption becomes prevalent the more that power is separated from integrity, and the loss of integrity in leaders and institutions undermines the realization of most of the points above.

Across the board we try to address ways of leading commonality-in-diversity. The Geneva Leadership Alliance co-produces leadership learning experiences with multicultural, multidisciplinary, and multilateral participants, organizations, and dynamics. Sometimes representatives of inimical national/cultural/tribal entities are in the same experience. We have learned from the self-evident and paradoxical commonalities of the diversity in our rooms. We recognize that learning is derived to a large extent *from the sharing, bonding, and insights between participants far over and above any "training" per se.*

HOW WE "DO IT"

We approach learning by differentiating leading at individual, group, organizational, and societal identity levels. We cocreate systematic, action-learning explorations, and exercises of leadership challenges in workshop settings. We use experiential learning that helps people form "bring-it-in" rather than "bring-it-on" attitudes. We engage in action-research projects that help us and our client organizations emergently learn how to leverage commonality-in-diversity, together. In many ways, this is the history of Geneva as an international peacebuilding center itself.

IMPLICATIONS FOR THE FUTURE

Leader development in peace and security is under transformation. Our view is that there are two "colliders" in Switzerland; one at the atomic level (at Cern) and the other at the Geneva Center for Security Policy (as Ambassador Christian Dussey casts our work). Both colliders work to accelerate and harness the energy derived from safe, semi-controlled collisions.

In our collisions, the Geneva Leadership Alliance focuses on facilitating shared understanding, and building action-oriented collective wisdom, based on recognizing diversity AS WELL AS developing skills and paradoxically bringing self-evident, common humanitarian values back into each group, organization, and societal identity our participants encounter after working with us. This sounds "large." It is not. It is actually awakening something simply essential and present in all of us.

Our humble suggestion is that governments, religious, educational, health, in short, *all* institutions, teams, tribes, and individuals should recognize both the tension and needed facilitation in leading practices of diversity through ever-emergent forms of shared, adaptive commonality stemming from these self-evident elements of humanity listed here. We see these common elements and tensions as a common foundation to address tensions of reconciliation with justice, independence with interdependence, short-term security imperatives with long-term security reform, and the security of a core culture with the adaptiveness of an open culture. In short, learning to embrace tensions collectively and to turn to common values to lead a constant evolution of social justice and equilibrium.

To learn more, visit www.GCSP.ch and www.ccl.org or contact the author at sweetp@ccl.org.

ACKNOWLEDGMENTS

The author expresses humble gratitude to the vision and people collaborating at Center for Creative Leadership Geneva Center for Security Policy, especially Mr Peter Cunningham, and to the International Leadership Association for its initiatives and recognitions.

PART III

INTERNATIONAL LAW AND SOCIAL JUSTICE

H. Eric Schockman, Vanessa Alexandra Hernández Soto and Aldo Boitano de Moras

The ensuing chapters explore the conditions and foundational basis for leaders and followers in achieving peace, reconciliation, and social justice, in particular contexts. In them, can be found a wonderful cast of academics and practitioners from various disciplines across the world who examine and question our current leadership and followership models and paradigms capacity and effectiveness to face the challenges of the twenty-first century.

New leadership approaches are needed to address the root causes of conflicts and building inclusive societies that resist violence and more critically prevent it. The world order and the structures of international law that were forged after the World War II seem to be unraveling. In times of heavy attacks on multilateralism and the rules-based order, the rise of populism and nationalism, we must call out and question the poor leadership (and their enabling followers) that we see around us.

That inclusive followership and transformational leadership can be successful under the most daunting circumstances such as post-conflict societies and war-ridden societies are evidenced through examples in the chapters that follow. The authors of this subsection invite us to pay greater attention to the roles of those who with little or no formal authority initiate, give momentum and deeply influence critical changes in their communities.

Initiating their leaders' agenda, some of them became leaders themselves championing for human rights and social justice.

Edin Ibrahinefedic and Randal Joy Thompson's chapter provides an interesting study of the power of women, who turned victimhood into social action, to build a grassroots civil society that is fostering reconciliation and peace. The chapter offers an example of how victim leaders who emerged during the war continued to heal and empower other victims. Many of them then became leaders themselves and continued to heal and empower other victims, despite being prevented from fully participating in the peacemaking processes and facing political marginalization in public life and decision-making. Douglas Castro, likewise, grapples with the gender dimensions of climate justice and aims to raise awareness of the urgency of increasing meaningful women participation and leadership in efforts to address climate change. The potential of climate change to induce conflict, exacerbate instability, and becoming a threat to peace, disruption of cultural heritages and diversity has led the United Nations to recognize climate change as one of the greatest long-term challenges to international peace and security. To be up for the challenge, leaders need to encourage followers and especially empower women as agents of change who must equally be part of the solution toward a sustainable future. Regrettably, despite the vital role of women in preventing conflict and helping to forge peace, women remain grossly unrepresented informal peace processes and negotiations, to the detriment of society. Women, however, continue to be at the forefront of informal peace processes and peacebuilding efforts at grassroots levels, leading peaceful movements that are at the origin of post-conflict community recovery. Their agency is a crucial part of healing and easing the suffering of affected communities.

These chapters assert that building new paradigms of international law and sustaining peace need women's voices and leadership. Investing and developing women leadership is essential for lasting peace and security. If leadership is going to be an enduringly transformative force, then we need to be creative and courageous in tackling one of the world's toughest challenges: women's exclusion from power and decision-making processes. We will never achieve sustainable peace and security if half of the population is excluded. It is only when women are participating in a meaningful way that we can bring about change. Comprehensively overcoming barriers to women's leadership and influence requires that the harmful gender stereotypes and norms that underlie women's unequal status be dismantled. Leaders need to listen and learn from women on the frontlines of peacebuilding and those who are fighting against injustice and inequality. Leaders with a seat at the table must look around and ask: Who is not here and how can we bring them in? The inclusion of women, in particular, those from minority and marginalized communities, is one mission which our generation of leaders cannot afford to fail.

We need to do all we can to cherish and nurture a culture that resists and prevents violence as well as encourages intelligent disobedience. The authors herein examine the role that followers have had in mass atrocities, gross human rights violations and authoritarian regimes as well as the role that intelligent disobedience and "upstanders" play in responsible and ethical followership when leaders have failed their followers. Lorraine Stefani makes a strong and compelling call advocating for a transformational leadership based on a paradigm of social justice facing the challenges of toxic leadership and countering the rising nationalist populism and extreme supremacist ideologies that is infecting our politics. This chapter uses Brexit, the British referendum on remaining or leaving the European Union as a focal point from which to observe the failures of Britain's political leaders in the lead up to and the execution of 'the will of the people' to exit the European Union. Stefani argues that at this critical moment in the history of Britain, essential leadership characteristics including honesty, integrity, authenticity, and courage are not in evidence. It further contends that if we are to move forward to heal the wounds in society, we must find the courage to examine leadership failures in order to re-envision leadership and followership through the lens of inclusion, diversity, and civility, as a matter of social justice. The author poses the question: Would Brexit have happened at all if a wider range of voices were heard, their real issues and grievances understood by the politicians, in addressing the different challenges within our own multicultural and multi-ethnic communities? In this chapter, it is a powerful call to arms to everyone involved in leadership studies, conflict resolution, leadership education, scholarship, and research to address the question: How do we make an active contribution to improve the status of leadership and followership in fractured societies? What are our responsibilities as a multi-layered community of practice? Are we really practicing what we preach in supporting diverse, inclusive leadership and followership? Bruce C. Pascoe's chapter makes a cogent case for the need to further scrutinize the role that the followers and not only the leaders played in mass atrocities, against the backdrop of the Bosnian and Herzegovina war and genocide, *as one cannot lead without followers and one cannot accomplish genocide without obedient followers.* The author invites us to learn from upstanders, those who stand up for right in difficult situations, irrespective of the dangers. As well as the critical importance of developing a critical mass of upstanders to be trained in intelligence disobedience as a means to avoid vainly relying on individual leaders to prevent human cruelty.

The chapters in this section remind us that seeking justice for grave international crimes matters for peace. There cannot be peace without accountability. They also illustrate, however, the limits of the international justice system. Criminal trials help to establish social stability by removing perpetrators from leadership positions and neutralizing their capacity to incite hate and violence. They also play a vital role in establishing the historical truth as well as recognition of the harm suffered by victims. Notwithstanding, the very nature of the crimes under the jurisdiction of the International Criminal Court, coupled with the inherent limitations of many judicial mechanisms, makes inevitable that prosecutors focus on a few of the most responsible perpetrators. Accountability mechanisms and criminal tribunals are only one piece of the puzzle among a myriad of other responses and actors. It is just a starting point toward peace.

Lastly, Fátima Martínez-Mejía and Nelson Andrés Ortiz Villalobos likewise examine the leadership of the Vicariate of Solidarity, an organization of the Catholic Church during the dictatorship in Chile (1973–1990). Just a few days after the *coup d'état* that brought Pinochet to power, the Cardinal and Archbishop of Santiago and a group of churches declared themselves against the devastating violence that was gripping the country. Immediately, religious leaders took up the defense of the most vulnerable, the persecuted, marginalized, and poor. The authors analyze the work of the Vicariate of Solidarity and its leading role in the fight against human rights violations, strengthening social reorganization, reconciliation, and the return to democracy in Chile. The chapter strongly illustrates the perilous work of those that with little or no formal authority, operating in the shadows, risking their lives, who choose to not remain neutral or silent in the face of injustice and cruelty. They, however, shared a vision and a spirit to serve their communities and to make the world a better place for us all.

The chapters of this subsection present case studies with profound implications for peace, reconciliation, and social justice leadership across the globe and in our own communities. Each of the chapters advocates from different perspectives and corners of the world for the importance of transforming the notions of authenticity of the leader and follower in our own societies, in addition to post- and pre-conflictual societies. Elements of mistrust, torn social fabric, and serious difficulties in working together toward common goals are not only specific to major or violent conflicts but often a prelude stage leading to social unrest. In confusing and disconcerting times, they invite us to reflect on how leadership can remain relevant amidst the global challenges of nationalist populism and anti-globalism? What role do followers play? Are new international justice structures needed for manifesting a just world? How do we learn from post-conflict countries in achieving reconciliation, and how to resist and prevent violence in our own communities? And how do we cultivate environments that promote the type of leadership that empowers and enable us to build lasting peace?

9

WOMEN'S POSTWAR ACTIVISM IN BOSNIA-HERZEGOVINA: A HUMAN RIGHTS APPROACH TO PEACEBUILDING AND RECONCILIATION THROUGH LIMINAL SPACE

Edin Ibrahimefendic and Randal Joy Thompson

ABSTRACT

Bosnia-Herzegovina has recovered slowly from the war of 1992–1995 partly due to the fact that the Dayton Accord that ended the war created a consociational state segmented by the three majority ethnic and religious groups, the Bosniaks, the Serbs, and the Croats. These "constituent peoples" live in divided spaces, rule the country separately, and have not yet reconciled their differences, impeding the creation of national identity. Women's nongovernmental organizations (NGOs) and women peacemakers are working toward reconciliation and peace through the construction of an alternative narrative to that of the government's and creating an increasingly influential civil society. These NGOs, comprised of women "victims" who became "empowered leaders," are fostering reconciliation and peace through the promotion of the human rights of five groups: (1) deceased victims of the war; (2) surviving victims of the war; (3) minority groups; (4) marginalized groups; and (5) women. By the construction of liminal space through civic art, psychosocial healing, and political action, these groups are creating a new future and building the momentum to push the country forward to a reintegrated society. Leadership of the groups is dispersed throughout the country and comprised of many ethnic groups who collaborate to meet the needs and demands of their followers, who, in effect, have created the leaders and lead inclusively with them. The chapter provides an interesting study of the power of women, who turned victimhood into social action, to build a grassroots civil society that is fostering reconciliation and peace.

Keywords: Bosnia-Herzegovina; reconciliation; peacebuilding; human rights; liminal space; women's leadership; post-conflict societies

In black clothes and silence, UDIK expresses the deepest respect for the civil victims of the war and the pain of the whole community because of it. With this act, UDIK provides strength to the victims, showing them that that they are not alone, that there is someone to fight for their rights and someone to stand for them on the street or square. Through conscientious objection, nonviolence, peace education, campaigns, civil disobedience, UDIK requests demilitarization of community [...] Blackness is what makes us tick and resistant to the mass that fosters a culture of violence. Darkness is our sign for movement [...] Silence is our invitation to the movement against violence in the community.

Association for Social Research and Communication ([UDIK], n.d.),
NGO member (Women's Network of BIH)

Bosnia-Herzegovina (BIH) inherited a culture of violence and ethnic discord at the end of the civil war that lasted from 1992 to 1995, a culture cemented by the General Framework Agreement (GFA) for Peace in Bosnia and Herzegovina, also known as the Dayton Accord, which created a consociational state divided among the three major ethic and religious groups, Bosniak, who are primarily Muslim, Croats, who are primarily Catholic, and Serbs, who are primarily Orthodox. The consociational state, reinforced by ethnically divided neighborhoods and schools teaching different histories, has stymied the process of reconciliation and the creation of a unified national identity and effectively functioning national government. Nonetheless, a number of cross-ethnic women's nongovernmental organizations (NGOs) and networks, as well as women peacemakers, have emerged that are working to address human rights issues, to help create a unified state, and to increase the involvement of women in the formal political system, from which they have been largely excluded. Women Citizens for Constitutional Reform, Women's Network BIH,[1] and Mothers of Srebrenica are such groups that have been mobilizing networks of women's organizations throughout the county promoting healing, human rights, and justice through their various activities and rewriting the Constitution to honor human rights of all. *Peace with a Women's Face: Women's Initiative for Dealing with the Past* (Horozonti, n.d.) has been one of their notable projects. Nusreta Sivac is one peacemaker who has stepped out across wounds and ethnic boundaries to help renew the cosmopolitan society Bosnia was prior to the war.

Women's groups function by inclusive leadership dispersed throughout the country and united by common goals and common values. The groups' leadership has responded to the needs and requests of a diverse group of women followers who have cocreated the leadership to meet their own needs and aspirations for the country. These groups have blended civic art with humanitarian and political action to create a liminal space of transformation (Parent, 2016; Simmons, 2010).

Although government remains frozen in ethnic conflict and nationalist politics (Hodzic, 2015; Perry, 2018), Women Citizens for Constitutional Reform, Women's Network BIH, Mothers of Srebrenica, Nusreta Sivac, as well as other women's groups and peacemakers are helping to build an increasingly effective alternative to the dominant ethnically divisive and nationalistic government discourse. These groups have persevered for over 20 years, understanding that changing an entrenched government takes time and dedication (Avramovic, 2017; Cockburn, 2013a; Mulaic, 2011). Their work is an example of reconciliation and peacebuilding through human rights, two concepts that have often been considered as antithetical (Norquist, 2008; Parlevliet, 2017).

WOMEN AS PEACEMAKERS

Women victims organized during the war to provide humanitarian assistance and to maintain the functioning of society while their men were doing battle

(Spahic-Siljak, Spahic, & Bavcic, 2012). After 1995, international donors provided significant funding to support women NGOs to fulfill their agenda for ethnic reconciliation and peace. As a result, controversy emerged in the academic literature regarding whether Bosnian woman were merely puppets of an international agenda or were actually authors of a reconciled reality. The discussion also ensued regarding whether viewing women as peacemakers stereotyped their supposedly "essentialist nature" as caregivers or whether they were driven by feministic values (Helms, 2003, 2010; Jansen, 2010; Parent, 2016; Spahic-Siljak, n.d.; Walsh, 2000).

Regardless of such debates, women NGOs have moved the reconciliation agenda forward as evidenced by the discussions and debates that take place prior to elections, and some women peacemakers are happy to embrace "essentialist" qualities (Siljak, 2014; Simic, 2009), while others are staunchly feminist (Cockburn, 2013a, 2013b). As Siljak argued (2014), "women have the capacity to build peace and reconciliation by creating webs of relationships and networks, establishing very strong and at times unexpected links" (p. 13). Women's NGOs, she wrote, "work to heal the physical and spiritual traumas of war. They attempt to re-knit the fragile web of inter-ethnic and inter-religious solidarity in BIH" (Siljak, n.d., p. 1).

REQUIREMENTS FOR RECONCILIATION

Reconciliation is a relational social process "where harm is repaired in such a way that trust again can be established" (Norquist, 2008, p. 32). Components of the reconciliation process include "acknowledgement, contrition, truth telling, reparation, and justice" (Norquist, 2008, p. 32). These components drive the reconciliation work via human rights of the women's groups and peacemakers considered in this chapter. According to the 2016 Social Cohesion and Reconciliation Index (SCORE) for BIH, the propensity for reconciliation is relatively high (IMPAQ, 2016).

LIMINAL SPACE

Women's NGOs and peacemakers work in liminal space to recreate social relations and reality. Liminal spaces are "transitional or transformative spaces [...] waiting areas between one point in time and space and the next"

(Better help, 2018, pp. 2—14). "Liminal" comes from the Latin root "limen" that means "threshold." In liminal space:

> our old world [is] left behind, while we are not yet sure of the new existence [...] a good space where genuine newness can begin [...] sacred space where the old world is able to fall apart, and a bigger world is revealed. (Liminal space, n.d., n.p.)

Women's NGOs and peacemakers create liminal space by working through relationships that are unsupported by the current governmental order; by using civic art to shake up the daily reality, shift perceptions and perspectives, and catalyze the emergence of a renewed vision of society; by psychosocial healing of victims to help them transition to a state of wholeness; by political action in the streets, at the grassroots; by legal action to change the Constitution and laws that discriminate against marginalized groups; and by constantly creating a discourse of peace and harmony. Women especially use the "'free zone' of art to encourage communication and mutual responsibility between the government and citizenry" (Simmons, 2010, p. 1). As Siljak (2014) concluded:

> These women dared to imagine a life beyond the imposed boundaries of violence and fear. They accepted the challenge to embark into the unknown; their "moral imagination" was strong enough to encompass the complexity of circumstances and provide space for new opportunities. They knew that when one comes to the edge, "one of two things will happen — there will be something solid to stand on, or one will be taught to fly." (p. 10)

LEADERS AND FOLLOWERS

Women leaders who emerged during the war were engaged in humanitarian and social activities that met the needs of their followers, and hence, there was a natural harmony between leaders and followers; followers "created" leaders. Leaders promote the rights and welfare of followers by offering them healing, recognition, and participation in an egalitarian society, and hence leaders and followers share purpose and hope. Victims are empowered to become leaders in their own right through healing, training,[2] organizing, and leading initiatives for reconciliation in their own communities, thus proliferating the web of influence. Some NGOs also provide loans or grants to women to establish businesses, thus empowering them to take control of their lives (Rose, 2018).

APPROACH TO HUMAN RIGHTS

Human Rights of Deceased Victims

Women's NGOs work to keep the memory of the deceased alive purposely in order to memorialize them, to ensure that the process to try war criminals continues, but most significantly to obtain acknowledgment from the Serbs, the first step in reconciliation, that their massacre of 8000 Bosniaks at Srebrenica in July 1995 was, in fact, a genocide. Both the International Criminal Tribunal for the Former Yugoslavia and the International Court of Justice determined that this massacre fulfilled the genocide criteria. However, Serb political parties still reject this judgment, and in June 2018, the Government of Republika Srpska announced that there is still a need to clarify this determination of genocide (Burdeau, 2018).

Art, which by definition creates a liminal space, has been a major medium used by women's groups to keep the memory of the victims alive (Jensen, 2017). Photographic exhibitions of the Srebrenica and other massacre victims and their families have been held regularly for more than 20 years since the war ended. Each year on the anniversary of the Srebrenica genocide, gatherings are held in Potočari cemetery where the dead are buried and memorialized. Names of the victims are read each year at places throughout BIH. Mothers of Srebrenica, especially, have kept the memory of the massacre alive.

Street installations also memorialize the war and its victims. On April 6, 2012, 11,541 red chairs were lined up on Titova Street in Sarajevo to remember the victims, whose names were and continue to be written on displays throughout the city (Cooper, 2012; Kamber, 2012). Women's NGOs continuously inculcate a culture of remembrance in the public through films, conferences, debates, and artists continue to write novels and poems and create paintings, sculptures, and installations to honor victims and heal the trauma of the past.

Documentaries such as that of the 2009 *It Cannot Last Forever* (Simic, n.d.) interview both Bosniaks and Serbs who seek healing and reconciliation. Many Bosnian films, such as *Gori Vatra* about preparations for a postwar visit by former President Clinton, employ dark humor as an effective approach to heal the past much as Sarajevans did during the siege of Sarajevo as a technique of survival (Thompson & Ibrahimefendic, 2017).

Scholar Cynthia Simmons (2010), who identified artists who have worked after the war to both create a culture honoring the past and reconstructing a new postwar reality, called the dialogue that lies at the center of the work of women NGOs to foster peace, justice, and reconciliation also as "art" since it imagines a future.

HUMAN RIGHTS OF SURVIVING VICTIMS OF THE WAR

Hundreds of thousands of surviving victims of the war seek healing and reconciliation, and recognition of their human rights. Two major groups, especially, seek recognition, namely women who were raped, and survivors who were forced from their homes and became refugees in BIH and internationally. Rape as a strategy of ethnic cleansing (Bell-Fialkov, 1993) was widely employed during the war and at least 20,000 women were raped (Simic, n.d.; Simmons, 2010). Women's groups have worked to expose rape as a war crime, to provide psychosocial healing services for survivors, and to mobilize large numbers of women to transform this individual grievance into a legitimate social concern. Women's groups seek the human rights of these victims, also, through continued pressure to bring rapists to justice and to counter the social denial of this crime. More than 20 years after the war, hundreds of war criminals have not been prosecuted and many women victims of rape still live in communities with their rapists.[3]

The International Criminal Tribunal for the former Yugoslavia found, for the first time in judicial history, that rape was "used by members of the Bosnian Serb armed forces as an instrument of terror" (Bassiouni & McCormick, 1996; Kunarac, Kovac, & Vucovik, n.d.; Simic, n.d.). Further, the United Nations finally recognized rape as a war crime in 2008 (Hodzic, 2015).

Despite these rulings, "rape camps" have not been properly commemorated, a necessary step so that acknowledgment can lead the way to reconciliation. Leadership to expose the horrors of the rape camps and rape, in general, is challenging due to denial and trauma and such leadership takes considerable commitment and personal sacrifice. Nusreta Sivac, a judge before the war, was a victim of the rape camp in Prijedor, an industrial town in northwestern Bosnia. After Prijedor was taken over by Serb forces, Sivac and 36 other women were taken to Omarska camp outside Prijedor, where they were held and raped until international exposure forced the closure of the camp. Immediately after her release, she and other survivors became active and committed themselves to gather information and stories of other victims, using any means possible to expose the scope of the suffering and calling for the prosecution of war criminals and justice for victims (United Nations, 2009, n.d.).

Bosnian filmmaker Jasmina Zbanic's films have confronted the sensitive story of women raped and tortured during the war. Her 2006 film *Gravica: Land of My Dreams* tells of the struggles of a rape victim after the war and her 2013 film *For Those Who Can Tell no Tales* tells the story of the torture and rape of over 200 women and the ethnic cleansing of over 3000 Bosniaks in Visegrad as a way to memorialize them and keep their memory alive until justice can be served (Hak, 2016). These films have used liminal space as an effective approach to mobilize followers who continue to demand acknowledgment by and the prosecution of war criminals.

Sivac was also an internally displaced person, having been forced to abandon her home in Prijedor. After the war, Sivac assumed the role of a leader of the returnees and returned to Prijedor to reclaim her home, a courageous but dangerous decision, given the fact that Priejedor was now part of the Republika Srpska and inhabited almost exclusively by Serbs. She suffered constant intimidation, even to the point that "Omarska"concentration camp name was carved on the door of her apartment.

Sivac and other returnees to Prijedor began to mobilize, starting with commemorations and then demanding recognition and memorialization of the atrocities that took place there. Some gestures of acknowledgment were made in 2013 by Serb Mayor Marko Pavić who visited a newly discovered mass grave of Bosniaks in Tomašica. The returnee community, local activists, and Bosnian and international supporters began commemorating "White Armband Day" each May 31 in memory of May 31, 1992, when Serb authorities ordered all non-Serbs to wear white armbands. Despite receiving international recognition and many honors, Sivac and many other victims are still marginalized in their hometown. But, their persistence to talk, organize, participate in public events, and constantly engage with authorities has created an environment in which there are open discussions so that the war crimes are not pushed aside. They have directly confronted the culture of silence that permeates Bosnia. As a consequence, survivors and supporters in Prijedor are working together for reconciliation and a redefinition of their future through liminal space.

Some victims have sought healing and reconciliation through psychosocial approaches that help women confront their enemies, heal their trauma, reconcile, and build a new narrative of peace and coexistence (Hart & Colo, 2014). Mixed ethnic groups of women tell their stories, seek compassion, understanding, and forgiveness, and reconciliation, rewriting the ethnically divisive narrative promulgated by the government and political parties. Their narrative is the liminal space of possible social transformation. Reaching people on a psychological level and building empathy and understanding have a major potential to encourage reconciliation (Avramovic, 2017) and to empower victims to assume leadership roles in helping others.

HUMAN RIGHTS OF MINORITIES

The fundamental challenge BIH currently faces is how to create a unified State with a stronger national government, which, until recently, was a requirement for accession to the European Union (EU) (Dapo & Ridic, 2015). A new Constitution must be written based upon unity rather than divisiveness, and recognition of the rights of all peoples, not only the constituent peoples. Since 1996, the BIH constitution has been questioned due to its failure to provide human rights for all. The country collective presidency and several other positions can be held solely by the three constituent peoples and only when they reside where these peoples are the majority.

In 2009, in the case of Sejdić & Finci filed by two members of Bosnian Jewish and Roma communities, the European Court of Human Rights declared these sections of the constitution discriminatory. It was expected that BIH would amend the discriminatory constitutional provisions and provide all citizens equal rights. Several attempts at reform have been made, including the April Package in 2006, the Prud Agreement of 2008, and the Butmir Process of 2009 (Kavish, 2012), but all have failed due to Serb, Bosniak, and Croat leaders who have been developed entrenched and powerful special interests.

Women Citizens for Constitutional Reform, established in 2013, are working on constitutional reform across ethnic and gender boundaries and at the grassroots level throughout BIH. The network upholds five principles that should be manifested in the new constitution, namely (1) application of gender-sensitive language in the revised Constitution; (2) introduction of affirmative measures in the Constitution in order to accomplish full sex and gender equality; (3) amendments to the existing Catalogue of Fundamental Rights with provisions regarding unique health, social, and family care; (4) affirmation of a higher level of judicial and legal protection of human rights and freedoms, and (5) introduction of the principle of direct democracy in the process of constitutional reform.

Women citizens have been meeting with senior officials, Ambassadors, political parties, and human rights advocates to promote their agenda and push change. On July 28, 2018, in Ethno Village "Stanišići" in Bijeljina, the Initiative organized a round table to discuss the need for a revised Constitution. Twenty-two participants in the round table included representatives of the political parties that comprise part of the city government and civil society organizations led by women working to improve the position of marginalized women. Representatives of the citizens' committees of political parties that will be on the candidate lists in upcoming general elections were interested in the discussion and expressed the desire to have a formal lecture on the issue in the future (GradjankeZaUstavnePromjene, 2018a).

The network works at the grassroots level also, talking to women on the streets throughout the country to inspire them to join the cause and make their positions known to the local political machinery. An example of this street action took place on July 4, 2018, in the city square in Zenica, where women supporters asked women on the street to sign a petition to change the constitution (GradjankeZaUstavnePromjene, 2018b). Street-canvassing is one way women leaders work to empower other women war victims to take charge of their future and become leaders.

HUMAN RIGHTS OF MARGINALIZED GROUPS

Women's NGOs have worked for the human rights of marginalized groups such as the Roma, LGBTI, certain religious groups considered as sects, and others that have suffered prejudice and exclusion.

The coauthor Edin worked on a case involving a Roma woman who needed emergency surgery because her fetus had died in her womb and would cause sepsis if not removed. Since she did not have state medical insurance, the hospital demanded the equivalent of 500 Euros, an amount far beyond the ability of her scrap metal dealer husband to afford. BIH has comprehensive laws on medical insurance which are available to everybody.

However, there are strict deadlines to register. Roma generally have problems with the bureaucracy because they move and often live for years in a place without identification or registration. The Office of the Ombudsperson received a complaint from the NGO that represented the Roma woman and, after conducting an investigation, issued a recommendation to authorities to adjust and implement programs in a way that suits groups whose lifestyle and circumstances are specific. By applying standards and procedures that look neutral to a group such as the Roma who are in an unequal position, the state is indirectly discriminating against them. The issue catalyzed extensive public discussion and news coverage. In 2013, Bosnian filmmaker Danis Tanovic made a critically acclaimed movie called *An Episode in the Life of an Iron Picker*, about the incident, again using liminal space to shake up the accepted reality and show the way to a possible new inclusive one.

HUMAN RIGHTS OF WOMEN

As in all wars, women in BIH were required to keep society running during the war, and consequently, they took on increased responsibility and had greater decision-making authority than prior to the war. However, also as in other wars, they were forced to return to a highly patriarchal society following the war and were totally excluded from the formal peacemaking process. There were no BIH women present at the negotiations or signing of the Dayton Accord (Spahic-Siljak et al., 2012). The challenge women are now facing, hence, is how to ensure the inclusion of gender language in the Constitution and their inclusion in the formal political process. Women's NGOs are working together to promote women's rights and to develop more influence in the official political system so that politicians listen to the demands of the grassroots. Violent demonstrations in 2014 throughout the country by the population discontented with the government's inability to solve problems caused by the transition from socialism to capitalism (Borger, 2012; Sejfija & Fink-Hafner, 2016) illustrate the tension that exists between citizenry and leaders that women NGOs are trying to bridge. Further, the thus far successful effort of the women of Kruščica to halt the construction of a hydropower dam by foreign investors, despite police violence, and to successfully elect their own representative in the community assembly illustrates that the women-created civil society is garnering political power (Save the Blue Heart of Europe, 2018).

CONCLUSION AND LESSONS FOR PEACEMAKERS

Despite ethnically oriented leadership in the government, women NGOs and networks and women peacemakers continue to build an alternative reconciliatory narrative and an increasingly strong inter-ethnic civil society. BIH offers an example of how victim leaders who emerged during the war continued to heal and empower other victims who then became leaders, established NGOs, and continued to heal and empower other victims, until all of BIH has been networked with collaborating NGOs, building a civil society whose influence has increased over time. Their alternative narrative of reconciliation is filling up larger liminal spaces and has the potential to create a civil society influential enough to push the government's divisive narrative aside and replace it with the narrative of unity and inclusiveness. The need for women's NGOs to construct an alternative narrative could have been assuaged had women been involved in the peace process. Left by their men to operate society during the war, they had the knowledge and experience to help re-establish the fabric of a recovering society and the country could benefit from their involvement in the development and implementation of post-conflict strategies. Treating women as victims justified their exclusion, but women proved that they could transform this victimhood into powerful action. Women's NGOs are influencing the public sector and the international community, pushing for structural and institutional reforms, enabling women's agency and decision-making. They are empowering women and girls to achieve their full and equal human rights and unsettling patriarchal, sexual hierarchies, customs, and the structural conditions that made violence possible.

NOTES

1. The 23 NGO members of Women Citizen's for Constitutional Reform include NGOs promoting women's rights and political activism, ending domestic violence, women's legal issues, peacebuilding, and psychosocial healing, cooperation between women and development of democratic processes, reconciliation, and peacebuilding. The 24 NGO members of the Women's Network BIH focus on women's equality and economic and political empowerment, safe houses for victims of domestic violence, promotion of culture and the arts, local-level political involvement, protection and promotion of human rights of all groups, mental health, and freedom of information.

2. The coauthor Edin interviewed, the President of the Women Citizens' for Constitutional Reform and member of Foundation CURE, and she gave examples of workshops and seminars they have organized for women's empowerment and how empowered women work to transform their communities. Workshops helped empower women "returnees" to Bratunac, for example. A war widow in Konjevic Polje who ran her farm alone opened a beauty salon after much wrangling with local officials who eventually gave her a grant to open the salon.

3. Rape is a highly stigmatized crime in BIH and women who were raped are blamed and often outcasts in their families and communities. Bosniak women, especially, are stigmatized due to the dictates of Islam. Many Serb children were born from raped Bosniak women, who were not allowed by the culture to keep them. Hence, the women who openly admit to being raped and who fight for criminality of rape and prosecution of their rapists are courageous leaders of this internationally important cause. Their efforts have resulted in the determination that rape is a war crime.

ACKNOWLEDGMENT

The authors would like to acknowledge Vildana Dzekman for her useful contributions to this chapter.

REFERENCES

Avramovic, I. (2017). Reconciliation in Bosnia and Herzegovina. *Beyond Intractability*. Retrieved from https://www.beyondintractability.org/casestudy/Avramovi%C4%87-Bosnia-Herzegovina

Bassiouni, C., & McCormick, M. (1996). *Sexual violence: An invisible weapon of war in the former Yugoslavia*. International Human Rights Institute, Strasbourg, France, Occasional Paper 1. Retrieved from http://mcherifbassiouni.com/wp-content/uploads/Sexual-Violence-an-Invisible-Weapon-of-War.pdf

Bell-Fialkov, A. (1993). A brief history of ethnic cleansing. *Foreign Affairs*. Retrieved from https://www.foreignaffairs.com/articles/1993-06-01/brief-history-ethnic-cleansing

Better Help. (2018). *Understanding how liminal space is different from other places*. Retrieved from https://www.betterhelp.com/advice/general/understan ding-how-liminal-space-is-different-from-other-places/

Borger, J. (2012). Bosnia war 20 years on: Peace holds but conflict continues to haunt. *The Guardian*. Retrieved from https://www.theguardian.com/world/ 2012/apr/04/bosnian-war-20-years-on

Burdeau, C. (2018). Rewriting history: Bosnian Serbs question Srebrenica genocide. *Courthouse News Service*. Retrieved from https://www.courthousenews. com/rewriting-history-bosnian-serbs-question-srebrenica-genocide/

Cockburn, C. (2013a). Against the odds: Sustaining feminist momentum in post-war Bosnia-Herzegovina. *Women's Studies International Forum*, 37, 26–33.

Cockburn, C. (2013b). When is peace? Women's post-accord experiences in three countries. *Soundings*, 53, 143–159.

Cooper, R. (2012). Bosnia remembers: Empty chairs laid out in Sarajevo in memory of the 11, 541 killed twenty years after bloody conflict began. *Daily Mail*. Retrieved from http://www.dailymail.co.uk/news/article-2126117/Bosnia-remembers-11–541-chairs-laid-Sarajevo-memory-dead-20-years-bloody-confli ct-began.html

Dapo, E., & Ridic, O. (2015). What does the European Union's new approach bring to Bosnia and Herzegovina (B&H). *Epiphany: Journal of Transdisciplinary Studies*, 8(2), 227–235.

GradjankeZaUstavnePromjene. (2018a). *Engendering constitutional changes: Center of women's rights from Zenica organized street action*. Retrieved from https://womencitizensforconstitutionalreform.wordpress. com/2018/07/17/engendering-constitutional-changes-center-of-womens-rights-from-zenica-organized-street-action/

GradjankeZaUstavnePromjene. (2018b). *Politicians from Bijeljina supported the initiative "women citizens for constitutional reform."* Retrieved from https:// womencitizensforconstitutionalreform.wordpress.com/2018/08/03/politicians-from-bijeljina-supported-the-initiative-women-citizens-for-constitutional-reform/

Hak, A. (2016). 5 Bosnian films you need to see. *Culture Trip*. Retrieved from https://theculturetrip.com/europe/bosnia-herzegovina/articles/5-bosnian-films-you-need-to-see/#

Hart, B., & Colo, E. (2014). Psychological peacebuilding in Bosnia and Herzegovina: Approaches to relational and social change. *Intervention*, 12(1), 76–87.

Helms, E. (2003). Women as agents of ethnic reconciliation? Women's NGOs and international intervention in postwar Bosnia-Herzegovina. *Women's Studies International Forum*, 26(1), 15–33.

Helms, E. (2010). The gender of coffee: Women and reconciliation initiatives in post-war Bosnia and Herzegovina. *Focaal-Journal of Global and Historical Anthropology*, 57, 17–32.

Hodzic, R. (2015). Twenty years since Srebrenica: No reconciliation, we're still at war. *ICTJ*. Retrieved from https://www.ictj.org/news/twenty-years-srebrenica-no-reconciliation-we're-still-war

Horozonti. (n.d.). *Peace with women's face: Women's initiative for dealing with the past*. Retrieved from http://horizonti.ba/en/peace-with-womens-face-womens-initiative/

IMPAQ. (2016). *Gender analysis report for Bosnia and Herzegovina*. USAID. Retrieved from http://www.measurebih.com/uimages/Edited20GA20Report20 MEASURE-BiH.pdf

Jansen, S. (2010). Of wolves and men: Postwar reconciliation and the gender of inter-national encounters. *Focaal-Journal of Global and Historical Anthropology*, 57, 33–49.

Jensen, L. (2017). Using film to empower youth reconciliation in Bosnia and Herzegovina. *Democracy Speaks* blog. Retrieved from http://www.democracyspeaks.org/blog/using-film-empower-youth-reconciliation-bosnia-herzegovina

Kamber, A. (2012). *Sarajevo's Red Line* [video]. Institute for War and Peace, London, England. Retrieved from https://www.youtube.com/watch?v=XSC1NWKoVmI

Kavish, D. (2012). *Constitutional reform in Bosnia and Herzegovina: State-nation theory and the spirit of the Dayton Accords*. Retrieved from http://juisblog.global.wisc.edu/wp-content/uploads/2013/10/Click-here-to-download-PDF.pdf

Kunarac, Kovac, & Vucovik (n.d.). *Centre for women, peace, and security.* Retrieved from http://blogs.lse.ac.uk/vaw/landmark-cases/a-z-of-cases/kunarac-kovac-and-vukovic-case/

Liminalspace. (n.d.). *What is liminal space?* Retrieved from https://inaliminal space.org/about-us/what-is-a-liminal-space/

Mulaic, M. (2011). Women's NGOs and civil society building in Bosnia-Herzegovina. *Epiphany, 4*(1), 40–55.

Norquist, K. (2008). *The crossroads of human rights and peacebuilding – An ongoing debate.* Research Paper Series No. 2. Stockholm School of Theology, Sweden. Retrieved from http://www.ehs.se/sites/default/files/general/paper_no2. pdf

Parent, G. (2016). Local peacebuilding, trauma, and empowerment in Bosnia-Herzegovina. *Peace and Change, 41*(4), 2–28.

Parlevliet, M. (2017). Human rights and peacebuilding: Complementary and contradictory, complex and contingent. *Journal of Human Rights Practice, 9*(3), 333–357.

Perry, V. (2018). Frozen, stalled, stuck, or just muddling through: the post-Dayton frozen conflict in Bosnia and Herzegovina. *Asia Europe Journal, 16*(57), 1–21.

Rose, E. (2018). *Brick by brick: The women helping Bosnia heal.* Balkan Transitional Justice. Retrieved from http://www.balkaninsight.com/en/article/brick-by-brick-the-women-helping-bosnia-heal-08–20-2018

Save the Blue Heart of Europe. (2018). *Another victory for the brave women of Kruščica.* Retrieved from https://www.balkanrivers.net/en/news/another-victory-"brave-women-kruščica"

Sejfija, I., & Fink-Hafner, D. (2016). Citizens' protest innovations in a consociational system: The case of Bosnia-Herzegovina. *Teorija in Praksa, 53*(1).

Siljak, Z. S. (2014). *Shining humanity: Life stories of women in Bosnia and Herzegovina.* Cambridge, England: Cambridge Scholars Publishing. Retrieved from http://www.tpo.ba/b/dokument/SHINING%20HUMANITY%20Introd.pdf

Siljak, Z. S. (n.d.). Women, religion, and peace leadership in Bosnia and Herzegovina. *Ewi Fellowship Programme Unpublished Report.* Retrieved from http://www.eiz.hr/wp-content/uploads/2014/12/Zilka-Spahic-Siljak-ENG.pdf

Simic, O. (2009). What remains of Srebrenica? Motherhood, transitional justice and yearning for truth. *Journal of International Women's Studies*, *10*(4), 220–236.

Simic, O. (n.d.). *Activism for peace in Bosnia and Herzegovina: A gender perspective*. Melbourne Law School Article 11. Retrieved from http://www. globalmediajournal.com/open-access/activism-for-peace-in-bosnia-and-herzegovina-a-gender-perspective.pdf

Simmons, C. (2010). Women engaged/engaged art in Postwar Bosnia: Reconciliation, recovery, and civil society, Pittsburgh, PA. *The Carl Beck Papers in Russia & East European Studies*. Retrieved from https:// carlbeckpapers.pitt.edu/ojs/ind ex.php/cbp/article/view/150/151

Spahic-Siljak, Z. (n.d.). Do it and name it: Feminist theology and peace building in Bosnia and Herzegovia. *Journal of Feminist Studies in Religion*, *29*(2), 176–188.

Spahic-Siljak, Z., Spahic, A., & Bavcic, E. (2012). *Women and peacebuilding in BH: Baseline study*. Sarajevo: TPO Foundation Sarajevo. Retrieved from http://www.tpo.ba/b/dokument/Baseline%20ENG%20Women%20and%20 Peacebuilding%20in%20BH.pdf

Thompson, R., & Ibrahimefendic. (2017). The cellist of Sarajevo: Courage and deviance through music as inspirations for social change. In S. J. Erenrich & J. F. Wergin (Eds.), *Grassroots Leadership and the Arts for Social Change* (Chapter 1, pp. 3–28). Bingley: Emerald Publishing Limited.

United Nations. (2009). Nusreta Sivac: Speech given at the Durban Review Conference, Geneva, April 2009. *Voices*. Retrieved from http://www.un.org/ en/durbanreview2009/pdf/Nusreta%20Sivac.pdf

United Nations. (n.d.). *The story of Nusreta Sivac*. Retrieved from https:// www.ohchr.org/EN/NewsEvents/Pages/StoryOfNusretaSivac.aspx

Walsh, M. (2000). *Aftermath: The role of women's organizations in post conflict Bosnia and Herzegovina*, Washington, DC. USAID Center for Development Information and Evaluation Working Paper No. 308.

10

CLIMATE JUSTICE: BUILDING OPPORTUNITIES FOR WOMEN'S PARTICIPATION AND LEADERSHIP IN THE CLIMATE CHANGE REGIME

Douglas de Castro

ABSTRACT

The International Climate Change Regime is important for the very survival of the humankind. However, the unimpressive results and escalation of the challenges are becoming very dangerous. By looking into participation at the international level, this chapter finds that women's participation is very low. The chapter relies on the Feminist Theory for International Law and Relations to argue that the international regime is lacking women's leadership traits as solidarity, creativity, and resilience. The cases of the El Nino in Peru, local farming in Brazil, and energy efficiency for cookstoves in Kenya present positive examples in which women's participation is essential, generating a model bottom-up that includes local and transnational levels that fill that gap that risks global environmental and human health and life itself.

Keywords: Climate change; feminist theory; participation; local and transnational networks; climate justice; leadership

INTRODUCTION

Castro (2018) points out that one of the causes of the failure of the International Climate Change Regime is the lack of women's participation and engagement. As such, current features of International Law present metanarratives that homogenize politics, law, and values based on the European model, which promotes a subtle form of domination by creating scenarios of non-existence and invisibility of the women (Eslava, Fakhri, & Nesiah, 2017; Lyotard & Jameson, 1984). As such, the climate justice surfaces as an important aspect for the Global South population, considering that they are the most affected parties by the growing climate disruptions around the globe (Nixon, 2013). To Sweetman (2009, p. 115), the inequality between women and men in participating connects with the concept of climate justice:

> [...] gender aspects are rarely addressed in climate-change policy, either at the national or at the international levels. Reasons include gaps in gender-sensitive data and knowledge about the links between gender justice and climate change; and the lack of participation of women and gender experts in climate-related negotiations.

Climate justice according to Heyward and Roser (2016) is connected to the fact that the climate changes affect the most vulnerable people in the planet, who are already in a situation of distress due to poverty and hunger to name a few social and economic variables. In this perspective, women are the most vulnerable group, along with children and the elderly that are usually under their care. For instance, Wouters, Dukhovny, and Allan (2007, p. 81) in reporting the array of environmental problems in the Aral Sea inform that "traces of pesticide were found in women's milk."

As such, according to the postcolonial feminist theory, women are "in a unique position to articulate the politics of lived reality in its theoretical and material forms" (Zuckerwise, 2014), which provides an empowering and critical intervention in the form we perceive the climate change regime to incorporate the missing concepts of hope, creativity, resilience, persistence, and solidarity.

Therefore, the objective of this chapter is presenting the central role of the women's participation and leadership in the climate change regime as necessary to increase the levels of climate justice and environmental security in the Global South.

THE LACK OF WOMEN PARTICIPATION IN THE INTERNATIONAL CLIMATE REGIME

Countries recognize that climate change is no longer a challenge that is far away but a phenomenon that requires immediate action (Alam, Atapattu, Gonzalez, & Razzaque, 2015; Warming World, 2018).

As a logical stance, nowadays as in any historical moment of mankind, dealing with global threats such as climate change requires a high level of cooperation to ensure survival itself. However, observing the engagement of the countries in dealing with climate change presents a disconcerting apathy vis-à-vis the magnitude of the threat and the potential spillover to another dimension.

As a form of addressing the challenge in the global dimension, the United Nations has to press on calling countries to implement a legal order capable of containing and reducing the anthropomorphic effects in the climate. As a direct result of the United Nations Conference on the Human Environment (Stockholm, 1972) and the United Nations Conference on Environment and Development (Rio, 1992), the legal backbone of the climate change regime is built: (1) the United Nations Framework Conference on Climate Change (1992); (2) the Kyoto Protocol (1998); and (3) the Paris Agreement (2015).

An analysis of the Provisional List of Participants in the preparatory meetings for signing these conventions shows a distressing view regarding the participation of women. The Lists selected randomly are the following: Geneva, 1991, section 2; Nairobi, 1991, section 3; Geneva, 1991, section 4; New York, 1991, section 5; New York, 1991, section 5-II; Geneva, 1992, section 6; New York, 1993, section 6; Geneva, 1993, section 8; Kyoto, 1997, section 3; Paris, 2015, section 20; and Marrakesh, 2016, section 22.

Figure 1 shows the participation of public officials in the preparatory meetings to build the legal structure for an international climate change order, in which the average of participation is 70% men and 30% women.

The participation of civil society through NGOs in the discussions of climate change presents a similar ratio as observed in Figure 2. This empirical

Figure 1. Participation of Public Officials.

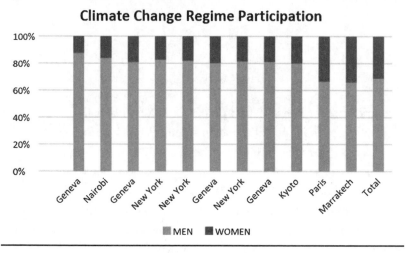

Figure 2. NGO Participation.

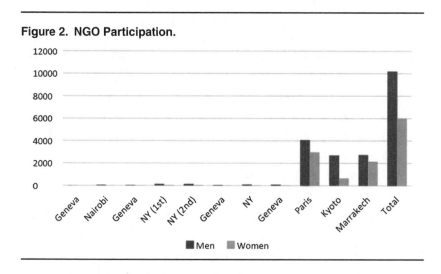

evidence contests the assumption that ONGs are spaces for more open and democratic participation of women than governments (Agarwal, 2009). However, rather than seeking the causes for this contradiction, this study presents the arguments for increasing women's participation as a form of increasing the distribution of climate justice.

WOMEN LEADERSHIP INTERVENTION IN THE CLIMATE CHANGE REGIME

As observed, there are spaces at the international and national levels in both government and non-government that need to be occupied by women.

However, before engaging in discussions regarding the importance of women's intervention and the available spaces for this intervention, it is worth making a general statement about climate ethics and more specifically how to account for the normative dimension of the climate change regime in which women are an essential part of distributing justice.

To Simon Caney, there are four dimensions in which agents have to act in order to ensure climate justice: (1) climate change policy must specify a particular target; (2) climate change policy should identify duty-bearers and specify who should perform how much of which climatic responsibilities; (3) climate change policy should not result in the imposition of unfair "burdens" on others; and (4) climate change policy should honor additional moral ideals (Heyward & Roser, 2016). Therefore, within this normative framework, women's participation and leadership traits at local and transnational level become essential to increase the results in dealing with the burdens imposed by the climate change and to push the discussions and action at the international level, which is marked by an unimpressive political response.

In the next part of the chapter, we present the empirical evidence that the climate change regime might gain powerful traction within the framework provided by Simon Caney and the women's leadership.

The Necessary Intervention — Leadership Traits

The existential threat posed by climate changes and the dubious results of the existing regime should be enough incentives for increasing women's participation by occupying spaces of leadership, as the feminine experience and nature intervene by incorporating to the discussions the concepts of hope, creativity, resilience, persistence, and solidarity, all central to feminist theories (McCann & Kim, 2013; Tickner, 2001; Tickner & Sjoberg, 2011). Translated into the lexicon of international politics, dealing with climate change requires a constructivist approach in which individual experiences and identities are important (Demeritt, 2006; Sweetman, 2009).

Figure 3. WordCloud – United Nations Framework Conference on Climate Change, Kyoto Protocol, and the Paris Agreement.

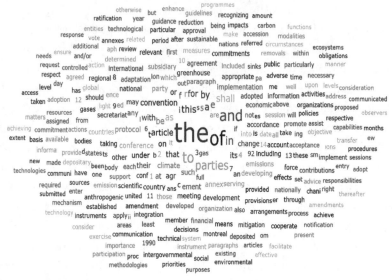

Source: Author using ATLAS.ti.

As observed in **Figure 3**, in the international dimension of dealing with climate change, the concepts do not show up even marginally or to some extent similar to important terms in the agreements, thus confirming the prescription uttered by Sweetman (2009) in regard to the need of higher participation of women.

In a survey conducted in 2008 by the Pew Research Center, the report "A Paradox in Public Attitudes Men or Women: Who's the Better Leader?" shows that there are eight important leadership traits in the public arena for men and women. As observed in **Figure 4**, women ranked higher than men in honesty, intelligence, compassion, creativity, and outgoingness. Thus, the concepts that are lacking in the international climate regime are exactly the ones present in the leadership traits of the women in both government and civil society dimensions. Villagrasa (2002, p. 43) in presenting a recommendation to deal with climate change states that "[...] aren't gender specific, but I believe they could appeal particularly to women, who tend to share knowledge more easily than men."

Figure 4. Leadership Traits Based on a Paradox in Public Attitudes Men or Women: Who's the Better Leader?

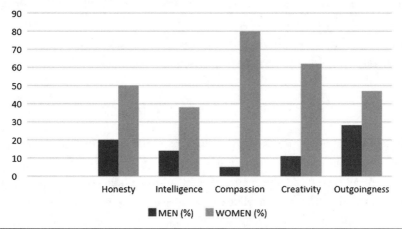

Figure 5. Co-occurrence Feminist Concepts X Leadership Traits.

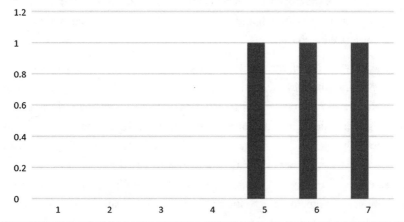

Figure 5 presents compelling empirical evidence to confirm our argument. The co-occurrence analysis of feminist concepts and leadership traits score in both aspects in the intersections of solidarity/compassion, creativity, and persistence/resilience/outgoingness.

Therefore, addressing the challenges posed by the climate change adequately and increasing its normative dimension in the climate justice concept is necessary to increase the women's participation in the international, regional, and national levels, as well as in the government and civil society initiatives. Thus, paraphrasing Sukarno in the Bandung Conference, this is necessary to "[…] inject the voice of reason into world affairs."

Spaces for Intervention – A Local-to-international Strategy

In terms of strategy to increase the participation, considering that the traditional space of production of International Law presents obstacles for participation as observed, the national and transnational spaces assume a fundamental role in the emancipatory and participatory locus for effective participation and leadership for women (Baksh-Soodeen & Harcourt, 2015; Gupta, Grijp, & Kuik, 2013; True & Mintrom, 2001). This bottom-up strategy is what Tétreault and Lipschutz (2009, p. 3) suggest:

> Each person has a history (upbringing, family-supplied resources such as emotional security, nutrition, and education), individual capacities (intelligence, health, energy, and attractiveness), interests (social and economic), and temperament (optimism/pessimism, initiative/passivity).

The complexity of the challenge in dealing with climate change is best handle in the microlevels, as the responses might be "[…] categorized into mitigation and adaptation – the former involving efforts to reduce greenhouse gas emissions, and the latter involving strategies to adapt to predicted changes" (Ingwersen, Garmestani, Gonzalez, & Templeton, 2014, p. 1). In this sense, while women in rural areas are considered part of the most vulnerable group to climate changes (especially in the Global South), they are the most prominent and efficient agents of positive transformation (Dankelman, 2002). Their influence over the alternatives and solutions to alleviate anthropogenic pressures to the environment and climate change is very high, thus essential for remodeling the phenomenological understanding of the human–object and human–human relationships in the contemporary society in the quest of the Aristotelian "good life" (Wilke, 2014).

There are many initiatives worldwide that we might offer to illustrate our point of view and reinforce our argument. However, we have selected some cases that evidence how important women's leadership is. The common trace for the cases is the location for the participation and specific target: rural areas and food security.

Women in Peru – Addressing El Niño Effects

The losses and damages sustained during the El Niño event caused household income to fall dramatically during 1997 and increased the exposure of rural households to acute food insecurity, hitting women and children disproportionally compared to men. The lack of appropriate governmental response to the crisis pushed the women in the Piura region to form local organizations to secure for themselves and children forms increasing food security. Among the organizations were the Comités de Vaso de Leche ("glass of milk committees"), Comedores Populares (popular canteens), and Clubes de Madres ("mothers club"), which associated with The Centre for Andean Advancement and Development (CEPRODA MINGA) and the Oxford Committee for Famine Relief (OXFAM), gained traction politically to face the challenges and promote a more equitable distribution of food and other goods necessary to survival and rebuilding.

The objectives of the CEPRODA MINGA network were to surpass mere discussions over risks and adaptation of climate changes but to consider "[...] how communities might build new kinds of social and political relationships and institutions" (Reyes, 2002, p. 67). Therefore, the goal was to go beyond survival to the more active participation of women in the political decision-making process, until then invisible regarding public participation. This active participation spilled over issues of education, health, violence, abuse, and other issues that although far from being accepted as normal, increased women's capacity-building and participation to intervene in the public arena and develop national and regional networks to increase the legitimacy (DeMars, 2005; Holton, 2007).

Family Farming Practices in Brazil – Women at the Center

Another dimension of the participation and leadership prominence at national and regional levels is the small farming practices. Local farming is more efficient regarding food production to increase food security and protect biodiversity, both systematically connected to climate change (Shiva, 2011). As stated by Bello (2009, p. 13):

> [...] a World Bank report on agriculture in Argentina, Brazil, Chile, Colombia, and Ecuador showed that small farms were three to fourteen times more productive per acre than their larger competitors.

In Brazil, some estimates account that 70% of the total food consumed by people is produced in local farming, which indicates a model that distributes food locally with no need to transport it in long distances, thus consuming fossil fuel as energy (Greenpeace, 2017). Despite the difference in data, spaces for participation and improvement are huge as the country is the eighth producer of food in local farms; however, as public policy, local farming does not receive the same incentives as monocultures for exportation receive (Secretaria Especial de Agricultura Familiar e do Desenvolvimento Agrário, 2018).

The participation of women in the Brazilian agriculture accounts for 14 million women, which was recognized in 2003 by the former president Luiz Inácio Lula da Silva by creating the National Secretary of Women's Rights. As one of the goals of the Secretary is to create programs and action plans to generate incentives and credit lines for women participation, such as the National Program for Strengthening Family Agriculture (PRONAF).

The PRONAF is part of the National Development Bank (BNDES) that possess a special line of credit for rural women (Pronaf Mulher) with an interest of 2.5%/year. Also, the Human Rights Secretary created in 2008 the Rural Women for Production Organization with the purpose of strengthening organizations, small farms, and cooperatives to access local and regional markets.

The National Union for Rural Workers possess chapters that include Family Farming and Gender that account for mobilization all over Brazil to increase women participation in the decision-making processes involving issues directly or indirectly connected to them by taking social relations to another level and working for the recognition of their rights. As stated by (Sales, 2007), women in Brazil are heavy:

> [...] engaged in family agricultural production. In spite of certain invisibility, women are occupying fields, planting, and harvesting. At the same time, they are longing for a free land where they can work.

The Contribution of Kenyan Women to Sustainable Energy and Climate Change Regime

According to the World Bank, there are approximately 3.04 billion people in the world that use biomass energy for cooking as well as for meeting other household energy needs. Despite technology and economic growth, estimates indicate that by 2030, 2.5 billion people will still cook with biomass-based fuels (Global Tracking Framework 2017 – Progress Toward Sustainable Energy 2017). For that reason, Makhabane (2002, p. 84) in debating the role of women stated that:

> […] gendered implications of climate change and energy policies need to be explored and addressed, and an understanding of women's particular knowledge and usage of energy resources should be integrated into mitigation initiatives.

Kenya relies heavily on its forest resources to steer economic growth through the provision of forest goods and services. Over 80% of Kenyans depend on forests for the provision of domestic energy in the form of charcoal and firewood (Kenya Economic Survey, 2016).

The problem presents a two-fold challenge. First, forests in Kenya are decreasing as indicates the World Bank, indicating that in 1990 the forest coved 8.3% of the territory, dropping to 7.8% in 2015 (World Bank, 2015). Second, due to decreasing the forest coverage and the reliance on coal for energy, the World Health Organization estimates that more than 15,000 die prematurely, and 13.000 become disable due to indoor air pollution in Kenya. Although data are scarce and to a certain point limited, it is reasonable to assume that the largest part of the deaths and disabilities hit women, children, and elderly in the household. The Mapping of the Impact of Unclean Cooking Technologies Report states that: "Aggravated Asthma, disproportionately affected more women than men and children in the region."

As such, due to the negative effects associated with the use of inefficient cookstoves for cooking and heating, GROOTS Kenya (a non-governmental organization founded in 1995 during the Beijing Conference) and the Clean Cook Stoves Association of Kenya (CCAK), supported by the Netherlands Development Organization, have initiated an Evidence-Based Policy Dialogue Project on clean cooking aimed at increasing the adoption rate of clean cooking practices in the Kitui County, Kenya.

According to one of the findings in the Mapping of the Impact of Unclean Cooking Technologies Report:

> [...] it would be critical that a number of youth and women groups
> be identified and trained in the production and repair of the
> improved cookstoves. By doing so, the county government and
> partners will equally be contributing to improved employment
> amongst the youth, and ensure that the supply of the clean cooking
> stoves is sustained. (p. 8)

Thus, part of the solution in securing clean air for the household, especially to women, children, and the elderly, is to make cookstoves more efficient in burning wood and releasing smoke. The efficiency rate of the cookstove is connected to less smoke released into the air and less wood burned, thus decreasing the wood extraction from forests that increase CO_2 absorption area. Due to the direct impact on women, the project receives investments from several financial institutions, including the most significant the Kenya Women Finance Trust, and the Women Enterprise Fund.

Working in connection to these institutions, the Global Network on Gender and Sustainable Energy (ENERGIA) has achieved since its foundation in 1995 the construction of a strong network:

> [...] one regional, two sub-regional, and nine national focal points,
> all of which are in Africa. These national and regional networks
> adhere to ENERGIA's basic principles, which are to empower
> women and engender energy for sustainable development.

Also, the Southern African Gender and Sustainable Energy Network (SAGEN) has become an important actor by "[...] advocating for the increased inclusion of the issue of income-generation in policies on energy provision, and the need to consider income-generation and energy together."

FINAL REMARKS

The unimpressive response at the international level to climate changes due to the barriers created by the traditional arena of production of International Law and the idiosyncrasies of international politics generates opportunities to local and transnational participation, especially for women.

Women's participation is much in need due to their unique leadership traits, which are developed considering the experiences and social encounters. Among those traits, solidarity, creative, and resilience form a stack strong enough to fight climate change bottom-up, thus filling the gap men are unable to address even though a life-and-death issue.

As observed, the bottom-up strategy is necessary to surpass the barrier of proper participation in the lawmaking and decision-making processes. The cases presented in this chapter show clearly that there is a lot to be done and much space for participation. At the local and regional level, the strong participation of women in NGOs and other organizations present significant and positive impacts on local overall well-being.

Therefore, the framework proposed in this chapter expects to contribute to address both urgent needs of humanity: climate and gender justice.

ACKNOWLEDGMENT

Thanks to Professor Michelle Ratton Sanchez Badin for continuous academic support and friendship.

REFERENCES

Agarwal, B. (2009). Gender and forest conservation: The impact of women's participation in community forest governance. *Ecological Economics*, 68(11), 2785–2799.

Agricultura familiar do Brasil é 8a maior produtora de alimentos do mundo | Secretaria Especial de Agricultura Familiar e do Desenvolvimento Agrário. ([s.d.]). Retrieved from http://www.mda.gov.br/sitemda/noticias/agricultura-familiar-do-brasil-%C3%A9-8%C2%AA-maior-produtora-de-alimentos-do-mundo. Accessed on August 28, 2018.

Alam, S., Atapattu, S., Gonzalez, C. G., & Razzaque, J. (Orgs.). (2015). *International environmental law and the global south*. New York, NY: Cambridge University Press.

Baksh-Soodeen, R., & Harcourt, W. (2015). *The Oxford handbook of transnational feminist movements* (1st edition). New York, NY: Oxford University Press.

Bello, W. (2009). *The food wars*. London: Verso Books.

Castro, D. de. (2018). The colonial aspects of international environmental law: Treaties as promoters of continuous structural violence. *Groningen Journal of International Law*, 5(2), 168–190.

Dankelman, I. (2002). Climate change: Learning from gender analysis and women's experiences of organizing for sustainable development. *Gender & Development*, 10(2), 21–29. doi:10.1080/13552070215899

DeMars, W. E. (2005). *NGOs and transnational networks: Wild cards in world politics*. London; Ann Arbor, MI: Pluto Press. Retrieved from https://doi.org/10.2307/j.ctt18fs3q9

Demeritt, D. (2006). Science studies, climate change and the prospects for constructivist critique. *Economy and Society*, 35(3), 453–479. doi:10.1080/03085140600845024

Eslava, L., Fakhri, M., & Nesiah, V. (Orgs.). (2017). *Bandung, global history, and international law: Critical pasts and pending futures*. New York, NY: Cambridge University Press.

Global Tracking Framework. (2017). 2017 – Progress toward sustainable energy. Text/HTML. World Bank. 2017. Retrieved from https://www.worldbank.org/en/topic/energy/publication/global-tracking-framework-2017

Greenpeace (2017). Segura este abacaxi! ([s.d.]). Retrieved from https://www.greenpeace.org/brasil/publicacoes/segura-este-abacaxi. Accesssed on August 28, 2018.

Gupta, J., Grijp, N. van der., & Kuik, O. (2013). *Climate change, forests and REDD: Lessons for institutional design*. Abingdon, UK: Routledge.

Heyward, C., & Roser, D. (Orgs.). (2016). *Climate justice in a non-idealworld* (1 ed.). Oxford: Oxford University Press.

Holton, R. J. (2007). *Global networks* (1st ed.). Basingstoke: Palgrave Macmillan.

Ingwersen, W. W., Garmestani, A. S., Gonzalez, M. A., & Templeton, J. J. (2014). A systems perspective on responses to climate change. *Clean Technologies and Environmental Policy*, 16(4), 719–730. doi:10.1007/s10098-012-0577-z

Kenya Economic Survey. (2016). Kenya National Bureau of Statistics (blog). Retrieved from https://www.knbs.or.ke/download/economic-survey-2016/

Lyotard, J.-F., & Jameson, F. (1984). In G. Bennington & B. Massumi (Trans.). *The postmodern condition: A report on knowledge* (1st ed.). Minneapolis, MN: University of Minnesota Press.

Makhabane, T. (2002). Promoting the role of women in sustainable energy development in Africa: Networking and capacity-building. *Gender & Development, 10*(2), 84–91. doi:10.1080/13552070215909

McCann, C., & Kim, S. (Orgs.). (2013). *Feminist theory reader: Local and global perspectives* (3rd ed.). New York, NY: Routledge.

Nixon, R. (2013). *Slow violence and the environmentalism of the poor* (Gld ed.). Cambridge, MA: Harvard University Press.

Reyes, R. R. (2002). Gendering responses to El Niño in rural Peru. *Gender & Development, 10*(2), 60–69. doi:10.1080/13552070215907

Sales, C. de M. V. (2007). Rural women: Establishment of new relations and recognition of rights. *Revista Estudos Feministas, 15*(2), 437–443. doi:10.1590/S0104-026X2007000200010

Shiva, V. (2011). *Monocultures of the mind*. New Delhi: Natraj Publishers.

Sweetman, C. (2009). *Climate change and gender justice*. Edited by Geraldine Terry. Warwickshire, UK: Oxford, UK: Practical Action.

Tétreault, M. A., & Lipschutz, R. D. (2009). *Global politics as if people mattered* (2nd ed.). Lanham, MD: Rowman & Littlefield Publishers.

Tickner, J. A. (2001). *Gendering world politics*. New York, NY: Columbia University Press.

Tickner, J. A., & Sjoberg, L. (Orgs.). (2011). *Feminism and international relations: Conversations about the past, present and future* (1st ed.). London: Routledge.

True, J., & Mintrom, M. (2001). Transnational networks and policy diffusion: The case of gender mainstreaming. *International Studies Quarterly, 45*(1), 27–57.

Villagrasa, D. (2002). Kyoto protocol negotiations: Reflections on the role of women. *Gender & Development, 10*(2), 40–44. doi:10.1080/13552070215902

Warming World. (July/August 2018). *Foreign affairs.* Retrieved from https://www.foreignaffairs.com/articles/2018-06-14/warming-world. Accessed on August 28, 2018.

Wilke, S. (2014). Anthropocenic poetics: Ethics and aesthetics in a new geological age. In H. Trischler (Ed.), *Anthropocene: Envisioning the future of the age of humans* (pp. 67–74). Munich: Rachel Carson Center for Environment and Society. doi:10.5282/rcc/6215

World Bank. (2015). Forest area (% of land area) | Data. Retrieved from https://data.worldbank.org/indicator/AG.LND.FRST.ZS?locations=KE

Wouters, P., Dukhovny, V., & Allan, A. (Orgs.). (2007). *Implementing integrated water resources management in Central Asia.* Netherlands: Springer. Retrieved from http://www.springer.com/gp/book/9781402057304. Accessed on August 28, 2018.

Zuckerwise, L. K. (2014). Postcolonial feminism. In *The encyclopedia of political thought.* John Wiley & Sons, Ltd. Retrieved from https://doi.org/10.1002/9781118474396.wbept0812

11

TOXIC TO TRANSFORMATIONAL LEADERSHIP: PEACE, RECONCILIATION, AND SOCIAL JUSTICE AS THE PARADIGM

Lorraine Stefani

ABSTRACT

In an unpredictable and volatile world, more than ever before we need transformational leadership based on a paradigm of social justice, peace, and reconciliation. Instead, what we are increasingly witnessing is toxicity in the actions and behaviors of leaders and followers. Political leaders in Britain are stirring up division instead of unity and causing serious damage to the fabric of society. Immigrants are a convenient cover for politicians rather than facing up to the real causes of anger in society many of which are due to the corrosive impact of austerity imposed after the global economic crisis of 2008. The toxic political environment is inciting a war on civility.

This chapter uses Brexit, the British referendum on remaining or leaving the EU as a focal point from which to observe the failures of Britain's political leaders in the lead up to and the execution of "the will of the people" to leave the EU. At this critical moment in the history of Britain, essential leadership characteristics including honesty, integrity, authenticity, and courage are not in evidence.

The final section of the chapter is a call to arms to everyone involved in leadership studies, conflict resolution, leadership education, scholarship, and research to address the question: How do we make an active contribution to improving the enactment of leadership and followership in fractured societies? What are our responsibilities as a multilayered community of practice? Are we really practicing what we preach in supporting diverse, inclusive leadership and followership?

Keywords: transformational leadership; social justice; Brexit; diversity; inclusion; followership; reconciliation

INTRODUCTION

Britain has long been a multicultural, multiethnic society. While the history behind this dates back to the era of the slave trade, during the world wars of the twentieth century, people from Commonwealth countries came to Europe to fight for Britain. In the period after the World War II, at the request of the British government, thousands of immigrants came to Britain from Caribbean countries to rebuild the country (Somerville, Sriskandarajah, & Latorre, 2009). Immigrants contribute hugely to Britain in a multitude of ways including business, entrepreneurship, manufacturing, the arts, food and hospitality, banking and other industries (O'Grady, 2014; Rodriguez, 2017).

Immigration has continued into the early part of the twenty-first century, particularly because of the 2004 expansion of the EU of which Britain is/has been a major player (Philipson, 2013). A significant issue relating to this wave of immigration is that many people, particularly from Eastern Europe, came to Britain in the hope of securing a better life through higher paid employment (Bush, 2016; Travis, 2017).

While immigrants make major contributions, bring diversity and vibrancy to a country and become part of the fabric of societies, sudden increases in numbers in Britain have led to increasing hostility, racism, and xenophobia (Gayle, 2018; Samuelson, 2018). A new narrative is prevalent in parts of Britain: "Immigrants from Central and Eastern Europe and the Balkans are 'flooding into the country'; taking jobs that British people should have. Immigrants are clogging up services such as the National Health and obtaining benefits that British people are not getting" (Bulman, 2017). It so happened that the peddling of this narrative coincided with the population feeling the full impact of the austerity agenda of the British government imposed in the aftermath of the 2008 Global Economic Crisis. The austerity agenda led to job losses, increases in the cost of living and the longest wage freeze in British history (O'Hara, 2015). Austerity hit the poorest in society the hardest. Aided and abetted by extreme right-wing politicians and a right-wing populist press, the angst over the impacts of austerity fed into a hatred of immigrants (Sims, 2016). This, in turn, led to the Prime Minister and leader of the ruling Conservative Party offering an ill-thought-out referendum on Britain's membership of the EU, with the voting public being asked to respond to a simplistic in/out statement: remain a member of the EU/leave the EU (Green, 2017). The shock result of the Brexit referendum was a narrow victory for the "Leave" campaign (Asthana, Quinn, & Mason, 2016). The consequences of the lead up to and of the outcome of the referendum are profound and catastrophic. There is the real prospect of disintegration of the United Kingdom as a unitary state (Hill, 2016); the country is heading toward xenophobic authoritarianism; there is a noticeable loss of tolerance of social, intellectual, and political diversity (Golec de Zavala, Guerra, & Simão, 2017). Thousands of immigrants currently working in Britain including those employed in the National Health Service, the catering and hospitality industry, the building industry feel uncertain about their right to live in Britain. Taken together it is a license to blame immigrants for all of society's current woes, which in turn led to a seismic event, the Brexit referendum.

At some point in the future, books and scholarly articles will examine Brexit in all its complexities. In this chapter, Brexit is examined through a lens with a fine focus on inclusion, diversity, and civility in leadership and followership. It is a focal point from which to observe the role played by leaders and followers in shaping a society now at war with itself, not a civil war creating bloodshed, but a war on civility.

Fifty-two percent of the British public who voted in the referendum voted for "leave," 48 percent for "remain." British society is seriously divided and polarized. Scotland voted 62% for "remain," Northern Ireland 56% for "remain," and London, the financial powerhouse of the world, 60% for "remain." Throughout Britain, cities, towns and even families are divided. Some "leave" voters did so as a protest over the consequences of austerity, many voted "leave" based on fear of thousands of more immigrants arriving on British shores (Singh, 2016).

Only now, over two years since the Brexit referendum, less than 100 days (at the time of writing) before our exit from Europe on March 29, 2019, are businesses in Britain, from farmers to finance, to manufacturers, and exporters and importers being heard when they speak out about the consequences for the labor market. The need for migrants is clear (Chu, 2016), but for the government to acknowledge this will spoil the pervasive, populist narrative.

Whatever the outcome of the ongoing Brexit negotiations between Britain and the other 27 countries comprising the EU, the wounds created within the British population in general and in societies across Britain and beyond will be a long time in healing. It will take courageous, authentic, evidence-based leadership and followership, a rational vision of what kind of country Britain aspires to be and coherent, accessible and honest narratives on social policy, to bring civil discourse back into British politics and to encourage civility throughout society.

This is a pivotal moment for everyone involved in what has become the "leadership industry" (Kellerman, 2018), in leadership studies, leadership education and scholarship, to address the questions: How do we make an active contribution to improving the enactment of leadership and followership in fractured societies? What are our responsibilities as a multilayered community of practice?

LEADERSHIP AND FOLLOWERSHIP TOXICITY

The twenty-first century appears to be a period marked by a vacuum of empowering, transformative global governance. Political leaders have forgotten, or perhaps choose to ignore, the idea that essential ingredients of (a) leader(ship) are a commitment to serve, to unite rather than divide and positive role-modeling as an example to the followers, and to show courage in the face of great turbulence (e.g., Avolio & Gardner, 2005). The Brexit referendum is a focal point from which to examine the failure of leaders and leadership at an immensely disruptive moment in the history of Britain.

Research on the EU referendum and its outcome highlighted the extent to which the "vote leave" result was a protest vote against the government by those who felt "left behind" (Harris, 2016), those who are suffering most as a result of years of austerity. David Cameron, the then Prime Minister and political leader who called the EU referendum, led a very weak campaign for remaining in the EU. There was no powerful narrative presented regarding the benefits of Britain being in the EU and no plan in the event of a "leave" vote.

The prejudices, assumptions, and arrogance of Britain's political leaders are constantly laid bare during this "Brexit moment." The condescension, dismissiveness, isolation, and finger pointing at swathes of the voting population have encouraged the growth of incivility across society.

The major failures of the political leaders pre-referendum were their unwillingness to recognize the downside of globalization, the negative impacts of austerity, and the rising levels of anger among ordinary working people (Sims, 2016). Middle-class, middle-aged, predominantly white, male leaders showed little knowledge or understanding of those they lead. They felt no need to look at the effects and impacts of their policies in and across wider society.

Britain is not alone in its political troubles. The policies in many countries across Europe and in the United States associated with globalization and profit-making have resulted in a shift from financial deficits to social deficits, with a concomitant threat to our understood social fabric (Elliott, 2016). The public sector in many countries is squeezed through funding shortfalls to the extent that there are few services left for the most vulnerable people in society. Power lies in the hands of big business and the financial markets ensuring that the rich get richer on the backs of the rest of the population (Jones, 2014).

At the time of the referendum, there was a lack of authentic, constructive, and inclusive leadership and in turn a lack of honesty, integrity, and courage. Those who strongly promoted a "leave" vote did so by peddling false information and presenting a vision based on lies and misinformation (Grice, 2017; Payne, 2018). According to this narrative: Leaving the EU would be easy and despite not being a member of the EU, we would all still have the same positive benefits, particularly with respect to free trade (Henley, 2017). Possibly the most powerful lie of all, the promise that numbers of immigrants would reduce by hundreds of thousands per year once Britain exited the EU (Chu, 2016; Thompson & Hunt, 2016): a compelling but entirely dishonest narrative. Those promoting a "remain" vote had no compelling vision, no easy but truthful soundbites that would play well with the electorate, while at the same time emphasizing the benefits of the EU and Britain's strong role within that Union. No effort was expended on the narrative of what Britain gains from its membership, only what we supposedly lose.

The referendum result was 52/48% to Leave and the Prime Minister resigned. In the face of one of the most historic and profound votes in British history, the political leader made manifest his lack of courage to lead the country through the crisis he precipitated.

Most Conservative or Tory Party Members of Parliament and the MPs of the main opposition Labour Party did not themselves believe that leaving the EU was a positive and beneficial move for Britain to make – but they put forward little challenge to their leaders, after all, the referendum result was "the democratic will of the people." This ignores the will of the people in Scotland and Northern Ireland. Immigration served as excellent cover for the deeper cause of anger in society, the consequences of austerity for all but the richest members (Jones, 2016).

If we are to move forward to heal the wounds in society, we must find the courage to examine leadership failures in order to re-envision leadership and followership through the lens of inclusion, diversity, and civility in leadership and followership, as a matter of social justice.

Diversity, Inclusion, Social Justice – A Noble Goal?

The lack of diversity in British politics leads to voter apathy for some sections of society (Bulman, 2018). Government has little to say about poverty and lack of opportunity for huge sections of the population. It could address voter apathy and shape the sorts of policies we desperately need if our political leaders and leadership were more reflective and representative of the population they serve. In the senior leadership team of the current Prime Minister, most of the key office/portfolio holders attended fee-paying schools and/or were educated at Oxford, Cambridge, or other high-profile, elite universities (Bulman, 2018; Reland, 2018). Notwithstanding the Prime Minister herself, membership of this team is almost all white, middle-class, middle-aged, heterosexual men, who appear to have little experience of life beyond their own social, economic, and intellectual spaces. In relation to Brexit, there is little concern among the ruling party of the consequences for the many of breaking away from the EU. Few briefings even from within government paint a bright future based on realities. Recently, in talking up a "no-deal" break with the EU because Britain won't get everything it wants from the EU after its exit, senior politicians/leaders of the British government suggested stockpiling medicines and food (Buchan, 2018)! Such threats are apparently intended to force all members of a divided government and the opposition to vote for a deal parliament rejects and the public doesn't actually understand. The political leaders are playing to the gallery of "leavers." No concern for almost 50% of the voting population.

Like other countries currently experiencing political turmoil, the primary opposition party in Britain seems incapable of offering viable approaches with an emphasis on what is best for the country rather than what might suit their careers. Political leadership has collapsed.

Since the referendum, there is an ongoing rise in anti-immigrant and xenophobic sentiments, particularly in "leave" constituencies within Britain (Coulter, 2018). The country appears to be led by the agenda of the increasingly right-wing media who in turn are being led by "armchair followers" posting anti-Europe, anti-immigrant, xenophobic comments on social media which in turn is leading to increased racism and street crime (Samuelson, 2018).

Honesty and Integrity?

Despite the fact that declaring the joys we will all experience once Britain exits from the EU, the Government has no vision for Britain post-Brexit, there is much talking up by one side of the divide and much scaremongering on the other (Enfield, 2017). The Conservative political party leadership team has shown itself to be at war with itself, with leadership challenges and different factions demanding different types of Brexit, hard, soft, or somewhere in between. Personal insults, derision, and open contempt for each other, all of the small wars played out endlessly in public, seen globally — but the leaders and followers appear oblivious to the damage being done, the potential danger of dividing rather than uniting the society. It is surely reasonable for the British population to expect their leaders to be role models for a civil society. Political leadership and followership in the context of Brexit are highly polarized, and the society is fractured; polls show "remainers" and "leavers" are wedded to their cause. The underlying message for all to see is that our political leadership and followers lack professionalism and integrity.

Having the courage to lead is critical in times of strife. When the Prime Minister resigned after the referendum result, the incoming Prime Minister of the Conservative government had an opportunity to take an extraordinarily powerful stand. The Referendum campaign was based on lies about extra funding to be poured into the National Health Service, about reducing the number of immigrants by hundreds of thousands per year. The new leader and the Prime Minister had the opportunity to take a principled stand, to open up a meaningful conversation about what it means to exit from the EU. To acknowledge and laud the contribution made to Britain by immigrants, to be truthful about the potential consequences, good and bad of leaving the EU and allow the electorate to reflect on realities before descending into the potential and actual chaos of Brexit.

The new Prime Minister did not challenge the validity of the referendum. She herself is at heart a "remainer," but nevertheless pledged to take Britain out of the EU by whatever means possible (Tolhurst, 2018). Political leadership is bound and constrained by popular sentiment. Addressing realities by showing integrity and honesty would have put the Prime Minister at odds with slightly more than 50% of her constituency, her mantra being that she will fulfill the democratic "will of the people." Going through with Brexit with a very slim majority obtained by dishonest and dishonorable means will not heal the wounds of a divided society and country. Just as important, what about her own moral integrity? Will this leader be comfortable with the consequences of the actions she is taking? Will we all wish that as our leader she had shown the moral courage to question the Brexit referendum and its aftermath?

There will be many accounts of Brexit in the future whatever the outcomes of ongoing deliberations may be. There will be many sides to debates, and much more detail than is possible in this chapter. Whether one is a leaver or remainer, it is difficult not to conclude that there is a lack of honesty, moral integrity, authenticity and courage on the part of leaders and followers throughout the Brexit debacle. Where divisions exist, the leadership and followership have fanned the flames rather than promoted unity. The responsibilities of holding the highest positions of service to the public are consistently flouted in favor of self-serving agendas.

FROM TOXICITY TO TRANSFORMATION

In the near future, it is unlikely there will be much change in the cultural homogeneity of the British government. However, demographics are changing and whether or not half the population wishes to acknowledge the fact, Britain will always be multicultural and multiethnic. A paradigm shift toward cultural diversity in government is inevitable but will undoubtedly be a painful journey. In a recent book on inclusive leadership, Melba Vasquez (as quoted in the study by Chin, Trimble and Garcia, 2018) states:

> the opportunity for citizenry to have a diverse leadership is a social justice issue. Leaders with varying ideologies and values that include prioritization of social justice can have a positive impact on racism, classism, sexism and other oppressions.

It is a privilege to lead one's country, but the role should not be open only to the privileged. A greater understanding of the population, the cultural, social and economic diversity within that population and its different types of society would provide the scope for evidence-based leadership and policy formation. Evidence-based leadership could enhance followership participation and encourage meaningful, civil engagement by being educative in both directions.

The journey toward diversity and inclusion has to begin with intentionality, and collective action is essential and vital. A white male, middle-class, heterosexual hegemony will not relinquish its privileged position easily. Being inclusive means being truly democratic; being participative and team-oriented; seeking multiple perspectives; being ethical; having high emotional intelligence; and being honest and transparent (Stefani, 2017). It will be a challenge to bring forward leaders from ethnic minorities, from the working class, from the LGBT community. Anyone new coming from outside the norm will be interrogated and scrutinized on their leadership credentials by a hostile press.

A serious question to be addressed is why are leadership scholars, researchers, practitioners not "calling out" the poor leadership we see all around us? Do we, as contributors to and consumers of the leadership industry, think so little of the importance of leadership and followership that we can afford to rest on our laurels with current approaches to leadership development? When will we acknowledge that Western, primarily North American, influenced leadership paradigms are not fit for purpose in the twenty-first century (Kellerman, 2018; Stefani, 2017). Our models are failing the world badly. As Alice Eagly and Jean Lau Chin (2010) state: "Our leadership models are primarily derived from traditional paradigms with little to say on diversity and difference [...]" Would Brexit have happened at all if a wider range of voices were heard, their real issues and grievances understood because the politicians, the leaders understood and addressed the different challenges within our own multicultural and multiethnic communities? "There is scant research on the shaping of leaders' behaviors by their potentially multi-identities as leaders and members of gender, racial, sexuality, ethnic or other identity groups" (Eagly & Chin, 2010).

Many parts of Britain with a high concentration of "leave voters" are likely to suffer the most economically as a consequence of Brexit (Parker, 2018). The government was not listening to the real anxieties, the impacts of austerity, the fear of immigrants, low wages. Those feeling "left behind," those in poorly paid jobs protested, they voted "leave" because they were not listened to.

Leadership and followership communities of practice, scholars, researchers, and practitioners in the vast field of leadership should act as role models and give form and meaning to new understandings of leaders and leadership. While it is without doubt a challenge, we should take our knowledge from its current exclusivity of scholarly journals, business schools, and the beneficiaries of the leadership industry into wider society and share it in accessible ways to enable a diverse audience to enact leadership in different ways.

Barbara Kellerman's recent call for the professionalization of leadership (2018) is a timely contribution to the many twenty-first-century leadership and followership challenges. The world sits too precariously in the twenty-first century to carry on voting in, promoting, elevating people to serious leadership roles based on privilege, money, social capital, and charisma. Brexit is but one manifestation of toxic leadership and followership in the twenty-first century, globally there are many examples. Leadership is too important to leave on the margins as merely a role, a title, but imbued with extraordinary power. Bold moves are required to bring forward better leaders and leadership encouraging responsible, respectful followers and followership.

We have a moral and ethical responsibility as followers of leadership to lead from behind to take a new generation of leaders from all backgrounds into spaces and places in government and all other organizations previously and currently closed to them. As followers, we can applaud their differences and diversity and what that brings to leadership. As followers, we can support them in upholding honesty and integrity by appreciating that they can communicate authentically across society. We can promote civil communication and show pride for commitment to the service of constituents. We can applaud their courage in taking on the challenges of complex political landscapes in a manner intended to mitigate conflict and promote peace.

This is a hopeful vision of leadership and followership in the twenty-first century. If we, the leaders and followers of leadership, take purposeful action and reexamine our research and scholarship, our practice, our influence, through a lens of peace, reconciliation, and social justice, we can and must shift our leadership from toxic to transformational.

POSTSCRIPT

At the time of completing this chapter, how Britain leaves the EU is unresolved. The political leaders have failed their constituents and are countenancing inflicting the hardships of a war-like environment on their own people in the event of a bad Brexit! How did it come to this? For the sake of power, Britain's political leaders forgot their constituents, they lost their moral compass, and they put a lid on their moral values. Did they relinquish the right to call themselves leaders?

ACKNOWLEDGMENT

Thanks to Eric, Aldo, and Vanessa for their encouragement to carry on and their positive comments when the discombobulation of Brexit seemed to defy attempts to squeeze out a coherent narrative on the roles of political leaders and followers.

REFERENCES

Asthana, A., Quinn, B., & Mason, R. (2016). UK votes to leave EU after dramatic night divides nation. *The Guardian*. Retrieved from https://www. theguardian.com/politics/2016/jun/24/britain-votes-for-brexit-eu-referendum-david-cameron. Accessed on June 24, 2018.

Avolio, B. J., & Gardner, W. L. (2005). Authentic leadership development: Getting to the root of positive forms of leadership. *Leadership Quarterly*, *16*, 315–338.

Buchan, L. (2018). Brexit: Government admits plan to stockpile medicines and blood in case UK leaves EU with no deal. *Independent*. Retrieved from https://www.independent.co.uk/news/uk/politics/no-deal-brexit-blood-medicine-stockpile-nhs-health-secretary-matt-hancock-a8462531.html. Accessed on September 20, 2018.

Bulman, M. (2017). Brexit: People voted to leave EU because they feared immigration, major survey finds. *Independent*. Retrieved from https://www.independent.co.uk/news/uk/home-news/brexit-latest-news-leave-eu-immigration-main-reason-european-union-survey-a7811651.html. Accessed on August 25, 2018.

Bulman, M. (2018). Theresa May's cabinet members now five times more likely to be privately-educated than British public. *Independent*. Retrieved from https://www.independent.co.uk/news/uk/politics/cabinet-ministers-private-education-reshuffle-public-schools-state-educated-uk-public-theresa-may-a8151106.html. Accessed September 18, 2018.

Bush, S. (2016). Divided Britain: how the EU referendum exposed Britain's new culture war. *New Statesman*. Retrieved from https://www.newstatesman.com/politics/uk/2016/06/divided-britain-how-referendum-exposed-britains-culture-war. Accessed on August 24, 2018.

Chu, B. (2016). What do immigrants do for the UK economy? Nine charts conservative ministers seem to be ignoring. *Independent*. Retrieved from https://www.independent.co.uk/news/business/news/immigration-uk-economy-what-are-the-benefits-stats-theresa-may-amber-rudd-tory-conference-speeches-a7346121.html. Accessed on September 22, 2018.

Coulter, M. (2018). UN official claims Brexit, austerity and immigration policy has 'made the UK more racist'. *Evening Standard*. Retrieved from https://www.standard.co.uk/news/uk/un-official-claims-brexit-austerity-and-immigration-policy-has-made-the-uk-more-racist-a3837161.html. Accessed on August 25, 2018.

Eagly, A. H., & Chin, J. L. (2010). Diversity and leadership in a changing world. *American Psychologist*, *65*, 216–224. doi:10.1037/a0018957

Elliott, L. (2016). Brexit is a rejection of globalisation. *The Guardian* Retrieved from https://www.theguardian.com/business/2016/jun/26/brexit-is-the-rejection-of-globalisation. Accessed on August 24, 2018.

Enfield, N. (2017). We're in a post-truth world with eroding trust and accountability. It can't end well. *The Guardian*. Retrieved from https://www.theguardian.com/commentisfree/2017/nov/17/were-in-a-post-truth-world-with-eroding-trust-and-accountability-it-cant-end-well. Accessed on July 14, 2018.

Gayle, D. (2018). UK has seen 'Brexit-related' growth in racism, says UN representative: UN special rapporteur on racism says 'extreme views' have gained ground in Britain since vote. *The Guardian*. Retrieved from https://www.theguardian.com/politics/2018/may/11/uk-has-seen-brexit-related-growth-in-racism-says-un-representative. Accessed on September 22, 2018.

Golec de Zavala, A., Guerra, R., & Simão, C. (2017). The relationship between the brexit vote and individual predictors of prejudice: Collective narcissism, right wing authoritarianism, social dominance orientation. *Frontiers of Psychology, 8*, 2023.

Green, D. A. (2017). The tale of the Brexit referendum question. *The Financial Times*. Retrieved from https://www.ft.com/content/b56b2b36−1835-37c6−8152-b175cf077ae8. Accessed on August 24, 2018.

Grice, A. (2017). Fake news handed Brexiteers the referendum − and now they have no idea what they're doing. *Independent*. Retrieved from https://www.independent.co.uk/voices/michael-gove-boris-johnson-brexit-eurosceptic-press-theresa-may-a7533806.html. Accessed on August 24, 2018.

Harris, S. A. (2016). Brexit 'Regretters' say they 'Weren't Really Voting To Get Out Of The EU': 'I based it on a false premise really'. *Huffington Post*. Retrieved from https://www.huffingtonpost.co.uk/entry/brexit-eu-referendum-people-regretting-leave-vote_uk_5770e6b3e4b08d2c56397a46. Accessed on July 25, 2018.

Henley, J. (2017). Britain's cake-and-eat-it Brexit routine wears thin with Barnier. *The Guardian*. Retrieved from https://www.theguardian.com/politics/2017/aug/31/britain-cake-and-eat-it-brexit-routine-michel-barnier. Accessed on July 20, 2018.

Hill, F. (2016). The "greatest catastrophe" of the 21st century? Brexit and the dissolution of the U.K. Retrieved from https://www. brookings.edu/blog/order-from-chaos/2016/06/24/the-greatest-catastrophe-of-the-21st-century-brexit-and-the-dissolution-of-the-u-k/. Accessed on August 10, 2018.

Jones, O. (2014). The establishment uncovered: How power works in Britain. *The Guardian*. Retrieved from https://www.theguardian.com/society/2014/aug/26/the-establishment-uncovered-how-power-works-in-britain-elites-stranglehold. Accessed on September 18, 2018.

Jones, O. (2016). It's a cruel deceit to blame all our problems on immigration. *The Guardian*. Retrieved from https://www.theguardian.com/commentisfree/2016/jun/09/cruel-deceit-problems-immigration-brexiters-truth. Accessed on June 10, 2018.

Kellerman, B. (2018). *Professionalizing leadership*. New York, NY: Oxford University Press.

O'Grady, S. (2014). Ten things that immigration has done for Britain. *The Independent*. Retrieved from https://www.independent.co.uk/voices/comment/ten-things-that-immigration-has-done-for-britain-9839549.html. Accessed October 3, 2018.

O'Hara, M. (2015). *Austerity bites: A journey to the sharp end of cuts in the UK*. Bristol: Policy Press.

Parker, G. (2018). Leave voting areas to be hit by Brexit. *Financial Times*. Retrieved from https://www.ft.com/content/33c51a40-0c5c-11e8−839d-41ca06376bf2. Accessed on September 23, 2018.

Payne, A. (2018). Boris Johnson says his £350 million a week Brexit claim was an 'underestimate'. *Business Insider*. Retrieved from http://uk.businessinsider.com/boris-johnson-says-his-350-million-a-week-brexit-claim-was-an-underestimate-2018-1. Accessed on June 14, 2018.

Philipson, A. (2013). Labour made a 'spectacular mistake' on immigration, admits Jack Straw. *The Telegraph*. Retrieved from https://www.telegraph.co.uk/news/uknews/immigration/10445585/Labour-made-a-spectacular-mistake-on-immigration-admits-Jack-Straw.html. Accessed on August 22, 2018.

Reland, J. (2018). How Diverse is the Government? *Full Fact*. Retrieved from https://fullfact.org/news/government-diversity/. Accessed on September 19, 2018.

Rodriguez, M. G. (2017). Migrants have helped make Britain. It's time to celebrate us. *The Guardian*. Retrieved from https://www.theguardian.com/commentisfree/2017/feb/20/migrants-britain-celebrate-markets-football-nhs-one-day-without-us. Accessed October 3, 2018.

Samuelson, K. (2018). 'We Fear Further Violence'. Far-right terrorism is growing in the U.K. *Time Magazine*. Retrieved from http://time.com/5180682/far-right-terrorism-on-rise-uk-hope-not-hate/. Accessed on April 2, 2018.

Sims, A. (2016). Austerity, not immigration, to blame for inequality underlying Brexit vote, argues Oxford professor. *Independent*. Retrieved from https://www.independent.co.uk/news/uk/politics/austerity-not-immigration-to-blame-for-inequality-underlying-brexit-vote-argues-professor-a7127751.html. Accessed on July 12, 2018.

Singh, R. (2016). Brexit referendum: Voting analysis. *The Parliament: Politics, Policy and People Magazine*. Retrieved from https://www.theparliamentmagazine.eu/articles/news/brexit-referendum-voting-analysis Accessed on September 24, 2018.

Somerville, W., Sriskandarajah, D., & Latorre, M. (2009). *United Kingdom: A Reluctant country of immigration*. Retrieved from https://www.migrationpolicy.org/article/united-kingdom-reluctant-country-immigration. Accessed on August 20, 2018.

Stefani, L. (2017). A multi-lens view of inclusive leadership in higher education. In L. Stefani & P. Blessinger (Eds.), *Inclusive leadership in higher education: International perspectives and approaches*. New York, NY: Routledge.

Thompson, M., & Hunt, K. (2016). Brexit's broken promises: Health care, immigration and the economy. *Money Magazine*. Retrieved from https://money.cnn.com/2016/06/27/news/economy/brexit-broken-promises/index.html. Accessed on August 25, 2018.

Tolhurst, A. (2018). 'HER HEART ISN'T IN IT' Theresa May 'is a Remainer who has remained a Remainer' claims Jacob Rees-Mogg as he blasts her Brexit plan. *Sun*. Retrieved from https://www.thesun.co.uk/news/6783130/theresa-may-is-a-remainer-who-has-remained-a-remainer-claims-jacob-rees-mogg-as-he-blasts-her-brexit-plan/. Accessed on September 23, 2018.

Travis, T. (2017). 80% of Britain's 1.4m eastern European residents are in work. *The Guardian*. Retrieved from https://www.theguardian.com/world/2017/jul/10/majority-of-britain-eastern-european-residents-are-in-work. Accessed on September 20, 2018.

Vasquez, M. J. T. (2018). Foreword. In J. L. Chin, J. E. Trimble, & J. E. Garcia (Eds.), *Global and culturally diverse leaders and leadership: New dimensions and challenges for business, education and society*. Bingley: Emerald Publishing.

12

BOSNIA AND HERZEGOVINA: UPSTANDERS AND MORAL OBEDIENCE

Bruce C. Pascoe

ABSTRACT

The 1990s war in Bosnia and Herzegovina is remembered for the atrocities committed by each of the ethnic groups involved. However, while it was mainly the leaders that were held to blame, the role of followers in these events also needs consideration. One cannot lead without followers. One cannot accomplish genocide without obedient followers. This study will examine the war in terms of three types of followers – participants, bystanders, and upstanders (those who stood up for their beliefs of right and wrong, refusing to obey orders from superiors or give in to the pressures of the situation). Studies in the past, such as the Milgram Experiment and the Stanford Prison Experiment, focused on the negative side of human behavior. We need to also focus research on the positive side of human behavior such as that displayed by the upstanders, so that such positive behavior can be encouraged and further developed in the interests of peace.

Keywords: Upstanders; bystanders; participants; followership; moral obedience; Bosnia and Herzegovina; Balkans War

Around 1,500 years ago, Slavic people migrated south and became the South Slavs. From 1389, those who became Serbs came under the religiously liberal rule of the Turks. The Serb's religion was predominantly Eastern Orthodox Christianity, and they looked east, being heavily influenced by the history and institutions of Constantinople. Many Bosnians and others conquered by the Turks adopted the Muslim faith. Croats and Slovenes, in the sphere of influence of the Austrian Empire, looked west to Europe in their attitudes and were predominantly Roman Catholics (MacLean, 2009). Still united by ethnic origin and a common language of three dialects, by the beginning of the twentieth century, the South Slavs had become very different in religion and culture. Created after World War I, the country of Yugoslavia fractured in a series of wars in the 1990s which saw many acts of genocide and other war crimes.

While it was mainly the leaders that were held to blame, the role of followers in these events also needs consideration. One cannot lead without followers. One cannot accomplish genocide without obedient followers. This study will focus on the behavior of followers in this war, not on the leaders.

LEADERSHIP AND FOLLOWERSHIP

Peter Drucker produced the most basic definition of a leader as a person who has followers (Drucker, 1988) – no followers and there is no leader. Success or failure of any venture is not only dependent on how well a leader leads, but on how well followers follow (Kelley, 1988). The two are inextricably interwoven. Although review shows that most leadership studies do recognize followers in some way, they tend not to focus on the follower in his or her own right (Uhl-Bien, Riggio, Lowe, & Carsten, 2013). James MacGregor Burns regarded this "bifurcation" (Burns, 2008, p. xii) between leadership studies and followership studies to be one of the most serious failures in leadership study. Too many studies assume that followers are all the same – amorphous (Kellerman, 2007). To almost anyone with experience in organizations, this is an oversimplification a major simplification of our experiences. Our experiences are also extremely likely to tell us that many followers lack neither influence nor power (Kellerman, 2007).

One goal of followership studies is to see leaders and followers not in terms of **Diagram 1** but rather in **Diagram 2**.

Diagram 1. One-way leadership.

Diagram 2. Two-way leader/follower interaction.

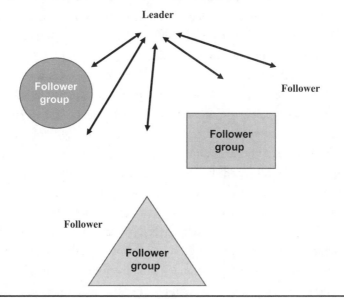

BOSNIA AND HERZEGOVINA

This study will consider three groups of followers during the war based on the behavior of different ethnicities toward each other during the war in Bosnia and Herzegovina (BiH). The terms "bystander" and "upstander" come from Svetlana Broz, whose book, *Good People in an Evil Time* inspired this study.

Participants were the followers of different military and paramilitary groups and others who were actively engaged in the atrocities. These might range from those whose hatred needed no encouragement to commit these crimes to those who believe that they were just following orders.

Bystanders were those who stood by and did not interfere with the atrocities. These might be military or paramilitary followers or civilians.

Upstanders were those people who stood up for what they knew was morally right, irrespective of the risk to them, displaying a high level of moral courage. Again, these might be military or paramilitary followers or civilians. "Morally right" means here conforming to generally accepted international principles of right. Paraphrasing seventeenth century Japanese scholar, Kaibara Ekken, the root of moral courage is in a humane and just mind (cited in Wilson, 2015, p. 16). Murder, genocide, and war crimes cannot be considered either humane or just. Even if a participant genuinely felt that acts he or she committed that constituted their war crimes were right, by breaking generally accepted standards of behavior, they cannot be considered upstanders or showing moral courage.

This participant/bystander/upstander typology of followers is structurally different from most other followership typologies. For example, Chaleff (2009) based his typology on two dimensions, according to the extent that a follower supported their leader and the extent to which the follower challenged their leader. Other two-dimensional typologies are those of Zaleznik (1965), Kelley (1988), and Potter and Rosenbach (2005). By contrast, Kellerman (2007) bases her followership typology on one dimension.

The typology of participant, bystander, and upstander is *not* a continuum but three discreet and mutually exclusive behaviors. In any situation, if a person is a participant, they cannot be a bystander or an upstander; a bystander cannot be a participant or an upstander; and an upstander cannot be a participant or a bystander. However, the same person might take on a different type in different situations. For example, a person who dislikes another group might verbally abuse members of that group, acting in this situation as a participant. If the abuse turns mildly physical, this person might believe this behavior wrong and refrain from acting in this way, but do nothing to try to stop the behavior, behaving as a bystander. However, if the treatment of members of the disliked group turns to torture or murder, the person might feel strongly enough to act to stop this from happening, becoming an upstander.

While at first this followership typology might seem similar to Hilberg's triage of perpetrators, victims, and bystanders (1993), it is very different and comes from a different perspective. First, victims are not considered in the followership typology. Second, this followership typology considers only those who were both directly involved and who were followers. For example, under bystanders, Hilberg considers neutral European states, the Allied countries, and the Pope. Third, Hilberg's examples of bystanders include those who actively worked with the Nazi (participants in the followership typology) and those who actively helped the Jews thereby endangering themselves (upstanders in the followership typology). This is not in any way meant to disagree with Hilberg, but rather to point out that his triage and this followership typology are structurally different.

By grouping such complex situations into only a few types, Hilberg's triage is a simplification of reality. However, it allows us to organize and focus studies (Vollhardt & Bilewics, 2013). Browning (2011) showed the utility of Hilberg's triage by focusing on perpetrators and breaking this grouping down into four categories. This limitation and advantage of Hilberg's triage also applies to followership typologies.

Participants

Kelman (1973) and Bandura (1999) both considered several ways in which people morally disengage when involved in inhumane conduct. Ways that Bandura researched of particular relevance to this study are stated in the forthcoming text.

Moral justification is where people self-justify their actions. For example, violence can be "justified" in the name of protecting religion, preserving peace, saving others from violence or subjugation, or by obeying their duty to their country.

Displacement of responsibility, an example of which is the Milgram experiment, the aim of which was to "find when and how people would defy authority in the face of a clear moral imperative" (Milgram, 2004, p. 4). A volunteer was ordered to give a "learner" increasingly strong electric shocks. While the shocks were not real, the volunteer believed them to be. Two-thirds of the volunteers continued to administer shocks to the full perceived level of 450 volts. Milgram's finding was that people tend to obey orders from an authority they see as legitimate (2004). Responsibility is directed to the authority directing the person, who then feels no responsibility for the action they are ordered to perform (Milgram, 2004). In military and bureau-cracies involved in sanctioned massacres, "unquestioning obedience to authoritative orders" (Kelman, 1973, p. 43) is shown not only in lower levels of the organization, but by also those of high levels as well. Even though the latter group has more power to intervene, they too tend to blindly follow orders, "without even feeling the need to ask questions" (Kelman, 1973, p. 43). As C. P. Snow wrote, "More hideous crimes have been committed in the name of obedience than in the name of rebellion" (as cited in Bandura, 1999, p. 207).

Diffusion of responsibility can be achieved through a division of tasks and responsibilities, or by group thinking. In these ways, no one person might be seen as solely responsible for an act.

Another example is in the findings of the Stanford Prison Experiment (SPE). This experiment, where volunteers were divided into prisoners and guards in a simulated prison, had to be stopped after only six days of what could have been a two-week study. Zimbardo wrote: "We had to do so because too many normal young men were behaving pathologically as pow-erless prisoners or as sadistic, all-powerful guards" (Zimbardo, 2009; Location 3439–3445). Zimbardo concluded that the significance of the experiment is that good people can be easily induced to do evil things to other good people "within the context of socially approved roles, rules, and norms, a legitimizing ideology, and institutional support that transcends individual agency" (Zimbardo, 2009; Location 3289–3296). The title of his book, *The Lucifer Effect: Understanding How Good People Turn Evil*, is a chilling reversal of the title of Broz's book, *Good People in an Evil Time*.

Dehumanization is achieved by denying others of their human qualities, seeing them as, for example, "mindless savages." The word "barbarian" comes from the Ancient Greek term for all non-Greek speakers.

There are therefore many possible explanations reasons that intend to account for why participants behave the way that they do. A key point, how-ever, is how do we stop their behavior, or, even better, change it for the better?

Bystanders

Bystanders need little explanation. We see them every day in small ways. Some may have total unconcern about what they see happening. Others may know that these things are wrong, and at least have the moral courage to refrain from participating but lack sufficient moral courage to act.

Upstanders

These are the people who stood up and acted for what they believed was right, refusing to be dehumanized by the situation, to follow orders that they considered to be wrong, or to succumb to the inertia of fear. They risked harm of many types and even death to do what they knew was right. Examples are the best way to describe them.

Salih Delić – a Muslim civilian – described how Serbs and Muslims had always lived amicably together in the village of Baljvine. He told of how the village was one of the very few not burned during World War II, because Serbs and Muslim neighbors protected each other. When forces including Muslims came to burn Serbs' homes, Muslims raised barricades in the street and didn't allow anyone through. When opposing forces of Serbs came, the Serbs of Baljvine protected the Muslims. When war came again in the 1990s, "No one was able to poison our good relations at any time during the war" (Broz, 2007, p. 6). When the village Serbs fled on hearing that Croatian Guard Corps fighters were coming, it was the Muslims who defended the Serb homes. The village was later destroyed by Croatian Defence Council forces. After the war, Muslims and Serbs helped each other to rebuild Baljvine (Broz, 2007, pp. 3–10).

Pero Simić, a Serb, lived in Gradačac, where he had Muslim and Croat friends. When there were few Serbs left after many had fled, these friends made sure that he was not harmed and was treated even-handedly. When he became sick, his friends helped him to be exchanged so that he could receive medical help. They gave him some of their scarce money to help him on his way. His son still lives in Gradačac, and people from all three ethnic groups work together there (Broz, 2007, pp. 44–45).

Stjepan Bradić, a Croat, tells of the time he was taken prisoner by Chetniks (Serbs who took up arms against other ethnic groups). After he was beaten by soldiers using their rifle butts, the uniformed Captain Mića came into the room in which they were held. Mića protected them, even having them moved because he knew they would be killed if they stayed where they were. Later they were moved in a bus. After being threatened with murder – and coming very close to it, they again came upon Captain Mića with six soldiers. With him and his men protecting them, the bus was driven to a place where prisoners were exchanged. Chetniks there wanted to beat them. Captain Mića ordered his men to shoot any Chetniks who came close. The men were safely exchanged – thanks to Captain Mića and his men (Broz, 2007, pp. 16–22).

Đuro Fišera, a Croat, told of how Miroslav, a Serb from Sarajevo serving with a Serbian special unit, helped his mother. Miroslav "was a man who helped everyone, not just Serbs" (Broz, 2007, p. 40). His attitude caused trouble with others in his army unit, and he had to flee to avoid being murdered. Fortunately, he survived the war (Broz, 2007, pp. 38–40).

Mile Plakalović spent every one of 1,440 days during which Sarajevo was besieged driving his battered and bullet-ridden taxi to help others of any ethnicity, usually in places others feared to go. He transported the wounded to help, brought food and clothing to the needy, and even took chocolate to children. As he calmly drove through gunfire, he would calmly say to his passengers, "Just put your head down" (Broz, 2007, pp. 87–88; http://www.gariwo.org/en/pages/miomir-mile-plakalovic).

When the Serb inhabitants of Čađavica evacuated it as the Muslim army came close, 69-year-old Radojka Umićević chose to stay behind. Two members of the Army of BiH moved into her house. They slept in her kitchen, allowing her to sleep upstairs. Fearing for her safety, they collected firewood for her; and when they left they gave her a note to ensure her safety if other units of their army came to the village (Broz, 2007, pp. 59–62).

The Milgram Experiment largely ignored upstanders who had the moral obedience to not carry out an immediate order that they saw as immoral, focusing on the obedient participants. Zimbardo (2009) wrote that he and Milgram did discuss the need to study these "dissidents, the rebels, the whistle-blowing heroes" (Zimbardo, 2009; Location 3326–3334), but found focusing on what made good people do evil deeds was more appealing to them. The focus of most such studies has been on the participants, omitting the bystanders, and ignoring the upstanders. This might help us understand the problems, but, apart from the importance of awareness of these issues, it has been less help in finding solutions. We need to research the behavior of the upstanders – what can we learn to help others to emulate their behavior? What makes upstanders of different ethnicities in Baljvine and Gradačac be good neighbors and friends irrespective of the war? What can we learn that might help us to find peaceful settlements between conflicting and ethnic groups?

Milgram, however, may well provide one key to the behavior of these upstanders. A deeply religious man refused to obey the experimenter's

orders. On being asked why he refused, his reply was: "If one has as one's ulti-
mate authority God, then it trivializes human authority" (Milgram, 2004, p. 49).
Milgram made a key observation – the man had substituted a good (in this case
divine) authority for a bad authority (Milgram, 2004). Put another way, the man
had a much more powerful allegiance to a higher authority (in this case religious,
but it doesn't have to be) than the one now giving him orders. Similarly, upstanders obeyed the dictates of conscience and right over wrong over any orders
given by a lesser authority and/or despite the dangerous situation in which they
found themselves. This is *moral obedience* – obeying a higher moral imperative
over behaving in a way that a person believes is wrong, irrespective of orders, the
situation, or the danger. Moral obedience is no more than moral courage given a
different title. Milgram showed how powerful obedience is in people, and the
powerful negative effects it can have. Using the term "moral obedience" rather
than "moral courage" seeks to tap into the power of obedience for the positive
effect of keeping people engaged with high moral values. For example, duty to
your country is a lower priority than obeying high moral principles.

Bandura (1999) noted the importance of "resolute *engagement* of the
mechanisms of moral agency" (p. 200) to regulate proactive moral action.
Examples of proactive morality include acting according to humane principles
when social situations dictate otherwise, renouncing social ends which justify
destructive means, forgoing personal welfare for convictions, understanding
that you are personally responsible for your own actions, continuing to be
empathetic to the suffering of others, and focusing on the similarity between
peoples rather than the differences (Bandura, 1999). These are important
behaviors exhibited by upstanders and embodied in moral obedience.

One tool currently available to help us develop moral obedience and to
combat mindless obedience is intelligent disobedience – doing right when
what you're told to do is wrong (Chaleff, 2015). Where we are brought up
to obey the rules and orders of authority, intelligent disobedience considers
when it is appropriate to obey an authority's orders and when that order
should be questioned, and how people can develop the ability to refrain
from doing something that they believe is wrong, even when they are
ordered and/or are under a powerful social pressure to do it (Chaleff, 2015).
This is something we are not trained in and is a higher level of training than
simple obedience – it requires critical thought and analysis. Intelligent disobedience – in this case disobeying an order that one believes is morally
wrong – can be an important tool in moral obedience.

Moral obedience can be learnt and strengthened by use. Chinese philosophers Mencius (2003), Xunzi (Nukariya, 2004), Yang Xiong (Bullock, 2011), and Su Shih (Nukariya, 2004) may have all disagreed about original human nature, but they, Confucius (1979) and Aristotle (2015) all believed that people can become better people by practicing good deeds. John McCain, who spent six years in a North Vietnamese prison camp wrote that: "Courage is like a muscle. The more we exercise it, the stronger it gets" (McCain, 2004b). If more people are to emulate the behavior of upstanders, we need to teach moral obedience. Cultural differences should not be an issue – as most cultures adhere to general principles of right and wrong. One key element in this training is being inspired by and identifying with the examples of others in the past. Every one of the upstanders that Broz interviewed knew of how others in the past in their cultural/social setting had behaved in a similar morally obedient way, usually in previous wars. This was the *only* point that was common to every one of the thousands of upstanders that Broz interviewed (S. Broz, personal communication, August 17, 2018). In international presentations Broz saw her audiences not only identify with her examples of upstanders but give their own examples of upstanders from their own cultural backgrounds in countries in Europe, America, Africa, and Asia (S. Broz, personal communication, August 17, 2018). John McCain also wrote that acts of extraordinary courage "can inspire us to emulate its author" (McCain, 2004a, p. 10) and that by learning about him or her, "our courage will not be wanting in the moment" (McCain, 2004a, p. 10).

Broz's goal is to educate the young in these issues so that they can reach a "critical mass" (S. Broz, personal communication, August 17, 2018) where their actions can help make the world a better place. Bandura (1999) noted that people cannot rely on individuals (who are leaders) to prevent human cruelty because of the power of moral disengagement devices. This critical mass is a means whereby reliance is not placed on individual leaders, but powerfully spread across a large group of followers.

Moral obedience can be also strengthened through practice – by exercising our "muscles" of moral obedience.

CONCLUSION

When we consider the war in Bosnia and Herzegovina, it would be a mistake to lay the blame totally on evil leaders and old quarrels. If we are to learn from this war and help achieve peaceful outcomes to future such crises we need to consider the role of followers involved in it as well.

A followership typology of participant/bystander/upstander is a means to focus on the behavior of these followers and to research and understand the behavior of each. Of particular importance is the need to help more people become upstanders – those who stand up for right in difficult situations, irrespective of the dangers. Developing a critical mass of upstanders is one means to avoid vainly relying on individual leaders to prevent human cruelty. Training in intelligent disobedience and moral obedience can help achieve this – where people obey the higher dictates of moral conscience and remain engaged with high moral values, rather than obeying a leader who orders them to commit an immoral act.

Amidst the horrors of war, BiH's upstanders are an inspiration to encourage others to emulate their feats. Future research needs to examine them and their behavior so that many more can emulate their upstanding courage and behavior in the pursuit of peace and friendship.

ACKNOWLEDGMENTS

The author would like to acknowledge Dr Svetlana Broz, whose book inspired this chapter, and whose help was vital to this work.

REFERENCES

Aristotle. (2015). *Nicomachean Ethics*. (W. D. Ross, trans.), Retrieved from https://ebooks.adelaide.edu.au/a/aristotle/nicomachean/

Bandura, A. (1999). Moral disengagement in the perpetration of inhumanities. *Personality and Social Psychology Review* [Special Issue on Evil and Violence], *3*, 193–209.

Browning, C. R. (2011). Revisiting the holocaust perpetrators. Why did they kill? Retrieved from https://bhecinfo.org/wp.../Revisiting-the-Holocaust-Perpetrators_Why-Did-They-Kill

Broz, S. (2007). *Good people in an evil time: Portraits of complicity and resistance in the Bosnian War.* New York, NY: Other Press.

Bullock, J. S. (2011). *Yang Xiong: Philosophy of the Fa yan: A confucian hermit in the Han Imperial Court.* Highlands, NC: Mountain Mind Press.

Burns, J. M. (2008). Foreword. In R. E. Riggio, I. Chaleff, & J. Lipman-Blumen (Eds.), *The art of followership: How great followers create great leaders and great organizations* (pp. vi–vii). San Francisco, CA: Jossey-Bass.

Chaleff, I. (2009). *The courageous follower: Standing up for and to our leaders.* San Francisco, CA: Berrett Koehler.

Chaleff, I. (2015). *Intelligent disobedience: Doing right when what you're told to do is wrong* [Kindle version]. Retrieved from Amazon.com.au

Confucius. (1979). *The analects – Sayings of Confucius.* (D. C. Lau, trans.). London: Penguin.

Drucker, P. L. (1988, January 6). Leadership: More doing than dash. *Wall Street Journal*, Section 1, 14.

Hilberg, R. (1993). *Perpetrators victims bystanders: Jewish catastrophe 1933–1945.* New York, NY: Harper Perennial.

Kellerman, B. (2007, December). What every leader needs to know about followers. *Harvard Business Review*, 84–91. Retrieved from https://hbr.org/2007/12/what-every-leader-needs-to-know-about-followers

Kelley, R. (1988, November–December). In praise of followers. *Harvard Business Review*, 142–148. Retrieved from https://hbr.org/1988/11/in-praise-of-followers

Kelman, H. (1973). Violence without moral restraint: reflections on the dehumanization. *Journal of Social Issues, 29*, 25–61.

MacLean, F. (2009). *Eastern approaches.* London: Penguin.

McCain, J. (2004a). *Why courage matters: The way to a braver life* [Kindle version]. Retrieved from Amazon.com.au

McCain, J. (2004b, September 1). In search of courage: Finding the courage within you. *Fast Company.* Retrieved from https://www.fastcompany.com/50692/search-courage

Mencius. (2003). *Mencius*. (D. C. Lau, trans.). London: Penguin.

Milgram, S. (2004). *Obedience to authority: The unique experiment that challenged human nature*. New York, NY: Perennial Classics.

Nukariya, K. (2004). *The religion of the Samurai: A study of Zen philosophy and discipline in China and Japan*. Retrieved from http://www.gutenberg.org/dirs/etext04/samur10.txt

Potter, E. H. III, & Rosenbach, W. E. (2005). Followers as partners: Ready when the time comes. In R. L. Taylor & W. E. Rosenbach (Eds.), *Military leadership: In pursuit of excellence*. Boulder, CO: Westview Press.

Uhl-Bien, M., Riggio, R. E., Lowe, K. B., & Carsten, M. K. (2013). Followership theory: A review and research agenda. *The Leadership Quarterly, 25*(1), 83–104.

Vollhardt, J. R., & Bilewics, M. (2013). After the genocide: Psychological perspectives on victim, bystander, and perpetrator groups. *Journal of Social Issues, 69*, 1–15.

Wilson, W. S. (Ed. And Trans.) (2015). *The pocket Samurai*. Boston, MA: Shambhala.

Zaleznik, A. (1965). The dynamics of subordinacy. *Harvard Business Review, 43*(3), 119–131.

Zimbardo, P. G. (2009). Reflections on the Stanford prison experiment: Genesis, transformations, consequences. In T. Blass (Ed.) *Obedience to authority: Current perspectives on the Milgram Paradigm* [Kindle version]. Lawrence Erlbaum Associates. Retrieved from Amazon.com.au

13

THE LEADERSHIP OF THE VICARIATE OF SOLIDARITY DURING THE DICTATORSHIP IN CHILE (1973–1990)

Fátima Esther Martínez Mejía and Nelson Andrés Ortiz Villalobos

ABSTRACT

On September 11th, 1973, started the darkest stage in the recent history of Chile. The military and the police, at the command of General Augusto Pinochet, executed the most atrocious acts against the human dignity that the country had witnessed. The martial and technocratic leaders of the dictatorship ripped apart and redesigned the institutions of the country at their will, through to the elimination of the opposition and the systematic violation of human rights, which reached any person or group. Just a few days after the coup d'état that brought Pinochet to power, the Cardinal and Archbishop of Santiago, Raúl Silva Henríquez, and a group of churches declared themselves against the devastating violence that was gripping the country. Immediately, the religious spaces took up the lead in the defense of the most vulnerable, the persecuted, marginalized, and poor. The major effort focused on the Vicariate of Solidarity, an organization of the Catholic Church in Chile that was tasked with the promotion and defense of human rights, which offered legal and social assistance to the victims and their families. The Vicariate quickly positioned itself as a leader in search of justice against the backdrop of repression, censorship, lack of representative institutions, and prohibition of popular movements. The purpose of the *present chapter is to analyze the work of the Vicariate of Solidarity and its leading role in the fight against human rights violations, strengthening social reorganization, reconciliation, and the return to democracy in Chile.*

Keywords: Vicariate of Solidarity; Chile; leadership; social reorganization; transitional justice; reconciliation

On September 4th, 1973, Salvador Allende, the first socialist president democratically elected in the world, took office. With the support of the Popular Unity (UP), Allende pushed the *Chilean road to Socialism*, a political agenda wherein the proposal was to achieve the development of the country in a noncapitalist way in the frame of bourgeois democracy, where middle classes and the people were represented in the Congress under the respect of the constitutional order, political pluralism, and freedom (De la Fuente, 2011, p. 1014). However, in the context of the Cold War, Allende's government sunk in a serious institutional crisis, as consequence of the complex political and economic relations originated in the mid-1960s. In this period, the Chilean society faced lots of challenges: on the economic side, there was a shortage of food and consumption goods and a constant economic and military pressure from the United States. On the political side, the society was highly polarized, the political actors were fragmented, there was ferocious anticommunism, and ultraconservative movements acted against the government. In this scenario, the political forces were unable to reach a consensus on an institutional solution that would prevent the breakdown of the democratic tradition.

TOTAL MILITARY POWER

On September 11th, 1973, the military and the police forces lead by Augusto Pinochet took control of the country. The martial and technocratic dictatorship's ranking officers acted by the *Junta de Gobierno*, which assigned itself and centralized the constituent, executive, and legislative powers. They then forced the country into a re-foundational process based on the neoliberal ideology. The authoritarian regime ripped apart the republic's institutions by dissolving the Congress; declaring political parties in recess and outlawing them; incinerating the electoral registers; suspending political and civil rights; establishing an interim public administration, except for the judiciary and the comptroller's office; declaring the cessation of duties to majors and councilors; ending labor relations of public civil servants; intervening and appointing the authorities of the universities; dissolving unions and popular organizations; repressing social mobilizations and protests; censoring the press and the media; pronouncing the state of siege; and finally imposing a new constitution in 1980.

Once the *Junta de Gobierno* controlled the country, they began the transformation of the political institutions, according to Valdivia Ortiz de Zárate (2010, p. 174), that intended not only to fight Marxism but also tried to solve the problems of underdevelopment. In the *Declaration of Principles* (1974), the military and the police forces committed to rebuild the political and economic structure of Chile. They attempted to do so through: (1) the organization of an authoritarian social order based on violence; (2) the implementation of the neoliberal economic model; and finally (3) the reshaping of the society through ideas like national unity, order, and discipline to form a generic cultural project (Tapia Valdés, 1980, p. 163). This transformation of the public order lasted over time under a legal scheme that was difficult to change, even though the dictatorship ended.

In the first days of the coup d'état, the violence and persecution focused on the UP collaborators, but as the months went by, it expanded to any person or group that could be considered a threat in the eyes of the repression organs: the National Intelligence Directorate (DINA) and the National Intelligence Center (CNI). Since 1977 onward, violence was more selective, but it intensified between 1983 and 1986 as a result of the national demonstrations that occurred those years. According to Monsálvez Araneda (2012, p. 42), the violations of human rights were sustained by the dictatorship through a legal and punitive architecture that justified arrests, murders, torture, exile, and other forms of repression.

In this setting of massive oppression, the Catholic Church was the only institution that kept autonomy and freedom to act, thanks to its moral authority and social legitimacy.[1] Immediately, it became a leading space for protection and assistance, whose work was based on the values of justice, freedom, peace, and truth (Vicaría de la Solidaridad, 1991). During the most difficult years (1973–1977), the Catholic Church was the only entity openly opposing the regime. It used various channels to influence the political and social spheres, casting from exhortations to the government and the public opinion, in the form of statements and pastoral letters, to even threats of excommunication (Veit Strassner, 2006, p. 78).

In response to the emergency, several organizations were founded: the *National Committee for Aid to Refugees*, the *Social Aid Foundation of Christian Churches*, and the *Cooperation Committee for Peace in Chile* (Pro-Peace Committee). The Pro-Peace Committee was born in October 1973 as an initiative of the Catholic, Jewish, and Christian Churches with the objective of offering legal, economic, technical, and spiritual assistance to political prisoners, exiles, tortured, dismissed workers, union members, university students, and relatives of disappeared or deceased. After two years of operation, the Committee was closed by direct order of Pinochet, who alleged that the ecumenical work was not welfare work but protection to Marxist–Leninist terrorists.

THE FORCE OF THE VICARIATE OF SOLIDARITY

After the Pro-Peace Committee was closed, Cardinal Raúl Silva Henríquez opened the Vicariate of Solidarity on January 1, 1976, an organization which continued with the same functions and personnel as the Committee, but belonged to the juridical order of the Catholic Church of Chile, under the command of the Archbishopric of Santiago. In addition to protecting victims of political persecution, as new national events arose, like an economic crisis, the Vicariate became a driver of social demands. Rodríguez Iglesias (2008, p. 130) points that the breadth of solidarity actions covered the issues of violence, insecurity, education, housing, health (drugs and sexually transmitted disease prevention), food (malnutrition), technical (self-management workshops), as well as economic and labor.

The work done by the Catholic Church was the first movement in favor of human rights committed to rearticulating the social fabric, the collective identity, and the reconstruction of a democratic culture (Bravo Vargas, 2016). Under the auspices and protection of the Vicariate, a second movement was formed that came from the initiative of the relatives of the victims of the dictatorship, the *Association of Relatives of Disappeared Detainees.* Right away, were formed *Association of Relatives of Executed Politicians* and *Association of Relatives of Political Prisoners, among others.* Subsequently, a third movement arose from the political field, the *Chilean Human Rights Commission* (Orellana & Quay, 1991, p. 12).

As a result of the lack of spaces for exercising freedom of expression and of the political representation void, the parish churches became places of non-partisan critical, supportive gatherings with aspirations for social justice (Arzobispado de Santiago, 1987). De la Maza and Garcés (1984, p. 16) argued that the parish churches formed a sort of para-state space of reunification, as they were the only spaces of regroupment tolerated by the authoritarian regime. In the temples, a set of initiatives of social, cultural, and political action were developed, coordinated by professional and religious personnel. This was done by the parish people together with the most politicized people and groups of the country (Garcés Durán, 2017). This caused the temples to begin to be surveilled and the religious and laity who carried out the solidarity work to be subject to suspicion, defamation, harassment, imprisonment, aggression, exile, and murder. Notwithstanding, the Church did not stop defending human dignity, justice, announcing the truth, and denouncing violence (Comité Permanente del Episcopado, 1980).

The Vicariate received international financial support from the World Council of Churches, the United States Conference of Catholic Bishops, and from the Nordic Lutheran Churches, as well as contributions from the government and political parties of Germany, Belgium, Canada, and The Netherlands, among others. Likewise, it received help through Amnesty International, the Ford Foundation, collections, and personal donations. However, the exiles played an important role in the dissemination of the country's internal situation and in the search for funding, as they were able to form a transnational network for the defense of human rights with representation in bodies like the United Nations and the Organization of American States (Ayala, 2014).

THE LIGHTS OF SOLIDARITY

During the dictatorship, jurisdictional matters were exercised normally in various areas; however, as far as the defense of human rights was concerned, the courts were notoriously insufficient and unwilling to prosecute the perpetrators of grave human rights violations. Judicial officials and judges (in theory independent) did not rule against the unconstitutionality or illegality of the laws and decrees enacted by the *Junta de Gobierno*, nor they ruled in favor of over 5,000 writs of *amparo* (is a rough equivalent of *habeas corpus*) pleas filled before Chilean courts (Matus, 2000). On the contrary, they accepted evidence issued by the repression organs, without evaluating its veracity (Comisión Nacional de Verdad y Reconciliación, 1991, p. 85). Most of the judicial proceedings were dismissed or terminated by the invocation of the 1978 Amnesty Law.[2] In addition to this denial of justice, the courts across the country gave no individual or collective procedural guarantees. Cardinal Silva Henriquez himself (1974) denounced that there were no legal safeguards for the people's security. This allowed arbitrary arrests, brutal interrogations, lack of information of the whereabouts of some detainees or charges that motivated arrest, limitations in the legal defense, unequal sentences for the same crimes, as well as restrictions to the right of appeal. In 1991 the Truth and Reconciliation Commission Report concluded that the courts could have saved lives and protected prisoners and defendants from mistreatment had they accepted them.

In the face of injustice, the Legal Department of the Vicariate gave legal support and assistance to those who faced charges in civil or "wartime" military courts for political reasons. This department developed programs to support detainees and defendants, lodging *habeas corpus* pleas, formulating the legal defense of the accused of crimes of opinion, carrying out administrative procedures for exiles, denouncing those responsible for violation of fundamental rights, locating and identifying the remains of disappeared detainees, among other tasks (Arzobispado de Santiago, 1987).

The Catholic Church and the Vicariate lead the reorganization of the marginalized population of squatter settlements, through the planning of collective activities and the delivery of technical tools for the execution of tasks; nevertheless, they always respected the rhythm and the internal process of social regrouping (Arzobispado de Santiago, 1987). The skills training was fundamental since the affected people were the ones who carried out the tasks themselves, with the purpose that the new organizations obtained autonomy, independence, and self-sufficiency for solving their problems, thus fostering followers and making room for other leaders.

In addition to the Legal Department, the Vicariate had two outstanding offices. First, the Rural Department, which encouraged the creation of autonomous farmers unions, trained the people on technical aspects to improve their products, and gave primary education. Second, the Zones Department focused on the progress of childhood and youth in the poorest, most vulnerable and marginal urban areas. It organized children's dining rooms, a job bank for unemployed, health programs, productive workshops, and economic aid. In addition, it coordinated cultural recreation programs with women's groups and youth centers.

At a time of lack of press freedom, when information was censored and the one allowed was biased, the Vicariate published the *Solidaridad* magazine, which was the only truthful mass media that informed, with a reflective character, on human rights violations and solidarity activity. Likewise, it also published rigorous monthly and annual reports that gave account of the situation of violence; these reports were sent to tribunals. Thanks to these materials, elaborated by lawyers and social workers, it was possible to elaborate maps of detention places, forms of torture, and the names of the agents responsible. Through the National Coordination Department and the Inter diocesan Covenant of Cooperation in Defense and Promotion of Human Rights, the supporting work coverage was extended to a national level. In this way, the Vicariate became "the voice of the voiceless."

In the early 1980s, economic measures propelled by the dictatorship unleashed a profound and devastating economic crisis causing massive dismissals, miserable wages, extreme poverty, and the closing of banks and enterprises. In 1983 the first demonstration against the dictatorship took place. The Confederation of Copper Workers called for a national strike that triggered the national days of protest. According to Cancino (2001, p. 49), the crisis became a catalyst of all the discontent produced by the system of domination, generating the deterioration of the social base supporting the dictatorship, questioned its legitimacy, criticized the leadership of the government, and placed the return to democracy at the discussion table.

Faced with the national demonstrations, the military regime reacted violently. There was a large number of deaths and hundreds were arrested; however, the more aggressive the government was, the greater were the number of mobilizations and the supporters of dissatisfied groups (university students, farmers, etc.). In this period, the Vicariate acted as a place for assistance and legal support for detainees and the relatives of deceased persons. In addition, the Vicariate along with the social organizations published informative booklets indicating how to act in the face of repression. This initiative intended the Church to be only a support since the aim was that people and collectives would the main promoters of their rights (Palet, 2002).

In the book *El Chile Perplejo. Del Avanzar sin Transar al Transar sin Parar*, Alfredo Jocelyn-Holt (2014) analyzes how the effect of protests escaped the dictator's grip on the country, forcing him to initiate the political liberalization. Such a process generated the alliance between the government and the moderate opposition since the dictatorship could not legitimate itself with violence and, likewise, the opposition could not impose itself over the institutional force. In this way, a logic of consensus began to operate: "the policy of agreements." According to Garretón (1987), the protests were insufficient elements to deepen the crisis of the regime and to advance in the transition process; consequently, they were absorbed by the political parties. Given that if social mobilization was not linked to a consensual institutional change, it would not have generated the end of the regime. De la Maza and Garcés (1984, p. 26) argue that after the protests, the opposing role of the Church changed to appear as a political mediator between the popular movement and the government, whose function was to ensure a non-aggressive departure of the regime.

In 1983 Cardinal Silva Henriquez's term as Archbishop of Santiago ended and was substituted by Cardinal Juan Francisco Fresno. The clerical renewal reaffirmed the commitment to encourage the dialog between the opposition and the government. On Cardinal Fresno's initiative, different political fronts were brought together and the *National Accord for the Full Transition to Democracy* (1985) was signed. During the second half of the 1980s, the Catholic Church continued to call for changes in politics as well as a peaceful process of return to democracy. Once the moderate opposition decided to abide by the transitional constitutional mandate, a period of social awareness began, in which the Catholic Church and the Vicariate carried out civic education campaigns and called to vote with conscience and responsibility in the plebiscites and elections of 1988 and 1989. Finally, in 1990 Chile made the transition to democracy, albeit with the shadow of an institutional framework protected by authoritarian enclave that limited the exercise of power.

THE FACE OF HORROR: SLIT-THROATED CASE
(DEGOLLADOS CASE)

On March 30, 1985, three corpses were discovered near the Santiago International Airport. The bodies belonged to the painter Santiago Nattino, the teacher and leader of the Professional Association of Teachers of Chile (AGECH) Manuel Guerrero, and José Manuel Parada, sociologist and chief of the Analysis Department of the Vicariate. They were members of the Communist Party on the underground. The triple murder was attributed to agents of the Directorate of Carabinero Communication (DICOMCAR). The victims were kidnaped in the street, tortured in the police station of 18 Street, and then they had their throats slit (Caucoto & Salazar, 2013). This murder became to be known as the "Slit-throated Case" (Degollados Case) and laid down a precedent for being the first one politically motivated which did not go unpunished. The case also showed the perilous work and the magnitude of the courage of those who fought for human rights, having proof that even the members of the Vicariate could be targeted.

The murderers' objective was to keep secret the crimes committed by the Joint Command that was being investigated by two of the victims. José Manuel Parada was leading a team in the Vicariate that gathered and pro-cessed information about the human rights violations to, when democracy returned, justice could be done in front of impartial courts (Insuza & Ortega, n.d.). This case generated great public pressure which forced an energic judi-cial investigation, by which the judge José Cánovas, four months after it began, indicted members of the National Police Force. It also caused the resig-nation of Cesar Mendoza, highest-ranking general of the police and member of the *Junta de Gobierno*, alongside with the dissolution of the DICOMCAR (Cavallo, Salazar, & Sepúlveda, 2008, pp. 529–539). The first years of the 1990s came with justice for the families of the victims. In 1991, the members of the police that had been involved in these murders were found guilty for kidnaping, murder, and terrorism. Five years later, the Supreme Court con-firmed their convictions and sentenced them to life imprisonment.[3]

FOR RECONCILIATION AND PEACE IN CHILE

Two days after the coup d'état, the Standing Committee of the Episcopate (1973) called for respect for human rights, the preservation of the rights gained by the workers and farmers, institutional normality, and the prompt restoration of democracy. In the document *Reconciliación en Chile*, Cardinal Raúl Silva Henríquez (1974) called for national reconciliation, a process by which everybody had to be handcrafters of peace. In addition, the basic condition for peaceful coexistence should be the full validity of the rule of law, where the Constitution and law would be a guarantee for everyone. Hereafter, a series of declarations came about such as *Reconciliación en la Verdad* (1985) and *¡Felices los constructores de la Paz!* (1986) pleading with the Chilean people to end violence, to dialog for a reasonable coexistence, and to allow political participation and the search for truth. Elizabeth Lira (2002, p. 101) argued that the Catholic Church and the work of the Vicariate anticipated the conditions for reconciliation in Chile; however, it has been a matter of time for institutions and the society how as a whole to bring about lasting meaningful reconciliation.

THE LEGACY OF THE VICARIATE FOR DEMOCRACY: SPEAKING TRUTH TO POWER

The Vicariate painstakingly gathered documentary material that has become evidence of a past that must not be denied, but above all must not be repeated. The testimonies that were built during 17 years of unspeakable horror served as evidence for the victims of gross violations of human rights, crimes against humanity, as well as for the families and survivors in judicial processes. However, they have been instruments in official and academic investigations as well as of truth-seeking mechanisms, such as the Report of the *National Commission of Truth and Reconciliation* and in the later instances of recognition and reparation for the victims, as well as relatives and survivors of the dictatorship.[4] In December 1992, the Vicariate closed its doors but created the *Documentation and Archive Foundation of the Vicariate of Solidarity* with the purpose of safeguarding and preserve the documentary and audio-visual heritage of the Pro-Peace Committee and the Vicariate.

CONCLUSION

The defense of human rights in Chile during the dictatorship cannot be understood without the tireless and at times perilous work of the Pro-Peace

Committee and the Vicariate of Solidarity. The efforts of these organizations to denounce gross violations of human rights, end the violence, seek the truth, and promote social restoration have historical value for the moral reconstruction of the country. In particular, its courageous groundbreaking work documenting evidence of human rights violations paved the way for the work of truth-seeking commissions, contributing to the fight against impunity, making justice and reparations for victims and relatives possible, and this way ending the silence and denial that often surrounds these atrocious crimes. The solidarity work carried out in this period has had an educational and reflexive contribution to the reconstruction of the social fabric once democracy is restored, since it promoted democratic actions to solve problems and to overcome divisions, beginning a long-term process of ethical and institutional transformation. Furthermore, its grassroots work empowering and leading among the most vulnerable and marginalized showed us that meaningful peace can only be achieved if we endeavor through the work and commitment of many hands.

Massive and systematic violations of human rights occur with the complicity of the entire institutional framework and the support of those manipulated by the propaganda or those who did not wish to know. The courageous work of the Vicariate is a reminder that we should not remain passive nor silent when human dignity and lives are in jeopardy. The 17 years of terror must be kept in the collective memory with the purpose that each person recognizes the consequences of violence and to acknowledge that human rights abuses and the prevention of its recurrence concern us all, the society as a whole.

NOTES

1. The Catholic social teaching is founded on the Second Vatican Council (1962–1965), the Conference of the Latin America Episcopate of Medellin (1968) and Puebla (1979), as well as in the Solidarity Pastoral letter (1975). The theological discourse of these documents shows human freedom in an integral sense (cultural, economic, and social), without depending on any social organization model based on any specific political ideology. The Vicariate worked on the parable of the Good Samaritan, which shows human rights in the heart of the Gospel and evangelization

beyond the spiritual, that is, it extends into the social field to defend the integrity and security of people (Precht, 2002, p. 30).

2. The Decree Law no. 2.191, art. 1 (1978) ruled that subject to certain exceptions, the Chilean amnesty applied to: "all individuals who performed illegal acts [...] during the state of siege in force from 11 September 1973 to 10 March 1978, provided they are not currently subject to legal proceedings or have already been sentenced." (United Nations, 2009, p. 7). At the present, the Amnesty Law is in force, but the courts do not apply it because is inconsistent with international law.

3. Noticiero Judicial (2017).

4. Since 1990, institutional changes have been made to offer transitional justice the State has drafted laws, judicial reforms, reparation measures, and public policies. Among them National Corporation for Reparation and Reconciliation; National Office of Return; Roundtable on Human Rights (known as *Mesa de Diálogo*); National Commission on Political Imprisonment and Torture; Human Rights Programs (in different governments); Program of Reparation and Comprehensive Health Care (PRAIS); and Restitution of Confiscated Property (Law no. 19.568). Furthermore, to the construction of memorial sites such as the Museum of Memory and Human Rights; Memorial to the Disappeared Detained and Executed Politicians; as well as commemorations and human rights campaigns.

ACKNOWLEDGMENTS

Special thanks to Alejandra Villalobos Sepúlveda for translating this chapter from Spanish and to Vanessa Hernández for her valuable and sensitive comments that enriched this chapter.

REFERENCES

Arzobispado de Santiago. (1987). *La Vicaría de la Solidaridad*. Santiago: Arzobispado de Santiago.

Ayala, M. (2014). Los exiliados argentinos en Venezuela, solidaridad, denuncia y construcción de redes regionales de derechos humanos (1976–1981). In S. Jensen & S. Lastra (Eds.). *Exilios: militancia y represión. Nuevas fuentes y nuevos abordajes de los destierros de la Argentina de los años setenta* (pp. 121–155). La Plata: Edulp.

Bravo Vargas, V. (2016). Iglesia liberadora, rearticulación de la política y protesta social en Chile (1973–1989). *Historia Crítica, 62*, 77–96.

Cancino, H. (2001). La Iglesia Católica y su contribución a la reconstrucción de la democracia en Chile. *Revista del CESLA, 2*, 40–62.

Caucoto, N., & Salazar, H. (2013). *La noche de los corvos. El caso degollados o un verde manto de impunidad.* Santiago: Ceibo Ediciones.

Cavallo, A., Salazar, M., & Sepúlveda, O. (2008). *La historia oculta del régimen militar. Memoria de una época 1973–1988.* Chile: Uqber Ediciones.

Comisión Nacional de Verdad y Reconciliación. (1991). *Informe de la Comisión Nacional de Verdad y Reconciliación.* Tomo I. Retrieved from http://bibliotecadigital.indh.cl/handle/123456789/170

Comité Permanente del Episcopado. (1980). *Carta a los católicos de Chile: "Yo soy Jesús, a quien tú persigues".* Retrieved from http://documentos. iglesia.cl/documento.php?id=227

Conferencia Episcopal de Chile. (1985). *Reconciliación en la verdad.* Retrieved from http://documentos.iglesia.cl/documento.php?id=315

Conferencia Episcopal de Chile. (1986). *¡Felices los constructores de la paz!* Retrieved from http://documentos.iglesia.cl/documento.php?id=342

De la Fuente, J. (2011). Salvador Allende, por la democracia y el socialismo. *Revista Latinoamericana de Ciencias Sociales, Niñez y Juventud, 9*(2), 1009–1018.

De la Maza, G., & Garcés, M. (1984). *La explosión de las mayorías. Protesta nacional 1983–1984.* Chile: Educación y Comunicaciones.

Garcés Durán, M. (2017). Los pobladores y la política en los años ochenta: Reconstrucción del tejido social y protestas nacionales. *Historia, 396*(1), 119–148.

Garretón, M. A. (1987). *Las complejidades de la transición invisible. Movilizaciones populares y régimen militar en Chile.* Santiago: FLACSO.

Insuza, A., & Ortega, J. (n.d.). *El día que la muerte llegó a la Vicaría*. Retrieved from http://www.casosvicaria.cl/temporada-uno/el-dia-en-que-la-muerte-llego-a-la-vicaria/

Jocelyn-Holt, A. (2014). *El Chile perplejo. Del avanzar sin transar al transar sin parar*. Santiago: Penguin Random House Grupo Editorial.

Lira, E. (2002). Enfrentar el futuro resolviendo los problemas del pasado. In Arzobispado de Santiago & Fundación de Documentación y Archivo de la Vicaría de la Solidaridad (Eds.), *Seminario. Iglesia y derechos humanos en Chile* (pp. 101–107). Santiago: LOM Ediciones.

Matus, A. (2000). *El libro negro de la justicia chilena*. Barcelona: Planeta.

Monsálvez Araneda, D. G. (2012). La dictadura cívico-militar del general Augusto Pinochet como proceso institucionalizado de violencia política. *Sociedad Hoy, 23*, 33–47.

Noticiero Judicial. (2017, October 12). Fallo Histórico-Caso degollados. *YouTube*, Poder Judicial Chile. Retrieved from https://youtu.be/EH7vUGMu6Rw

Orellana, P., & Quay, E. (1991). *El movimiento de derechos humanos en Chile, 1973–1990*. Santiago: Centro de Estudios Políticos Latinoamericanos Simón Bolívar.

Palet, E. (2002). Cómo y por qué se involucró la Iglesia en Chile en la defensa de los derechos humanos entre 1979 y 1990. In Arzobispado de Santiago & Fundación de Documentación y Archivo de la Vicaría de la Solidaridad (Eds.). *Seminario. Iglesia y derechos humanos en Chile* (pp. 33–46). Santiago: LOM Ediciones.

Precht, C. (2002). Del Comité Pro Paz a la Vicaría de la Solidaridad. In Arzobispado de Santiago & Fundación de Documentación y Archivo de la Vicaría de la Solidaridad (Eds.), *Seminario, Iglesia y derechos humanos en Chile* (pp. 19–32). Santiago: LOM Ediciones.

Rodríguez Iglesias, J. (2008). *Un misionero español en Chile. Miradas desde el pueblo, mensaje cristiano de justicia, memoria y vida*. Santiago: Editorial Tiberíades.

Silva Henríquez, R. (1974). *La reconciliación en Chile*. Retrieved from http://documentos.iglesia.cl/documento.php?id=152

Standing Committee of the Episcopate. (1973). *Declaración del Comité Permanente sobre la situación del país.* Retrieved from http://documentos. iglesia.cl/documento.php?id=147

Tapia Valdés, J. (1980). *El terrorismo de Estado. La doctrina de la seguridad nacional en el Cono Sur.* Mexico: Editorial Nueva Imagen.

United Nations. (2009). *Rule of law tools for post-conflict States: Amnesties,* 2009. Retrieved from http://www.refworld.org/docid/4a953bc82.html

Valdivia Ortiz de Zárate, V. (2010, enero-junio). ¡Estamos en guerra, señores! El régimen militar de Pinochet y el "pueblo", 1973–1980. *Historia,* *1*(43), 163–201.

Veit Strassner, M. A. (2006). La Iglesia chilena desde 1973 a 1993: De buenos samaritanos, antiguos contrahentes y nuevos aliados. Un análisis politológico. *Teología y vida,* *47*(1), 76–94. doi:10.4067/S0049–344920 06000100004

Vicaría de la Solidaridad. (1991). *Historia de su trabajo social.* Santiago: Ediciones Paulinas.

PART IV

PEACEBUILDING

H. Eric Schockman, Vanessa Alexandra
Hernández Soto and Aldo Boitano de Moras

The following chapters pay tribute to the peacemakers and peacebuilders who are transforming societies, by empowering others, challenging the status quo, and defending human rights. Each of these chapters, in their own way and from a multiplicity of perspectives, makes a case for leaders and followers to learn to collaborate actively for common good, with the ability to look beyond dividing lines – ethnic, social, or ideological – and with the capacity to find common goals. They show us that leadership can occur in a variety of roles and capacities and that the world needs each of our talents. The ensuing chapters further demonstrate that there is not a single way to engage peace leadership and that striving for building peaceful institutions, organizations, and communities is a collective endeavor not the privilege of a small notable few: a sobering reminder on the interconnectedness and interdependence of our fates, our inextricably shared humanity, in a global-ized yet divide world. In a modern world that often prizes, individualism, pride, privilege, and exclusiveness, these authors teach us to not be afraid to turn to the collective and in humbly accepting our shared humanity and responsibility for our common future.

Whitney McIntyre Miller and Miznah Omair Alomair's chapter provides an interesting study of the cases often women peacemakers operating in distinct areas of the globe. With the assistance of the Women's PeaceMakers program at the University of San Diego (San Diego, California), the authors invite us to learn about their stories. This chapter shares the findings from a study that helps to understand the work of these Women PeaceMakers through the lens of the Integral Perspective of Peace Leadership (McIntyre Miller & Green, 2015). The chapter helps to illustrate how women who take up peace-based movements in a variety of contexts may utilize peace leadership as a guide for sustainable change. It offers recommendations for others engaging in the leadership and followership work of creating, sustaining, and actualizing a movement with particular attention paid to the modern United States-based #Me Too and Time's Up™ movements.

Lyndon Rego, Katleho Mohono, and Gavin Michael Peter explore the understudied African models of leadership, going "beyond ubuntu" in their chapter. Despite the little attention that general global leadership literature has paid to African models of leadership, the continent of Africa has deep and rich traditions of relational leadership that have been practiced over centuries to honor individuality, broker differences, and foster unity. They place value on both the individual and the community. These practices, nurtured in village communities over centuries, are far from outdated in our modern world. The authors argue that they can help us build the kind of connection, mutual respect, and community that we lack today. This chapter shares a number of these practices and illustrates how they have been used to nurture community at the African Leadership Academy and the African Leadership University. Lastly, the authors explore how we may extend these practices in the wider world to cultivate greater well-being and stronger communities.

Sexual and gender-based violence continues to be a major problem in conflict and post-conflict countries due to gender discrimination embedded within all aspects of society and harmful cultural practices that marginalize and undervalue women survivor's voices, agency, and leadership. Due to the stigma attached to sexual violence, victims are often excluded from their communities and, consequently, do not have the possibility to influence decision-making processes or occupy leadership positions. Malini Laxinarayan and Benjamin Dürr engage with the theories around empowerment and argue that the resilience and strength of survivors not only helps them to deal with the harm they have suffered but also encourages them to become leaders and mobilize others within their communities who have suffered similar fates. Further, their chapter brings to light the work of the Global Survivor Network – a network of survivors of conflict-related sexual violence in over 20 countries – supporting women in making a change on a number of issues.

Through its survivor-led core, the Network ensures that the voices that can bring about the most change are made central, and the strength of women is reinforced. This chapter discusses the stigma faced by women and girls, the benefits of a global survivor network that thrives on leadership, and the impact such an initiative may have on reparations.

Josephine R. Marieta, Bagus Takwin, and Corina D. Riantoputra's chapter deals with the role that followers and leaders can play in conflict management in extractive industry companies. The chapter uses the analysis of case studies in Indonesia to argue that handling internal extractive company conflicts is a very important part in resolving conflicts between companies and communities in extractive industries. Indonesia as a country that is rich in natural resources has attracted various large multinational mining companies. The presence of these companies produces conflict-prone conditions, especially conflicts between companies and surrounding communities. For the last couple of years, natural resources have always surfaced on the top three conflict issues in Indonesia. The authors introduce a theoretical framework that allows them to explain how internal conflicts in extractive industry companies occur because of differences in views, orientation, and mindset between leaders and followers. These differences can be bridged by a common language of conflict resolution through an integrative and comprehensive conflict management program directed to the leaders in the head office, in Indonesia or overseas, and the followers in the area. Lastly, the authors reflect on the implications for the importance of involving and allowing followers to play an active and proactive role in conflict management in extractive industry companies.

Peacebuilding and peacemakers work for lasting peace in many different ways, in a variety of roles and capacities. They inspire us with their strength, resilience, selflessness of spirit, and dignity. They give us reasons to hope, leading by example in fighting inequality and injustice and building resilient peaceful communities driven by ethical values and mutual respect. With this publication, we want to honor the work of peacebuilders and peacemakers around the globe, by giving them a space to tell their story and by giving us the chance to learn from their experiences.

14

PEACE LEADERSHIP FOR SUSTAINABLE CHANGE: LESSONS FROM WOMEN PEACEMAKERS

Whitney McIntyre Miller and Miznah Omair Alomair

ABSTRACT

In many countries over the world, women have waged peace to challenge systemic oppressions and build societies that are reflective of women's voices, and in fact, all voices. Moved by the desire for change, and often even willing to put themselves at risk, these women have paved the way for societal change focused on peace, justice, and freedom. With the assistance of narratives from the Women's PeaceMakers program at the University of San Diego (San Diego, California), we can come to know some of these women and understand their stories. This chapter shares the findings from a pilot study that helps to understand the work of these Women PeaceMakers through the lens of the Integral Perspective of Peace Leadership (McIntyre Miller & Green, 2015). It also offers recommendations for others engaging in the leadership and followership work of creating, sustaining, and actualizing a movement with particular attention paid to the modern United States-based Me Too and Time's Up™ movements.

Keywords: Peace; leadership; women; movements; peacebuilding; change

In many countries over the world, women have waged peace to challenge systemic oppressions and build societies that are reflective of women's voices, and in fact, all voices. Moved by the desire for change, and often even willing to put themselves at risk, these women have paved the way for societal change focused on peace, justice, and freedom. With the assistance of the Women's PeaceMakers program at the University of San Diego (San Diego, California), we can come to know some of these women and understand their stories. This chapter shares the findings from a study that helps to understand the work of these Women PeaceMakers through the lens of the Integral Perspective of Peace Leadership (McIntyre Miller & Green, 2015). It offers recommendations for others engaging in the leadership and followership work of creating, sustaining, and actualizing a movement with particular attention paid to the modern United States-based *Me Too* and *Time's Up*™ movements.

WOMEN PEACEMAKERS

Beginning in 2003, the Women's PeaceMakers program at the University of San Diego hosts four women building peace in their home countries to live in residence at the university for a fall semester. As part of this program, women PeaceWriters work with the PeaceMakers (WPMs) to document their lives in narrative form. Between 2003 and 2016[1], the program hosted 48 WPMs and their writers. The written narratives produced during their time on campus contain the personal journey of each of the WPMs and serve as excellent opportunities to understand the manifestations of peace leadership all over the world. For this study, a pilot project that analyzed ten narratives, the following WPMs were selected, as they represented a range of countries, publication dates, and expertise: Samia Bamieh of Palestine (de Langis, 2007), a leading women's rights advocate in, and for, Palestine; Shukrije Gashi of Kosovo (Batanda, 2006), a journalist and lawyer working for human rights and conflict resolution; Thavory Huot of Cambodia (Ezer, 2005), community-based conflict resolution specialist who works against domestic and other forms of violence; Hyun-Sook Kim Lee of South Korea (Meeks, 2003), a domestic violence awareness and unification of the Korean peninsula advocate; Sarah Akoru Lochodo of Kenya (Thornquist, 2010), an assistant district chief working for nonviolence; Olenka Ochoa of Peru

(Morales-Egan, 2008), a women's and human rights activist; Manjula Pradeep of India (Choi, 2011), a human rights lawyer; Christiana Thorpe of Sierra Leone (McIntyre, 2004), the first female minister of education, a women's education activist, and the chief of the National Electoral Commission; Zahra Ugas Farah of Somalia (Dyck, 2003), a women's health and food advocate; and Claudette Werleigh of Haiti (Das, 2011), an advocate for structural change, the first female prime minister, and secretary general of Pax Christi International.

RELEVANT LITERATURE

These women are just ten of the 48 women who have participated in the program and just a few of the many women working to bring about peace at home and abroad. There has been a significant amount of literature written discussing the role of women in peacebuilding and women in leadership. The narratives discussed herein in many ways bridge this literature, which is less common. The next section in this chapter points to some of the relevant literature that can help to contextualize the role of women in peacebuilding and in leadership.

The Role of Women in Peacebuilding

Gender plays an important role in peacebuilding and peacemaking, as affirmed, and reaffirmed, by United Nations Security Council Resolution 1325 on women, peace, and security (S/RES/1325, 2000; S/2004/814, 2004). Numerous studies (e.g., Bridges & Horsfall, 2009; Mlinarevic, Isakovic, & Rees, 2015; Moore & Talarico, 2015; Unit, 2000) illustrated how women contribute to guiding communities and societies to peaceful change. Women, in fact, are seen as being crucial to sustainable peace as they comprise half of the population, are often survivors of conflict and violence, and have particular concerns that should be addressed (Hunt, 2005; Onyido, 2013). Also, women's inclusion in peacebuilding efforts tend to yield greater attention to gender equality and stronger relationship building (Onyido, 2013; Porter, 2007).

Women can play both official and unofficial roles in peacebuilding. Informally, women serve as advocates, organizers, protestors, educators, facilitators, relationship builders, and provide direct assistance to those in need

(Issifu, 2015; Onyido, 2013; Porter, 2007). In formal capacities, women serve as negotiators, consultants, participants in commissions, members of mass movements, and leaders of non-governmental organizations that provide services such as counseling, education, and training (Justino, Mitchell, & Müller, 2018; Paffenholz, Ross, Dixon, Shluchter, & True, 2016).

Women peacebuilders often face as many challenges as they have opportunities for success. They still have limited involvement in the peacekeeping and peacemaking operations (S/2004/814, 2004) and patriarchal societies and gendered stereotypes limit formal peacebuilding roles in many countries (Berkley & Lackovich-Van Gorp, 2015; Justino et al., 2018; Moosa, Rahmani, & Webster, 2013; Onyido, 2013). Women are also limited in their participation due to economic priorities, low literacy, limited educational programs, and limited self-confidence (Berkley & Lackovich-Van Gorp, 2015; Justino et al., 2018; Moosa et al., 2013; Porter, 2007). Therefore, the literature presents a story of the benefits to women's peacebuilding and peacemaking, but demonstrates the challenges and barriers to women's participation in many instances of this work.

The Role of Women in Leadership

The literature of women in leadership is often separated from its sister literature on women in peacebuilding. There are multitudes of studies, literature reviews, and meta-analyses that discuss women in leadership from various perspectives and in different contexts (e.g. Adler, 1998; Eagley, 2005; Eagly, Johannesen-Schmidt, & van Engen, 2003). As with the women in peacebuilding literature, these studies demonstrate a wide range of barriers that limit women's participation and representation in leadership roles (Diehl & Dzubinski, 2018; Ely & Rhode, 2010; Longman & Lamm Bray, 2018). In fact, women represent only 5% of heads of government, and only 18.3% of government ministers (UNGA, 2018; UN Women, 2017).

Evidence points, however, to the fact that women's influence over public policy improves the quality of life of their constituents (Goryunova, Scribner, & Madsen, 2018). Therefore, it is important work to lessen the barriers to women's leadership. This is why Maria Fernanda Espinosa Garcés, the President of the United Nations General Assembly (UNGA), focused the work of the UNGA on gender equality and the empowerment of women (UNGA, 2018) and why organizations such as the International

Leadership Association have created documents such as the *Asilomar Declaration* to campaign to increase women's leadership status worldwide (ILA, 2015).

Peace Leadership

While much of this aforementioned literature sets the stage for understanding the Women PeaceMakers and their role in societal change, a new and growing body of leadership studies literature, peace leadership, may help further elucidate some understanding of their experiences and the practices and skills the WPMs utilize in their efforts. There are numerous emerging perspectives of peace leadership in the literature that build from the amalgamation of leadership studies, peace studies, and conflict transformation literature. Some of these theories and ideas include Dinan's (2012, 2018) Ubuntu approach, Ledbetter's (2016) leadership for peace in business, Schellhammer's (2016, 2018) examination of peace leadership for a culture of peace, Amaladas's (2018) transformation to peace through will and love, and Chinn and Falk-Rafael's (2018) Praxis, Empowerment, Awareness, Cooperation, and Evolvement model. This chapter, and pilot study discussed herein, focuses on McIntyre Miller and Green's (2015) Integral Perspective of Peace Leadership (IPPL) and McIntyre Miller's (2016) definition of peace leadership as "the intersection of individual and collective capacity to challenge issues of violence and aggression and build positive, inclusive social systems and structures" (p. 223).

The IPPL (McIntyre Miller & Green, 2015) builds on Wilber's (2000) four-quadrant integral theory by plotting relevant leadership studies, peace studies, and community development literature into the quadrants. Each quadrant, while focusing on its own tasks, also functions as part of a whole, which provides the dynamic space to reach progressive goals such as peace leadership. The included quadrants are the I, or the Innerwork quadrant, which focuses on individual, self-based experiences; the WE, or the Communities quadrant, which focuses on collective, group-based experiences; the IT, or Knowledge quadrant, which focuses on internal knowledge-based experiences; and the ITS, or the Environment quadrant, which focuses on systems-based experiences (McIntyre Miller & Green, 2015; Pacific Integral, 2003). The IPPL creates a space where leadership capacities, relationships between and among groups, and networks and systems meet to shift the patterns of thinking and action in our world for the better (McIntyre Miller & Green, 2015; McIntyre Miller & Wundah, 2018).

In the context of this volume, the notion of collective seen in the IPPL (McIntyre Miller & Green, 2015) and McIntyre Miller's (2016) definition is extremely important. The authors take a constructionist view (DeRue & Ashford, 2010; Fairhurst & Grant, 2010; Uhl-Bien, Riggio, Lowe, & Carsten, 2014) that leadership is a shared relationship (Chaleff, 2010) and existing among all participants, those that might otherwise be classified as leaders or followers. In this case, although a focus is put on the Women PeaceMakers themselves, the role of all participants in the endeavors of peace leadership is seen as essential for success. It is the role of each of those engaged in such movements to both work within their individual capacities, while also serving to move forward for the collective good.

STUDY METHODS AND FINDINGS

The bodies of literature discussed above – women in peacebuilding, women in leadership, and peace leadership – often exist separately from each other, with limited overlap and opportunities to inform jointly theory, research, and practice. The study discussed herein served as a way to bridge those gaps by utilizing the narratives of 10 Women PeaceMakers to understand how the skills, practices, and experience of peace leadership were present in the work of each of the women. Briefly discussed in this section is the methods and findings of the forthcoming study.

Methods

The research study discussed herein aimed to answer the research question: In what ways does the Integral Perspective of Peace Leadership (IPPL) inform the understanding of the lives and work of Women PeaceMakers? The study was conducted through deductive qualitative analysis (DAQ) (Gilgan, 2010, 2015, 2017), which takes existing concepts, themes, and theories to test qualitative data with a focus on confirming and disconfirming these extant concepts and refining theory (Gilgan, 2010, 2015, 2017); in this case, the IPPL. For this project, the analyzed qualitative data was 10 of the 48 Women Peacemaker narratives described above. As aforementioned, selected pilot narratives accounted for a wide range of publication dates, geographic regions, and areas of focus.

The narratives were analyzed using hypothesis coding (Saldaña, 2013) and open coding (Gilgan, 2017; Strauss & Corbin, 1998), which enabled the researchers to both understand the IPPL through the narratives and see elements of the narratives, which may disconfirm or further illustrate the IPPL. Both researchers coded the narratives independently and then worked toward coder reliability through utilizing set hypothesis codes and discussed each incident of open coding when analyzing the data to ensure coding agreement was in effect (Richards, 2009).

Findings

The findings of the forthcoming study are presented in terms of the four areas of the IPPL below. For the purposes of this chapter, the findings below are broad representations of the detailed findings of the study. The study reveals the in-depth analysis of the ten narratives and how they serve to confirm and expand upon the IPPL and contains lengthy quotes and descriptions as evidence. Due to this chapter's brevity, however, the study's experiential quotes and descriptions are represented as categories instead.

Innerwork

In terms of Innerwork, three overarching findings were clear. These were the WPMs' connection to purpose and their externally and internally focused innerwork practices. WPMs were able to connect to their peace leadership purpose through the influences of role models; the drive of fear and anger; the need for safety and security; and the desire to challenge the status quo, predominantly in terms of the role of women in society and the culture of silence. The externally focused innerwork practices that were present for the women included listening, forgiveness, and respect for differences. The innerwork practices that were internally focused included self-awareness, being reflective of worldview and identity, and having courage, integrity, and hope.

Communities

The findings revealed that in terms of Communities, two elements were essential: community development and coalition building. Community development activities were those that organized communities and brought them together to do peace work, such as strengthening neighborhood ties and needs-based organizing, which often served to empower women. Coalition building activities were those which united sometimes disparate groups working toward the same goal and served to build social capital and consensus across a variety of stakeholders. Evidence demonstrated that benefits of both of these efforts were an increased feeling of solidarity, a sense of trust within the community, and the creation of appreciation for inclusivity and diversity.

Knowledge

The findings in the Knowledge area focused on the transfer of skills and practices in the work of the WPMs, particularly in conflict transformation and peacebuilding. Evidence pointed to efforts in the area of conflict transformation, including a commitment to nonviolence through dialogue, mediation, negotiation, and reconciliation. The second category of efforts in this area was in terms of peacebuilding practices. These practices included direct action such as nonviolent protests and marches, peace education, skills training, microfinance, and peace communication.

Environment

In the environment area, the findings revealed commitments to change linked to negative and positive peace and efforts of advocacy and activism. The commitments to challenge negative peace included a societal notion of challenging of status quo and efforts to stop corruption. The commitments to build positive peace included the desire for freedom, human rights, and justice for all peoples. Finally, societally focused efforts of advocacy and activism played a role in the efforts of WPMs to make systems and societal change. These included media and reporting strategies, building international networks, mobilizing international assistance, and strengthening national governmental systems.

The IPPL (McIntyre Miller & Green, 2015) did indeed serve to provide an in-depth understanding of WPMs' practices, skills, and experiences in peace leadership. As the IPPL suggests, each WPM worked within each of the four areas of peace leadership, often with practices overlapping in time and effort. This was expected, as the IPPL posits that peace leadership exists when all four of the areas are present and working in tandem. With a range of practices, skills, and efforts available to WPMs, it is no surprise that each woman had what could be considered a unique formula for peace leadership. The way each area manifested in each WPM was different, but all areas of work were present in each case and there were several key overlaps as outlined above.

While the study confirmed the presence of each area of peace leadership and demonstrated many of the expected skills and practices for each area, new ideas also emerged to help further develop the model, including the notion of connecting to purpose in Innerwork, the role of education in Knowledge, and the influence of media in Environment. This study helped to reveal the actions of peace leadership in specific contexts, particularly in the way the women build peace at the grassroots level by challenging society as it stands and working to put in place more peaceful and justice systems and structures. In fact, these cases help to confirm McIntyre Miller's (2016) aforementioned definition of peace leadership.

LESSONS FOR PEACE LEADERSHIP

This study can do more, however, than help to understand the cases of 10 Women PeaceMakers operating in distinct areas of the globe. It can help to paint a picture of how women who take up peace-based movements in a variety of contexts may utilize peace leadership as a guide for sustainable change. Herein we argue that some of these lessons may be particularly relevant to the emerging *Me Too* and *Time's Up*™ movements in the United States and rapidly spreading throughout the globe.

ME TOO AND *TIME'S UP*™ MOVEMENTS

Founded by Tarana Burke in 2006, *Me Too* is a social movement at the grassroots level that is focused on helping survivors of sexual violence, particularly young women of color from marginalized communities, find a path toward healing (Me Too, 2018; Wexler, Robbennolt, & Murphy, 2018). Stated in its vision, the movement's "[…] work continues to focus on helping those who need it to find entry points for individual healing and galvanizing a broad base of survivors to disrupt the systems that allow for the global proliferation of sexual violence" (Me Too, 2018). According to Wexler et al. (2018), Burke's vision of healing includes connecting with and sharing empathy with

survivors, community's recognition of victims, holding perpetrators accountable, and collectively dismantling the systems that enable violence against girls,
women, and even men. In their analysis, Wexler et al. (2018) indicated that
post-conflict societies could draw valuable lessons from the Me Too movement as it works to eliminate structural inequalities, bring an end to the denial
and normalization of violent behavior, create pathways for healing, and utilize
restorative and transitional justice. In this case, we argue the opposite is also
true, that the lessons of women in post-conflict countries may also provide
advice to the Me Too movement.

As the Me Too movement's work continues to spur social change, both
locally and globally, the Time's Up™ organization was established in 2017
by a group of women in Hollywood to address "[...] the systemic inequality and injustice in the workplace that have kept underrepresented groups
from reaching their full potential" (Time's Up, 2017). The organization
aims to change the workplace culture by creating safe workplace environment and improving laws and corporate policies, as well as providing legal
support for victims of sexual violence in the workplace (Time's Up, 2017).
Wexler et al. (2018) noted that the Time's Up organization focuses on sexual harassment, assault, and gender inequality in the workplace and aims
to continue building a momentum that amplifies the believability of survivors' voices and stories. As with many of the women in the Me Too and
Time's Up movements, women in post-conflict societies are survivors of
sexual violence or are working on behalf of those who are.

Lessons from the IPPL and WPM Study

In many ways, the Me Too and Time's Up™ movements already embrace
many of the lessons of the IPPL and WPMs pilot study. As nonviolent social
movements, they are a call to challenge the structures of misogyny and sexism
and creating spaces of equity for women in communities, organizations, and
other social systems. They are, as McIntyre Miller (2016) suggested, challenging violence and aggression and working to build systems, structures, and
institutions that are more positive. Much of this work is in the realm of
Communities and Environment, as they are able to build strong groups of supporters at various levels of influence and seek to challenge the status quo of
sexual abuse, harassment, and other forms of gender-based violence.

The role of Innerwork may be less present in these movements, however much of the drive may be based on the personal experiences of the people involved — it is perhaps their call to purpose. The role of hope, courage, and forgiveness may therefore be seen in these movements as they seek to create change from personal challenges. This may also be the case as the movements utilize some of the practices from the Knowledge area. Direct action practices are present as protests, demonstrations, and marches bring the work to the forefront of the public consciousness. In many cases, the work seen in these movements highlight notions of peacebuilding practices over those of conflict transformation.

As we learn from the experiences of the WPMs, engaging in all areas of the IPPL may be essential for the work of peace leadership. While the Me Too and Time's Up™ movements may be working already in each area of the IPPL, much of the public face of the work seems to be focused on the Communities and Environment arenas. Strengthening the work of Innerwork and building up areas of Knowledge may help solidify the efforts of Me Too and Time's Up™ to create long-term, sustainable change. As we learned from the aforementioned study, there is no one, formulaic way to engage in peace leadership. The Me Too and Time's Up™ movements have, and must continue to, pave their own paths as they aim to making lasting, systemic change in the treatment of women in the United States and beyond.

This study and discussion, therefore, paints an important picture for those engaged in leadership and followership work in women's movements, or in any peaceful nonviolent movement. The WPMs taught us that leadership can occur in a variety of roles and capacities, as these women spent their lives in formal and informal leadership positions. They helped to motivate what Chaleff (2010) might call courageous followers ready to engage in the work of creating better communities and societies. Striving for positive, sustainable change is the work of us all, not a small notable few. Only when we can engage in this work together can peace leadership be the way we move closer to the world we want to see.

NOTE

1. In 2017, the program was redesigned and changed to be more action-research based. Therefore, the narratives of the discussed study were only those in the original program formation.

ACKNOWLEDGMENTS

The authors would like to thank the University of San Diego's Joan B. Kroc Institute for Peace and Justice and its Women PeaceMaker Program for access to the narratives and the ongoing support for this research.

Miznah Omair Alomair: I would like to thank Whitney McIntyre Miller, PhD for the opportunity to co-author this chapter.

REFERENCES

Adler, N. J. (1998). Societal leadership: The wisdom of peace. In S. Srivastva & D. L. Cooperrider (Eds.), *Organizational change and executive wisdom* (pp. 205–221). San Francisco, CA: The New Lexington Press.

Amaladas, S. (2018). The intentional leadership of Mohandas Gandhi. In S. Alamadas & S. Byrne (Eds.), *Peace leadership: The quest for connectedness* (pp. 46–61). Abingdon: Routledge.

Batanda, J. (2006). Seeking freedom amid ruins: A narrative of the life and work of Shukrije Gashi of Kosovo. *Women PeaceMakers Program*, University of San Diego, San Diego, CA.

Berkley, L. A., & Lackovich-Van Gorp, A. (2015). Female leadership for peace and human security: Case study of Israel/Palestine. In S. R. Madsen, F. W. Ngunjiri, K. A. Longman, & C. Cherrey (Eds.), *Women and leadership around the world* (pp. 23–41). A volume in the International Leadership Association series, Women and leadership: Research, theory, and practice. Charlotte, NC: Information Age Publishing, INC.

Bridges, D., & Horsfall, D. (2009). Increasing operational effectiveness in UN peacekeeping. *Armed Forces & Society (0095327X), 36*(1), 120–130.

Chaleff, I. (2010). *The courageous follower: Standing up to and for our leaders.* San Francisco, CA: Barrett-Koehler Publishers, Inc.

Chinn, P. L., & Falk-Rafael, A. (2018). Critical caring as a requisite for peace leadership. In S. Alamadas & S. Byrne (Eds.), *Peace leadership: The quest for connectedness* (pp. 195–211). Abingdon: Routledge.

Choi, A. S. (2011). Broken can heal: The life and work of Manjula Pradeep of India. *Women PeaceMakers Program*, University of San Diego, San Diego, CA.

Das, B. (2011). Building bridges, building peace: The life and work of Claudette Werleigh of Haiti. *Women PeaceMakers Program*, University of San Diego, San Diego, CA.

de Langis, T. (2007). "They never left, they never arrived": The life and work of Samia Bamieh of Palestine. *Women PeaceMakers Program*, University of San Diego, San Diego, CA.

DeRue, S., & Ashford, S. (2010). Who will lead and who will follow? A social process of leadership identity construction in organizations. *Academy of Management Review*, *35*(4), 627–647.

Diehl, A. B., & Dzubinski, L. (2018). An overview of gender-based leadership barriers. In S. R. Madsen (Ed.), *Handbook of research on gender and leadership* (pp. 271–286). Cheltenham: Edward Elgar Publishing Limited.

Dinan, B. A. (2012). "Ubuntu leadership", presented at the Barrett Values-Based Leadership Conference, Cape Town, September.

Dinan, B. A. (2018). Conscious peace leadership: Examining the leadership of Mandela and Sri Aurobindo. In S. Alamadas & S. Byrne (Eds.), *Peace leadership: The quest for connectedness* (pp. 107–121). Abingdon: Routledge.

Dyck, C. (2003). Building the base of the community: A narrative of the life and work of Zahra Ugas Farah of Somalia. *Women PeaceMakers Program*, University of San Diego, San Diego, CA.

Eagley, A. (2005). Achieving relational authenticity in leadership: Does gender matter? *Leadership Quarterly*, *16*(3), 459–474.

Eagly, A. H., Johannesen-Schmidt, M. C., & van Engen, M. L. (2003). Transformational, transactional, and laissez-faire leadership styles: A meta-analysis comparing women and men. *Psychological Bulletin*, *129*(4), 569–591.

Ely, R., & Rhode, D. (2010). Women and leadership: Defining the challenges. In N. Nohria & R. Khurana (Eds.), *Handbook of leadership theory and practice* (pp. 377–410). Boston, MA: Harvard Business Publishing.

Ezer, O. (2005). Peace between banyan and kapok trees: Untangling Cambodia through Thavory Huot's life story. *Women PeaceMakers Program*, University of San Diego, San Diego, CA.

Fairhurst, G. T., & Grant, D. (2010). The social construction of leadership: A sailing guide. *Management Communication Quarterly*, 24(2), 171–210.

Gilgan, J. F. (2010). A primer on deductive qualitative analysis as theory testing & theory development. *Current Issues in Qualitative Research*, 1(3), 1–6.

Gilgan, J. F. (2015). *Deductive qualitative analysis as middle ground: Theory-guided qualitative research*. Amazon Online.

Gilgan, J. F. (2017). *Coding in deductive qualitative analysis and other essays on grounded theory and deductive qualitative research*. Amazon Online.

Goryunova, E., Scribner, R. T., & Madsen, S. R. (2018). The current status of women leaders worldwide. In S. R. Madsen (Ed.), *Handbook of research on gender and leadership* (pp. 3–23). Cheltenham: Edward Elgar Publishing Limited.

Hunt, S. (2005). Moving beyond silence: Women waging peace. In H. Durham & T. Gurd (Eds.), *Listening to the silences: Women and war* (pp. 251–271). Leiden: Brill/Nijhoff.

International Leadership Association. (2015). *The Asilomar declaration and call to action on women and leadership* (2nd ed.). Silver Spring, MD: ILA Women and Leadership Affinity Group. Retrieved from http://www.ila-net.org/Communities/AG/Asilomar_Declaration2015.pdf

Issifu, A. (2015). The role of African women in post-conflict peacebuilding: The case of Rwanda. *The Journal of Pan African Studies*, 8(9), 63–78.

Justino, P., Mitchell, R., & Müller, C. (2018). Women and peace building: Local perspectives on opportunities and barriers. *Development and Change*, 49(4), 911–929. doi:10.1111/dech.12391

Ledbetter, B. (2016). Business leadership for peace. *International Journal of Public Leadership*, 12(3), 239–251.

Longman, K. A., & Lamm Bray, D. (2018). The role of purpose and calling in women's leadership experiences. In S. R. Madsen (Ed.), *Handbook of research on gender and leadership* (pp. 207–222). Cheltenham: Edward Elgar Publishing Limited.

McIntyre Miller, W. (2016). Toward a scholarship of peace leadership. *International Journal of Public Leadership*, 12(3), 216–226.

McIntyre Miller, W., & Green, Z. (2015, April). An integral perspective of peace leadership. *Integral Leadership Review*, 15(2). Retrieved from http://integralleadershipreview.com/12903-47-an-integral-perspective-of-peace-leadership/

McIntyre Miller, W., & Wundah, M. (2018). Integral peace leadership: The case of Christiana Thorpe of Sierra Leone. In S. Alamadas & S. Byrne (Eds.), *Peace leadership: The quest for connectedness* (pp. 62–74). Abingdon: Routledge.

McIntyre, W. (2004). Time to make history, time to educate women: A narrative of the life and work of Christiana Thorpe of Sierra Leone. *Women PeaceMakers Program*, University of San Diego, San Diego, CA.

Meeks, A. J. (2003). Color from shadows: A narrative of the life and work of Hyun-Sook Lee Kim of Korea. *Women PeaceMakers Program*, University of San Diego, San Diego, CA.

Me Too. (2018). *Vision*. Retrieved from https://metoomvmt.org/home

Mlinarevic, G., Isakovic, N. P., & Rees, M. (2015). If women are left out of peace talks. *Forced Migration Review*, 50, 34–37.

Moore, C., & Talarico, T. (2015). Inclusion to exclusion: Women in Syria. *Emory International Law Review*, 30(2), 213–260.

Moosa, Z., Rahmani, M., & Webster, L. (2013). From the private to the public sphere: New research on women's participation in peace-building. *Gender & Development*, 21(3), 453–472. doi:10.1080/13552074.2013.846585

Morales-Egan, B. (2008). Paving the path to peace: The life and work of Olenka Ochoa of Peru. *Women PeaceMakers Program*, University of San Diego, San Diego, CA.

Onyido, O. (2013). Reconceptualizing women's role in peacebuilding. *African Peace and Conflict Journal*, 6(1), 74–91.

Pacific Integral. (2003). *Introduction to Integral Theory and Practice: IOS Basic and the AQAL Map*. Retrieved from http://www.pacificintegral.com/docs/integralsummary.pdf

Paffenholz, T., Ross, N., Dixon, S., Shluchter, A.-L., & True, J. (2016). *Making women count-not just counting women: Assessing women's inclusion and influence on peace negotiations*. [Research Paper]. United Nations Entity for Gender Equality and the Empowerment of Women. Retrieved from http://www.unwomen.org/en/digital-library/publications/2017/5/making-women-count-not-just-counting-women

Porter, E. (2007). *Peacebuilding: Women in international perspective*. New York, NY: Routledge.

Richards, L. (2009). *Handling qualitative data: A practical guide*. London: Sage Publications.

Saldaña, J. (2013). *The coding manual for qualitative researchers*. London: Sage Publications.

Schellhammer, E. (2016). A culture of peace and leadership education. *International Journal of Public Leadership*, *12*(3), 205–215.

Schellhammer, E. (2018). Authentic peace leadership. In S. Alamadas & S. Byrne (Eds.), *Peace leadership: The quest for connectedness* (pp. 75–91). Abingdon: Routledge.

Strauss, A., & Corbin, J. (1998). *Basics of qualitative research: Techniques and procedures for developing grounded theory*. Thousand Oaks, CA: Sage Publications, Inc.

Thornquist, S. (2010). Empowered to hope: The life and peacebuilding work of Sarah Akoru Lochodo. *Women PeaceMakers Program*, University of San Diego, San Diego, CA.

Time's Up. (2017). *Our mission*. Retrieved from https://www.timesupnow.com/#ourmission-anchor

Uhl-Bien, M., Riggio, R. E., Lowe, K. B., & Carsten, M. K. (2014). Followership theory: A review and research agenda. *The Leadership Quarterly*, *25*, 83–104. doi:10.1016/j.leaqua.2013.11.007

Unit, L. L. (2000). Mainstreaming a gender perspective in multidimensional peace operations. *DPKO, July*.

United Nations General Assembly. (2018, September 25). *President of General Assembly addresses general debate, 73rd session* [video]. Retrieved from http://webtv.un.org

United Nations Security Council. (2000, October 31). *Resolution 1325* (S/RES/1325). Retrieved from https://documents-dds-ny.un.org/doc/ UNDOC/GEN/N00/720/18/PDF/N0072018.pdf?OpenElement

United Nations Security Council. (2004, October 13). *Women and peace and security: Report of the Secretary General*(S/2004/814). Retrieved from https://documents-dds-ny.un.org/doc/UNDOC/GEN/N04/534/14/PDF/ N0453414.pdf?OpenElement

United Nations Women. (2017, July). *Facts and figures: Leadership and political participation*. Retrieved from http://www.unwomen.org/en/what-we-do/leadership-and-political-participation/facts-and-figures

Wexler, L., Robbennolt, J. K., & Murphy, C. (2018). # MeToo, Time's Up, and Theories of Justice. University of Illinois College of Law Legal Studies, Research Paper No. 18-14. Retrieved from https://papers.ssrn.com/sol3/ papers.cfm?abstract_id=3135442

Wilber, K. (2000). *A theory of everything: An integral vision for business, politics, science, and spirituality*. San Francisco, CA: Shambhala Publishing.

15

BEYOND *UBUNTU*: WHAT THE WORLD CAN LEARN ABOUT BUILDING COMMUNITY FROM AFRICA

Lyndon Rego, Katleho Mohono and
Gavin Michael Peter

ABSTRACT

The general global leadership literature has had little to say about African models of leadership. Despite this, the continent of Africa has deep and rich traditions of relational leadership that have been practiced over centuries to honor individuality, broker difference, and foster unity. This chapter shares a number of these practices and illustrates how they have been used to nurture community at the African Leadership Academy and the African Leadership University. We conclude with our perspective on the relevance of these practices to building community in the wider world.

Keywords: Africa; emotional intelligence; relational leadership; interdependent leadership; collaboration; *ubuntu*

> If you want to go fast, go alone. If you want to go far, go together.
>
> — African proverb

INTRODUCTION

In the book *Community: The Structure of Belonging*, Peter Block observes that unity and community have eroded even as our world has gained in material wealth. Community, Block says, is where we feel a sense of spiritual, emotional, and psychological belonging (Block, 2018). As the world looks to reestablish community, there is much that can be learned from Africa about fostering respect and relationship.

Traditional leadership practices in Africa are deeply relational. They place value on both the individual and the community. These practices, nurtured in village communities over centuries, are far from outdated in our modern world. We believe that they can help us build the kind of connection, mutual respect, and community that we lack today. Here we explore these traditional practices and their connection to key leadership concepts. We illustrate how these practices have been leveraged to build a vibrant pan-African community at two sister organizations – the African Leadership Academy (ALA) and the African Leadership University (ALU). Finally, we finally explore how we may extend these practices in the wider world to cultivate greater well-being and stronger communities.

THE AFRICAN LANGUAGE OF LEADERSHIP

Much of the leadership literature has been generated in the West and the East. Far less is known globally about African models of leadership. One African idea that has gained currency is *ubuntu*. *Ubuntu* has been translated as "I am because you are" but it has much more depth and nuance. Desmond Tutu explains that *ubuntu* expresses the essence of being human: "My humanity is caught up, is inextricably bound up, in yours" (Tutu, 2000). We belong in a bundle of life. We say, "A person is a person through other persons."

Ubuntu isn't a solitary idea but part of a larger construct of how to live in community. This starts with acknowledging people. In Southern Africa, tradition calls for people to be formally greeted and asked about their well-being. Gavin, one of the coauthors and a native of Zimbabwe explains, "We ask how is your spirit, how is your body? In asking, we express a sense of care and connection that is embodied in *ubuntu* – I am only okay only if you're okay."

The common Zulu greeting *sawubona* embodies this ethos. It translates as "I see you" and expresses the idea that I see you as a person, I recognize your humanity, and I offer you respect. The traditional answer to *sawubona* is *ngikhona*. It means, "I am here." It communicates that you are seen and acknowledged. This exchange is not a passing greeting but rather an investment in relationship-building. It contrasts to the casual greetings we often exchange elsewhere, where we might say hello or "how are you doing?" but not stop to truly see or hear.

Acknowledgment opens the door to relationship. It leads to the exploration of who we are together. The word *tirisano* in Tswana means working together. It comes from the proverb, *Tirisano motheo wa tswelopele*, which means working together is foundation of progress (South African Languages). *Tirisano* helped Botswana navigate the colonial era and create peace and prosperity. Centuries ago, Botswana's kings set aside differences to unite to repel invading Boers and broker treaties with the British. It enabled them to get through the colonial age without the horrors that their neighbors suffered. Post-independence, this philosophy enabled the nation to sidestep coups and civil conflict and sustain one of the fastest growing economies for decades (The World Bank In Botswana, 2019).

Tirisano is practiced in the tradition of the *kgotla* in Botswana. The *kgotla* is a public and inclusive means of dialog and debate used for key community decisions. A *kgotla* can be a public meeting, community council, or traditional court. In the *kgotla*, anyone may speak, and no one may interrupt others. The idea is to make community decisions through greater consensus. Although the chief often gets the last say, the practice recognizes the "chief is chief by grace of his tribe" (Botswana Public Assembly, 2010). Here, the spirit of *ubuntu* shines through. Even the highest leader, the chief, is the chief because of the people.

A related expression of collective engagement is *harambee* which means pulling together in Swahili. Susan Njeri Chieni of Moi University explains "The harambee concept embodies the ideas of assistance, joint effort, mutual self-responsibility and community self-reliance" (Chieni, 1999). It is a traditional principle by which people join to plant and harvest, build houses, and raise money for those in need. *Harambee* has been adopted by the Kenyan government as a national slogan and appears on the national coat of arms.

Another tradition elevated to a national practice is *umaganda* in Rwanda. Here people take to the streets on the last Saturday of each month to sweep the roads, fill potholes, and spruce up public spaces. The streets of Kigali are spotless because *umaganda* extends beyond the monthly cleaning to a mindset about the role of the individual in caring for the nation.

In all these African traditions, we see a recognition of individual dignity and well-being in the context of community. The practices also engender harmony by creating spaces for dialog and working through differences. They harness the collective power of people to overcome challenges and foster growth. The practices recognize that community exists when people feel cared for by each other. They reflect core leadership models for building relationships, cultivating interdependence, and getting things done, together.

THE CONNECTION TO LEADERSHIP THEORY

Leadership is about relationships. Relational leadership is a process of people working together to create a common good. Komives et al. (2013) state "Relationships are the connective tissue of the organization [...] over time, these new relationships, built on trust and integrity, become the glue that holds us together."

Emotional intelligence offers that we must understand others in order to know how to treat them. Emotional intelligence correlates with leadership effectiveness. From data gathered from more than 5,600 people across 77 organizations, Boedker (2011) of the Australian School of Business reported that the ability of a leader to be empathetic and compassionate had the greatest impact on organizational profitability and productivity. Belinda Parmar (2016) in *Harvard Business Report* states that "The top 10 companies in the Global Empathy Index 2015 increased in value more than twice as much as the bottom 10, and generated 50% more earnings." Emotional intelligence and relational leadership represent the very ethos of *ubuntu*.

The Center for Creative Leadership (McCauley et al., 2008) defines interdependent leadership as a collective activity that requires mutual inquiry and learning. This involves dialog, collaboration, building networks, valuing differences, and a focus on learning. Interdependent organizations and communities work effectively across organizational boundaries. Here we can see the link to practices such as *tirisano* and *kgotla*.

The framework of boundary-spanning leadership emerged from the Center for Creative Leadership's global research into effective ways of spanning differences and leveraging diversity (Ernst & Chrobot-Mason, 2011). The process of boundary spanning flows from: (1) managing boundaries to (2) forging common ground to (3) discovering new frontiers.

Boundary-spanning leadership maps well to the African leadership (AL) practices we shared. Managing boundaries is about recognizing identity and honoring differences. The term *sawubona* reflects the idea of seeing the other for who they are. *Tirisano* and *kgotla* recognize the second stage of fostering interdependence and forging common ground. *Harambee* harnesses the collective effort of a community.

We believe that these traditions reflect that essential leadership practices can be leveraged for how we can build organizations and nurture communities. We offer examples from the ALA, in South Africa, and the ALU, in Mauritius and Rwanda, to illustrate how these traditions have been used to build a pan-African community.

CREATING A PAN-AFRICAN COMMUNITY: AN AL CASE STUDY

There is a well-known African saying that it takes a village to raise a child. It follows then that the village becomes your family and those you care for in return. ALA and ALU set out to create a pan-African community that would claim the larger continent as home.

ALA and ALU were founded with a mission to develop leaders for Africa. The institutions are grounded in the belief that a pan-African approach can catalyze growth and development in Africa. African leaders must understand and collaborate with peers across the continent to remove barriers to trade, end conflict, and stimulate positive change.

Many of our students chose ALA and ALU because of the pan-African identity. Yet, what does it mean to live in a diverse community; how are bonds of unity forged? ALA and ALU drew inspiration from the wealth of African rituals and practices to build a community that would be diverse and united. These rituals and practices, described below, have become the fabric of AL culture.

Check-ins

At ALU classes and meetings often begin with a check-in ritual. People stand in a circle and respond to the question, "how are you feeling?" While a stand-up meeting in a tech company focuses solely on what are you doing, the ALU stand-up focuses first on feelings. This evokes the spirit of *sawubona* – of being seen. We may know that a person is tired because they didn't sleep well, or restless because they have a lot on their mind, or distracted because of a family concern. With this awareness, we engage differently. We know better how to read each other better.

Taalaw/Opening Ceremony

Taalaw which comes from the Arabic "come together" is the name for the colorful opening ceremony which marks the beginning of every school year, typically in mid-September at ALA. The key elements integral to a *Taalaw* are authentic African cultural fashion, movement, music and words, and the fire lighting. It evokes the traditional ways of welcoming guests to a home. The cultural rituals that the community performs together at a *Taalaw* ceremony are rich in history and recognizable in a manner that has no words. The ceremony, usually an hour or so in length, conjures elements that are tribal, ancient, and connecting [...] and familiar. To close the ceremony, after all the noise and energy, a new energy comes – fire. Fire is integral to so many African ceremonies and way of life and symbolizes the removal of the former status in order to allow the new to form. Following the dry season and before the rains, many lands will be burnt to cleanse and clear the land for the new shoots. The moment of lighting the torch of the new members in the community symbolizes that same start. The past is burnt away, and its layers now fertilize this new present. A fresh start, together. The design emerged over several years and evolved into a vibrant ritualized welcome into our community. The whole academy arrives dressed in their national attire, acknowledging our different roots. Students enter the room via a "parade of nations" – often accompanied by dance and music – to the cheers of other students to each other's traditions. The day ends with a vibrant night festival, celebrating the diversity and spirit of unity, family, and warmth that represents Africa.

One year a student from Senegal arrived late in the year. In November, two months after the start, we checked to see if anyone had not yet settled into the community. The new student had not, in spite of having completed all the academic and orientation programs. Like a visitor in a village, or in a new city, you can feel present and yet always looking in from a window pane, aware that another world and community are behind that glass. For the new student, we decided to do the ceremony again just for her. It changed everything for her. Later that year she led the creation of a summer school teaching project in her former school in Senegal. Her community strength was so powerful that she was joined, voluntarily, by five faculty members and 10 students, most of whom were not Senegalese.

My Story

When we tell a personal story, it reinforces our common humanity. In 2009 "Under the Baobab" was an informal gathering at ALA, used as a tool for students to share their life experiences as a means to get to know each other. One of the students shared a story so passionate that they were asked by ALA co-founder, Fred Swaniker, to share their story with the whole community at an assembly. Upon hearing their inspirational story, Fred suggested that more students share their stories in assembly. Thus, the birth of "My Story." Over the years, there have been countless numbers of staff and students who have inspired our community through their stories. The tradition has also given birth to variants such as "My Message" and "My Failure."

A key element in "My Story" is the moment when the storyteller lets the audience look into her soul. This can be just for a few moments, but their trust of the community to see their deep, and most guarded side, ripples through the room. In a phrase, "you had to be there." Storytelling is part of the African way of doing things. Oral storytelling, though often criticized as limited and limiting as compared to written storytelling, is where the magic of connection happens − hearing the story in the person's own voice and words, sharing their vulnerability, pride, pain, joy, and passion.

An ALA student we will call D announced one day that he wanted to tell his story, but he needed one month to complete it. It was an unusual request to have such a distant but specific timeline, but when he told the story, we knew why. D survived the Rwandan genocide. His parents and half his siblings did not. He was nine years old and hid with two sisters in the forests, eating leaves and berries for sustenance, terrified. When the killings stopped they emerged far from home, a home now lost. D found a way into a school, into a space to live, into a new life, one where he was the breadwinner. He wrote poetry for competitions and pumped fuel to earn the money for school. His spirit remained optimistic, so optimistic that it glowed, and he won scholarships, placements, and opportunities. He told his story that afternoon to a silent audience. His voice was steady and calm, the depth of his grief and struggle visible under the surface. He had needed a month, not to write the story, but to find the way to tell the story for the first time, to us, his new family. Most importantly, D did not want us to feel pity or get lost in the tragedy of the circumstances of his past. He ended with the title, "Tough times make tough minds." We have printed and published the written copy of his story many times as it is equally well written, but those who were in the room that day felt something different. D trusted us, he felt we were his family and so we should know his true past.

Assembly/Townhalls

Many organizations and academic institutions have team meetings and assemblies. We wanted to make these gathering different. We reached back to the ancient fireside gatherings of the village. Why had everyone come out of their huts, what had drawn them to sit together? How could you get a community to come to a meeting, even look forward to it? We aimed to include elements that made the best of ourselves reflect at our assemblies, even with bad news. We wanted the assemblies to be a reflection of the institution and bring everyone to reconnect to the warmth of community that can be lost during the routine and frustration of the regular week. Eventually, we scheduled all campus visits from outside guests to be on assembly days as we knew they gave an authentic snapshot into our culture and community. There are many stories, like the university recruitment agent who insists on speaking in assembly each year because "there is nowhere else in the world he has felt that warmth so intensely he could almost touch it;" or the student who had received a Commonwealth Award from the Queen and insisted on waiting for weeks before telling the community, as he wanted it done at assembly.

Nelson Mandela's work and example played a large role in our direction and teaching. We would often tell students "Leave your room as if one day you will meet Nelson Mandela in these corridors." For years it was always possible that Tata Madiba could actually visit, and he almost did on several occasions. It was also inevitable that one day this dream would be lost. In the six months leading to his death, everyone had the possibility in the back of their minds. Yet, nothing could have prepared us for the late-night news of his passing. In the early morning staff and students emerged, sad, solemn, and lost. The natural thing to do was to call an assembly. We all moved to the auditorium and took our regular seats. The Dean formally acknowledged the moment and event with a retelling of the news we already knew. Then, as with all assemblies, we share. So, he gave a semi-impromptu "My Story" of his love of Madiba and his own grief. Then, as if by routine, our choir was called up. They had met 10 minutes before assembly and decided to perform a freedom song. We played some images and then sat together. After some time, people left at their own pace and we could begin the day. The routine of assembly was not what saved us that dark day. It was that our assemblies are rituals, they are the way that we commune, and touch a higher place for all who participate. We were all amazed and grateful in how that impromptu assembly had turned into the memorial we needed to mourn and honor Tata Madiba in a way that was authentic to us.

Gratitude/Washing Hands

Izandla ziyagezana is an isiZulu idiom, also found in other Nguni languages, which can be translated as "hands wash each other together." Its literal meaning suggests that one hand cannot clean itself, rather both hands require one another to cleanse themselves. Wider meanings of the term can be linked to the concept of communal being linked to *ubuntu* — we cannot exist without each other. A similar idiom is *ukuph' ukuziphakela* meaning to serve others is to serve oneself (literally — to dish out for others is to dish out for oneself).

Gratitude and respect are African qualities that have served our growth. We included this ceremony to allow us space and silence to let gratitude be expressed. The washing allows for the natural uncomfortableness of the moment to be overcome. It is essential because these moments rarely happen in real-time interactions. The person offering gratitude has to be below the eye level to be able to wash the hands; this also allows for a break in eye contact, which again allows for the honesty to be free. We started the ceremony a few years ago and were unsure of the success. Even in our small community, which has so many regular touch points for one-on-one interaction, the outpouring of real gratitude is overwhelming. It allows the introvert, the person one does not regularly interact with, and the person one does not even know one has impacted the opportunity to come forward.

A student named G was always involved in our community, but in a very unemotional way. He was very athletic and action driven. He had a no non-sense and no emotion manner in planning programs and activities, though he was always involved. He was the one we could rely upon to get things done, but without open displays of emotion. When he appeared in the line, it was a surprise to most of the other students, even staff. We all thought it would be a brief, structured moment, sincere but quite matter of fact. His eyes welled up as he explained how he was so grateful for this place where he could finally feel free to be himself and express the other emotions he felt. He had often not been able to say thank you with emotion and humility. This simple gesture, with its stillness, proximity, finally allowed the unbot-tling of emotion. It remains one of the most moving moments for those who witnessed it.

Gratitude Waterfall

This tradition often concludes closing gatherings in our community, like an end-of-year party. Jugs of a beverage are passed around along with cups. Participants are invited to find others whom they are grateful to and fill a bit of their cup from a pitcher and offer a few words of thanks. Invariably we find we have many people to thank for support, for the learning they have provided, or simply for who they are. Unlike ceremonies where some people are singled out or people are thanked at large, the gratitude waterfall cere-mony is personal, democratic, and diffused. There is plenty of gratitude to go around for big and small things that made a difference. Giving thanks invokes the spirit of *ubuntu* – we are who we are because of each other.

Student N came from Turkey and had chosen to spend her two years of senior school at ALA. She was an introvert by nature and her origins played against her settling and finding friends. In truth her journey was about find-ing herself. N returned to campus after graduating from college. She pulled me aside to describe the evening of the waterfall exercise from her perspec-tive. On the day of the waterfall ceremony, she disclosed, she had been in a state of depression and resolved that she would commit suicide. The water-fall of gratitude from an endless line of students filled her cup to overflowing. She told me she only remembered her plan days later. Sometimes, a human connection can mean the difference between life and death.

Truth and Reconciliation

We all do things that sometimes break trust. Sometimes these can be serious missteps that draw reprimands or punishment. But a misstep, no matter how grievous, does not fully characterize a person. Failure can provide pivotal learning opportunities for an individual and the community to grow.

One year two students wished to spend their last evening together by going to a nice restaurant and then a hotel for the night. As they were still underage, they needed their parents' consent which was not granted. Not letting this stop them, they found a student who could disarm the campus security system and arranged for it to be deactivated so they could leave and return quietly. The news of the deactivation spread, however, and more students decided that it was their opportunity to take advantage of the situation. When preparing for how to deal with this breach of conduct the leadership team adopted a *truth and reconciliation* approach. Instead of applying the rule book, everyone in the community was allowed to come forward and be heard. This allowed students to speak in a safe way and others who had violated the trust to hear. As a community, we were able to collectively find the root problem of the incident. The victims felt their voices had been heard and as a group, we were able to provide discipline and punishment, while enabling learning and bringing closure. It was modeled on similar trials conducted in South Africa and Rwanda. A community wound needs the community to solve it. Like the *kgotla*, the gathering allowed for all voices to be heard.

In another incident, Student G made a mistake. As CFO of his student business he stole funds from the profits. The enterprise was so successful that he had reasoned that no one would notice. It was noticed and, as integrity is one of our values, a hearing was called. A decision was made that his enrollment be terminated and his college acceptance revoked. He was then booked to leave to return home within a few hours. As African educators, we then organized one of our rituals for expelled students. It comes from the village idea where when a member disappoints the community their "expulsion" is not permanent. More importantly, the belief that this one incident is not the sum total of all the character of this young leader. The ritual starts with everyone gathering around the student, just before he is due to depart. One by one people recount the good he has done – the positive actions, the moments where he showed the values we uphold. It ends with a summary that we hope he takes away. Our actions must have a firm consequence so that we learn from failure, but we are not here to break each other down. G went home, and after a long period of reflection started an initiative there to help young people jumpstart their entrepreneurial ideas based off the lesson he had learned. He made integrity as the principal value to be deliberately lived, sharing his story. We still see G as part of our community. He is still an agent of positive change active on the continent, the sum of more good values, than one mistake. A person is not only their faults but the good that they also are.

Collections for Colleagues/Harambee

In a village, when someone is in financial need, they can place a pot outside their hut for others to give what they can. The root idea is that everyone has something, no matter how small, and all those small contributions add up. It is an African version of crowdfunding. It allows the person in need to retain their dignity.

T graduated from ALA in 2010. She attended university and returned to South Africa to work. T dreamt of doing her masters one day, but she had a student loan to repay first. Ten years later she attended our 10th anniversary reunion. After meeting with her former classmates and hearing of their progress, she applied to read for her masters. She was successful in being selected and even earned a scholarship, but she was short US$10,000. She reached out to her classmates. Within a week, they had filled her pot. They were all young, recent graduates but their small contributions added up. *Harambee* works when a real community exists.

Departures/Praise Singing

A community is not static. People come, and people go. When the ones we love leave, there is a sense of loss. At ALU, this transition is marked by a praise singer, someone close to the person leaving who stands up to share. These reflections can be elaborate, sometimes funny, and often sad, but are always heartfelt. They typically are a recollection of memories, challenges, and happy times shared. If I am because we are, the departure of a member of the community changes who we are.

At ALU, on one occasion, a long-time staff member was leaving to return to her home country, get married, and begin a new phase of her life. Her boss stepped up as the praise singer. He laughed and wept as he recounted his earlier memories of their relationship, how they had gotten through difficult times, and how much he would miss her. For the community, the testimony celebrated the value of a dear colleague who had made her mark not only on the work but on people's hearts.

In these and other practices at the AL organizations, the workings of community are ritualized and repeated in a structured way. How we enter and how we leave is marked with ceremony. Each person forms a piece of the fabric of the community. Their contributions are noted with gratitude, and when they exit, they are celebrated by the community with a recollection of appreciation and praise.

The AL rituals and practices we shared exist in the boundaries of an educational institution but an institution made up of strangers from distant lands. Community is not left to chance but cultivated. We believe that deliberate practices such as these can be used to cultivate a sense of community in our organizations and cities. This, we believe that it is more essential now than ever. For as we are swept by the surge of globalization and rapid technological change, these African practices can help us reclaim the humanity and sense of kinship that has unraveled.

IMPLICATIONS

We are creatures of blood and bone, idealism and suffering.
Though we differ across cultures and faiths, and though history has
divided rich from poor, free from unfree, powerful from powerless
and race from race, we are still all branches on the same tree of
humanity.

— Nelson Mandela

Our world is deeply polarized and building understanding is critical to addressing our political, economic, environmental, and health challenges. In the *Radius of Trust*, Realo, Allik, and Greenfield (2008) observe that

one inevitable consequence of modernization is the growth of
selfishness and egoism, which poses serious threats to the organic

unity of individuals and society by paving a road to social atomization, unbounded egoism, and distrust.

As we look to the future and the emerging technology-driven "4th Industrial Revolution," Rob Elkington (2018) states, the type of leadership needed to thrive is Leadership 4.0. This is much less about technical savvy, and much more about inclusion, meaning, and social capital. He states that we must see ourselves as part of a complex adaptive system where everything we do is connected to others and the planet. This is an expression of *ubuntu*, a recognition that I am because we are.

Many great changemakers such as Mandela, Gandhi, and Mother Teresa were clear that we must ourselves be the change we wish to see in the world. Changing our organizations and the wider world starts with developing ourselves and our communities. The following are thoughts for how we might bring the spirit of AL into the wider world to build a stronger sense of connection and community.

Bring People Together

We need spaces for convening. Coworking spaces and meetups offer opportunities to connect with new people. Many organizations are also creating more open workspaces that enable more interaction. This is also happening in cities. Arts festivals and community events bring people together temporarily into a common space for a shared experience, but they don't necessarily encourage people to interact with those who they don't already know. The need is to build *bridging* social capital across identity groups – connecting people who aren't already connected. *Bonding* social capital is about strengthening existing group ties while bridging social capital is about creating social networks across dissimilar groups (Panth, 2010). The latter enables people who don't ordinarily connect to build relationships and trust. This widening of the "radius of trust" creates stronger and more innovative communities.

We have experimented with some bridging approaches. Katleho Mohono, one of the authors, hosted garden parties in Mauritius where he invited local Mauritians and expats, two groups that don't often mix, to connect socially. Lyndon Rego, another author, conducted a series of hackathons in South Africa that brought in people from business, government, and the social sector to rapidly cocreate possibilities for enhancing energy, finance, and the arts in their communities.

Create Platforms for Storytelling

The TEDx movement and *Pechakucha* are growing practices that encourage personal storytelling. These formats, like the AL "My Story" tradition, give voice to the stories of people in ways that often break assumptions and stereotypes. We need more channels for individual voices in our communities to be expressed and heard. Everyone has a story to tell and when we hear each other's stories, we are no longer strangers.

Mobilize Collective Action

In the United States, Lyndon was involved in inclusive urban revitalization efforts that brought together a broad coalition of stakeholders in an ecosystem to dream and work together on a common economic vision (Rego & Gergen, 2017). The creation of social capital and bridging networks in the community was foundational to growing jobs, attracting investment, and changing policy. Networks can extend beyond local communities via virtual platforms. Peer-to-peer platforms and social networks are part of the new sharing economy. They shift the vehicles of commerce and communication from brokers to everyday people. Crowdfunding is a digital form of *harambee*. Strangers give to strangers to help in times of need.

As we look into the future, we have a personal choice to make. We can retreat to our technology-insulated cocoons or reach out to build thriving hubs of community. We can choose to create a village that recognizes our humanity and raises all of us with respect and caring. The African practices of seeing and acknowledging each other (*sawubona*), working together (*tirisano*), resolving differences in community (*kgotla*), and helping each other (*harambee*) are practical ways to build community. Building community takes effort. If it takes a village to raise a child, it also takes every man and woman to build the village of belonging and caring. We must all get personally involved — for I am because you are.

ACKNOWLEDGMENTS

The authors offer our appreciation to the students and staff of ALA and ALU who live the leadership practices we've described.

REFERENCES

Block, P. (2018). *Community: The structure of belonging.* Oakland, CA: Berrett-Koehler Publishers.

Boedker, C., Cogin, J., Langford, P., Meagher, K., Mouritsen, J., Runnalls, M. et al. (2011). *Leadership, culture and management practices of high performing workplaces in Australia: The high performing workplace Index.* Sydney: Society for Knowledge Economics.

Botswana Public Assembly. (2010). Kgotla. Retrieved from https://participedia.net/de/methods/kgotla-public-assembly

Chieni, S. (1999). *The harambee movement in Kenya: The role played by Kenyans and the government in the provision of education and other social services. (n.d.).* Retrieved from http://boleswa97.tripod.com/chieni.htm

Elkington, R. (2018). *Are you developing effective leadership for the 4th industrial revolution (Industry 4.0)? Why it matters!* Retrieved from https://www.linkedin.com/pulse/effective-leadership-4th-industrial-revolution-40-dr-rob-elkington-/

Ernst, C., & Chrobot-Mason, D. (2011). *Boundary spanning leadership: Six practices for solving problems, driving innovation, and transforming organizations.* New York, NY: McGraw-Hill.

Komives, S. R., Lucas, N., & McMahon, T. R. (2013). *Revisiting the relational leadership model: Perspectives from the third edition of exploring leadership.* Eugene, OR: The University of Oregon.

McCauley, C. D., Palus, C. J., Drath, W. H., Hughes, R. L., McGuire, J. B., O'Connor, P. M. G., et al. (2008). *Interdependent leadership in organizations: Evidence from six case studies.* Greensboro, NC: Center for Creative Leadership.

Panth, S. (2010). Bonding vs. bridging. Retrieved from https://blogs.worldbank.org/publicsphere/bonding-and-bridging

Parmar, B. (2016). *The most empathetic companies, 2016.* Retrieved from https://hbr.org/2016/12/the-most-and-least-empathetic-companies-2016

Realo, A., Allik, J., & Greenfield, B. (2008). Radius of trust. *Journal of Cross-cultural Psychology, 39,* 447–462.

Rego, L., & Gergen, C. (2017). Fostering inclusive innovation ecosystems. In A. Boitano, R. L. Dutra, & H. E. Schockman (Eds.), Breaking the zero-sum game building leadership bridges (pp. 43–57).

South African Languages. Retrieved from http://salanguages.com/munnames.htm

The World Bank in Botswana. (2019). Retrieved from https://www.worldbank.org/en/country/botswana/overview

Tutu, D. (2000). *No future without forgiveness.* New York, NY: Doubleday.

16

ENGAGING SURVIVORS OF CONFLICT-RELATED SEXUAL VIOLENCE IN SOCIAL MOVEMENTS: THE CASE FOR REPARATIONS

Malini Laxminarayan and Benjamin Dürr

ABSTRACT

Conflict-related sexual violence, primarily affecting women, has become synonymous with the notion that stigmatization and dominant male power relations lead to the suppression of female voices when speaking about their experiences. Yet theories around empowerment argue that the resilience and strength of survivors not only helps them to deal with the harm they have suffered, but also encourages them to become leaders and mobilize others within their communities who have suffered similar fates.

A platform must exist that can facilitate and promote the efforts of survivors who are actively engaged in bringing about change. One means to achieve such a goal is to provide those who have been victimized with a mechanism to connect, share experiences, and engage in advocacy in large groups. SEMA: The Global Network of Victims and Survivors to End Wartime Sexual Violence represents one such platform that supports women in making a change on a number of issues. This chapter will discuss the stigma faced by women and girls, the benefits of a global survivor network that thrives on leadership, and the impact such an initiative may have on reparations.

SEMA and its focus on reparations is both influenced by and influences survivor leaders, who entail a crucial part of decision-making. Through its survivor-led core, SEMA ensures that the voices that can bring about the most change are made central, and the strength of women is reinforced.

Keywords: Conflict-related sexual violence; survivors; reparations; peacebuilding; women empowerment; transitional justice

INTRODUCTION

Sexual violence in conflict leads to far-reaching consequences that impact victims, families, communities and even subsequent generations (Leatherman, 2011). In addition to the medical and psychological effects of sexual violence, victims suffer from stigmatization by the society at large, which deeply affects their well-being. The trauma that ensues has severe implications on one's resilience and empowerment, and therefore steps must be taken to remedy such harmful outcomes.

Providing these women with these tools to express their voice and become agents of change must be made central throughout their recovery process. Greater decision-making power has been reflected in international mechanisms such as the Security Council Resolution 1325 (S/RES/1325) on Women, Peace, and Security. Particularly where these women are organized within social movements, they are more willing and inclined to voice their experiences, needs, and grievances. Expressing this type of information can be the catalyst for real social change, such as advocating for reparations and altering the existing stigmatizing culture that often exists.

Social movement theory aims to understand why and how social mobilization occurs, in addition to the political and social consequences that result. Within social movement theory, particularly in recent decades, there has been a focus on leadership. This area of scholarship more specifically examines how leadership roles may impact a movement's effectivity, exploring how women are able to inspire and organize others to mobilize and engage in strategic processes.

This chapter will apply this framework to an emerging initiative of the Mukwege Foundation, that aims to take the form of a social movement. SEMA: The Global Network of Victims and Survivors to End Wartime Sexual Violence who themselves have become or are becoming agents of change, situating themselves in a leadership role within their local contexts. The following pages will address two links. First, SEMA can facilitate leadership and engage supporters in order to create common goals and become empowered, especially when they return to their communities and act as leaders. Second, lobbying for and achieving political objectives, namely reparations, can lead to policy change; where women are psychologically, socially and economically empowered (through reparations), they are also more capable of acting as leaders.

SEXUAL VIOLENCE IN CONFLICT AND THE ROLE OF WOMEN

Sexual and gender-based violence (SGBV) continues to be a major issue in conflict and post-conflict countries due to gender discrimination embedded within all aspects of society, harmful cultural practices, and low status of women and girls (Leatherman, 2011). The position of women as second-class citizens in a patriarchal society makes them extra vulnerable and they are often seen as property of men. Particularly, rape in conflict is considered to be an attack not only on the woman's body, but on the men in her life whose masculinity is questioned, on her children who are often forced to witness the violence, and on the entire community that was unable to protect her.

Rape as a weapon of war has affected millions of women. Though the true number of sexual violence crimes cannot accurately be assessed, reports give an estimation of the prevalence of such crimes. In South Korea, the number of women are estimated to have been forced in the "comfort women" system is up to 200,000 (Soh, 2000). In Bosnia estimates are between 20,000 and 40,000 boys, girls, men, and women, while in Sierra Leone 200,000 to 260,000 women and children were victimized during the 11-year conflict (Ten Bensel & Sample, 2017). In only nine months during the Liberation War in Banglasdesh in 1971, it has been estimated that between 200,000 to 400,000 Bengali women were sexually assaulted and impregnated by Pakistani soldiers.

Survivors from every conflict ranging from Kosovo to Democratic Republic of the Congo (DRC) to Colombia have reported the stigmatization that results from victimization (Clark, 2019; Kelly, Betancourt, Mukwege, Lipton, & Van Rooyen, 2011). Stigma can have lifelong and lethal consequences for survivors and for children born of rape (UN Security Council, 2018). Victims are ostracized and rejected by families and communities, often encountering victim-blame and abandonment. This stigma contributes to the silence on sexual violence, which further exacerbates the structural inequalities within political, economic, cultural, and social structures. Furthermore, there is a massive "hidden figure" because survivors are unable to speak out without the support of their families and communities, having detrimental consequences on their access to legal and psychological services. This stigmatization has obvious repercussions on survivors' ability and willingness to break the silence.

Though women are disproportionately targeted and subsequently are more likely to suffer the consequences of sexual violence, they are also key players in conflict resolution and peacebuilding, where their leadership is invaluable to greater society. Security Council Resolution 1325 (S/RES/1325) on Women, Peace, and Security reflects the significance of empowered women, recognizing the crucial participation of women to promote peace and security through greater decision-making power in matters related to conflict prevention and resolution. While this Resolution represents an achievement in the struggles women face following violence, it does not provide guidance on *how* to provide space for women to demand their rights and create change both within their countries and globally. A network that provides this space is the first step to a larger movement to end sexual violence and engage in peace negotiations.

SOCIAL MOVEMENT THEORY AND LEADERSHIP

Citizens often take to movements in order to voice their grievances to the government, policymakers, and even the general public. Justice, and social justice more specifically, is undoubtedly an area that has received much attention from civil society. The anti-war movement, the battered women's movement, the civil rights movement, and more recently, the Black Lives Matter movement all represent the power of the citizenry to demand its rights after facing injustices.

The resource mobilization theory is helpful in understanding under what conditions a movement is likely to occur (McCarthy & Zald, 1987; Staggenborg, 2016). According to this theory, not only are grievances experienced by a community necessary, but groups should be able to mobilize resources in order to demand their rights. Societal support is emphasized, in addition to linkages of social movements to other groups and the dependence of movements on external support. At the individual level, the theory assumes that people are rational. A movement is more likely to result where resources such as money, solidarity, knowledge, skills and access to media are available.

Social movements are both collective and organized. For social movements to grow and maintain structure, leadership is crucial. Leaders are not only responsible for themselves, but also for the collective. Social movements will occur once leadership has been identified and developed. Movements can reinforce individuals' empowerment, making them agents of change who can return to their communities to further spread their messages.

Five practices have been outlined within social movement leadership (Snow, Soule & Kriesi, 2004). First, relationship building requires that members are mobilized through their commitment to future participation and with shared values. Ties must be strong to enhance trust and solidarity. Second, leaders should develop a narrative that articulates a story of self and "us," enabling leaders to link with others not only in the group but also the public. Narratives can help to guide others toward understanding how the world *should be*. Third, strategy within leadership converts resources into power, often in response to dealing with people who are in (more) powerful positions. Leadership teams are likely to be crucial for effective strategizing. Fourth, structure related to decision-making, coordination, and accountability are important to address. Again, leadership teams help to ensure structure and promote broadening of decisions and values. Thoroughly considering teams can help to prevent the emergence of isolated groups making decisions unilaterally for the larger group. Fifth, action must accompany the leadership practices in order to galvanize the movement. These actions must be strategic and focused.

IMPACT OF MOVEMENTS ON SURVIVORS OF CONFLICT-RELATED SEXUAL VIOLENCE

As noted earlier, rape can have debilitating consequences for survivors, leading to self-blame, lower self-esteem, and feelings of disempowerment, all of which impact their psychological well-being (Campbell & Raja, 1999; Herman, 2003). Their voices have been silenced, and they made to believe their needs or opinions have no value. Secondary victimization from those around survivors only serves to reinforce negative self-perceptions. Rape victims have been rendered powerless, an outcome that has obvious implications for remaining silent. Moreover, the stigma victims face is rampant, exacerbating the already immense trauma suffered.

While such experiences have been reported among countless rape victims, evidence also suggests that their resilience may be amplified through speaking out. By doing so, they are communicating to society that their rape is unacceptable and must be punished accordingly. Speaking out can also help victims become survivors, as they are no longer accepting the passive, injured role, but rather are fighting back against their aggressors and those who facilitate such aggression.

Indeed, by placing women in leadership roles, they are able to internalize their identity as one of an enabled and influential person. Through social movements, women may gain an increased sense of power and self-assurance, as was the case in women's suffrage and abolitionist movements (Klenke, 1996). Not only do these movements enhance collective identity, they also assert public voice, which is crucial for survivors of sexual violence who have been silenced, and whose needs often go unheard and unmet. They may learn they are not the only ones who have suffered, but rather that such abuse is part of a systematic attempt to destroy women and communities, and victims are not to blame.

At the national level, victims and victims' or women's groups have already been involved in successfully demanding and achieving their rights on topics related to reparations and inclusion in peace processes. For example, in Colombia, victims have been integral in peace negotiations, organizing themselves and arguing that victims of sexual violence should also be recognized in the measures that are being taken to compensate victims. In Kosovo, victim groups were pivotal in petitioning the government for reparations, leading to the amendment of a law that already provided support for combatants and other civilian war victims (Amnesty International, 2017). Furthermore, ongoing movements have been taking form, for example in DRC, where a protest of approximately 800 survivors took place in April 2018 in response to mass rapes and the inaction of the government (La Prunelle RDC, 2018). Undoubtedly, we cannot forget the role of the so-called "comfort women," who sparked their own movement in their fight for justice against the atrocities of the Japanese military sexual slavery system during WWII.

THE IMPACT OF REPARATIONS ON THE WELL-BEING OF SURVIVORS

Key to the formation of a social movement is the aim to fulfill common political objectives through mobilization. This mobilization — whether through demonstrations, marches, legal activism, or other forms — emphasizes respect for basic rights and helps to represent marginalized groups. Movements may "engage in coalition-building with other movements, political parties and politicians with the aim of influencing policy, or if possible the institutional framework of their countries" (Vergara-Camus, 2016). Social movements demand government action, which can take a number of forms, but which all aim to provide redress for the harm suffered and ensure that similar crimes do not occur in the future. More specifically, we are interested in understanding the impact that movements can have on achieving reparations as a form of justice for survivors of conflict-related sexual violence.

At the individual level, reparations can have an impact on the well-being of victims, leading to both empowerment and transformation following sexual violence. At least from a normative perspective, claims have been made that reparations indeed can repair and recognize the harm by restoring the dignity that has been violated (Couillard, 2007; Ní Aol'ain, O'Rourke, & Swaine, 2015; Walker, 2016; Yepes, 2009). The victim feels acknowledged, and victim-blame is reduced helping to combat the victim status and turn one into an agent of change. Rather than the disempowered, victim role, those who have been harmed are more likely to adopt a survivor role characterized by strength and resilience.

The transformative function also presents itself more acutely when the participation of victims is emphasized. For example, the Nairobi Declaration recognizes that exactly those who have suffered human rights violations are in the best position to inform policymakers how reparations should be offered, particularly in cases of sexual violence (Couillard, 2007). Such participation has obvious implications for their empowerment, allowing, particularly women, to be involved in decision-making and addressing their own wounds themselves.

In addition to the psychological well-being of victims, the socioeconomic benefit of reparations should not be underestimated. When reparations are more than a one-time cash payment, they can have a positive impact on gender equality and economic empowerment, for example when women get access to land, credit, employment, education, or health services (Freizer, 2016). By providing income-generating opportunities and activities, women can begin to rebuild their lives and strengthen their position in society.

At the societal level, reparations can support the process toward a stable and peaceful society by addressing root causes of conflict and in particular sexual violence, such as gender inequalities and stigmatization. For example, by publicly acknowledging the harm done to women, the blame that often falls on rape victims can be lifted and they may be able to return to their communities. Reparations can also take the form of Guarantees of non-repetition, which can include security sector and law reforms, human rights, and sex education in schools. This idea was highlighted in the Guidance Note of the UN Secretary-General on Reparations for Conflict-Related Sexual Violence which states that reparations for conflict-related sexual violence should "unsettle[e] patriarchal and sexual hierarchies and customs" (United Nations, 2014).

Experts have highlighted that:

> [m]aterial forms of reparations are necessary to address the economic needs of survivors, who often become heads of household and sometimes have to take care of children born of rape. Symbolic reparations are necessary to address the social stigma that survivors of sexual violence are subjected to, such as their exclusion from the community or abandonment by their spouse. (Rubio-Marín, 2006)

Reparations therefore may have positive implications on the financial and psychological well-being of survivors. At the same time, however, we would like to explore the role of survivors in obtaining reparations. A platform that provides a space for survivors to demand their rights may subsequently lead to reparations, as will be explained in the following section (Figure 1).

WOMEN MAKING CHANGE: THE GLOBAL SURVIVOR NETWORK AND REPARATIONS

SEMA: The Global Network of Victims and Survivors to End Wartime Sexual Violence, led by the latter, and aimed at building solidarity and advocating for the rights of survivors. Since 2017, women from 20 countries have been developing this network, and forming leadership roles. The leaders in the network have the goal of raising awareness, involving other survivors, and leading efforts in achieving the five goals of the network. These goals include (1) the creation of a global reparations fund, (2) developing a safe space for survivors to share their stories, (3) challenging stigma and raising awareness, (4) implementing days of memory in honor of survivors, and

Figure 1. From Victim to Agent of Change.

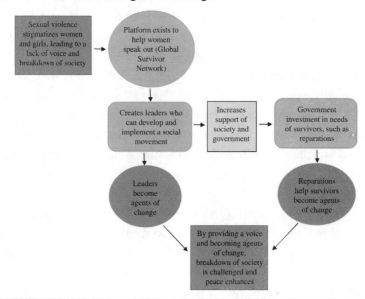

(5) launching a campaign demanding justice. The first goal, the creation of a global survivors' fund, will be linked to social movement theory in the following paragraphs.

WHAT CAN THE NETWORK LEARN FROM LEADERSHIP THEORY?

Tilly (1978) would likely characterize SEMA as currently falling between the preliminary stage and the coalescence stage (Tilly, 1978). According to the author, the preliminary stage is when citizens become aware of an issue and leaders begin to emerge. People then join together and organize themselves with the goal of raising awareness and setting the issue on the agenda. As was briefly noted, resources are a key factor to the success of the network. While the Mukwege Foundation plays a crucial role in currently gathering and providing resources to the network, the long-term vision will see the Foundation as an external supporter, where the survivors are driving the movement.

A focus on repairing the harm and strengthening the position of women can also lead to members of a movement to become agents of change. This is the case where the political objective itself – namely reparations – can serve as a catalyst of empowerment. For SEMA, it is evident that the members are clear on their mission and objectives, but leaders are still in the phase of mobilizing themselves. These women must take the role of strategic decision-makers who can inspire others to take part in the movement.

The practices related to social movement leadership that were identified earlier can be applied to the Survivors' Fund. Relationship building is key and for this reason members from 20 countries gather together multiple times a year in order to show solidarity, discuss the future, and devise initiatives that will improve their position. Through their strategic messaging, the network has been able to formulate a narrative of "us," depicting the notion that they stand together, the silence must be broken, and remedies must be provided (e.g., reparations). Furthermore, the structure of the network has been implemented, with two survivor coordinators per country, taking a leadership role and playing a key role in decision-making and coordination, also to reach out to others in their own countries. Finally, the network takes part in different activities, such as speaking out at international events (e.g., UN Human Rights Council), developing statements of solidarity, and taking part in knowledge-sharing activities.

APPLICATION TO THE SURVIVORS' FUND

When developing a clear strategy, survivors have the possibility to achieve systemic changes. The leaders of the Global Survivor Network identified the need for reparative justice as one objective, which the women share across generations, countries, and cultures. The need for and the right to reparations has been widely acknowledged.[1] However, in most countries, implementation of programs for reparative justice remains hugely challenging (United Nations Office of the High Commissioner for Human Rights). Both at the national and the international level, the issue of reparations has been neglected.

In 2018, SEMA established a working group on reparations. In the same year, The Mukwege Foundation started the first phase of planning of the The International Fund for Survivors of Conflict-Related Sexual Violence (Survivors' Fund), spearheaded by Dr Denis Mukwege and Nadia Murad, 2018 Nobel Peace Prize Laureates. The Fund aims to provide reparative justice through a reparations mechanism, advocate the prioritization of reparations internationally, and build up knowledge on the topic.

Though some survivors may be able to naturally a carry out a leadership role without too much guidance or assistance, others first require economic independence or livelihood support. They may also lack self-confidence as a result of their victimization. The acknowledgment by a Fund like this that they have been victimized and deserve redress can help overcome this obstacle because it teaches other members of their communities that survivors are not to blame. When this recognition comes with practical support, such as economic assistance, they can shift their attention from the struggle of daily survival to taking active roles in society.

So far, however, only a very small number of victims of conflict-related sexual violence worldwide have received reparations, for example in countries such as Colombia and Kosovo. In the absence of an adequate mechanism, the core of the Survivors' Fund will provide a platform where governments, corporations, and individuals can contribute. The role of survivors will become key in the Fund's upcoming committee, which will consist of survivors and distinguished experts. Survivors are best suited to understand how reparations should be dispersed, and can also play a key role in encouraging other States to participate.

The Survivors' Fund thus provides the basis for the transformation from survivor to agent of change by fulfilling the necessary preconditions in terms of practical and financial backing and societal acceptance and reintegration. Such support can have immense implications for their well-being, both financially and psychologically. Concerning the latter, where they receive the recognition through reparations that acknowledge the harm caused to them, the self-blame victims feel is likely to decrease or disappear. Like SEMA, the Survivors' Fund depends on the openness to change of society and governments in order for it to be fully effective.

Leadership theory is useful in understanding the steps necessary to realize the Survivors' Fund. From the framework developed by Marshall Ganz and outlined earlier, building relationships, developing a narrative, strategizing, and creating a structure are of particular importance for the Initiative. First, the leaders of SEMA and the Initiative need to build political support with governments and experts. In 2018, they met ambassadors and representatives of six countries (Dr. Denis Mukwege Foundation, 2018a, 2018b).

Second, their advocacy efforts must contain a compelling narrative which not only attracts more survivors to join the movement, but, more specifically, convinces political actors and the public on why governments should support the initiative financially and politically. So far, the stories of sexual violence survivors have largely been absent in the public discourse – a gap SEMA can fill. Third, a strategic approach is necessary to achieve systemic change. SEMA employs a dual approach by lobbying at the national and the international level. The national movement in DRC, for example, started to organize public demonstrations to bring the topic to the attention of the public. Leaders of the group also specifically petitioned the Congolese government to provide reparations (Dr. Denis Mukwege Foundation, 2018a, 2018b). Fourth, well-designed leadership teams are being created by designating survivor national coordinators within the global network and forming working groups on a diverse number of topics.

CONCLUSION

Reparations have been identified as an effective peacebuilding tool to rebuild societies and support individuals after an armed conflict. The combination of acknowledgment and practical – often financial – assistance provides an opportunity for individuals to take the role of survivor, characterized by strength and resilience, rather than disempowerment.

The transformative power is even stronger when victims participate in the development of policies and mechanisms for reparations. This idea has been recognized by international actors, for example in the Nairobi Declaration, which stresses that those who have suffered human rights violations are best positioned to inform policymakers about the effective provision of reparations.

However, due to the stigma attached to sexual violence, victims are often excluded from their communities and, consequently, do not have the possibility to influence decision-making processes or occupy positions of power. A international platform like the Global Survivor Network enables them to address these issues by lobbying for the means necessary to become agents of change and participate as leaders in policy and peacemaking processes. Survivors reach out both at the national and local levels, depending on the activity and the needs in the country.

NGOs can support this process by providing the necessary resources, such as communication tools or a space to meet. They also play an important role in assisting survivors in their advocacy, for example by helping to develop strong advocacy messages or by organizing trainings in public speaking or similar leadership skills.

NOTE

1. See for example 2014 United Nations "Guidance Note of the Secretary-General: Reparations for Conflict-Related Sexual Violence" (retrieved from http://www.ohchr.org/Documents/Press/GuidanceNoteReparationsJune-2014.pdf; accessed on August 27, 2018) and "Draft Articles on Responsibility of States for Internationally Wrongful Acts" (Report of the International Law Commission, 53rd session, 2001).

REFERENCES

Amnesty International. (2017). Wounds that burn our soul. Retrieved from https://www.amnesty.org/download/Documents/EUR7075582017 ENGLISH.PDF. Accessed on August 22, 2018.

Campbell, R., & Raja, S. (1999). Secondary victimization of rape victims: Insights from mental health professionals who treat survivors of violence. *Violence and Victims, 14*(3), 261–275.

Clark, J. (2019). 'Leaky' bodies, connectivity and embodied transitional justice. *International Journal of Transitional Justice, 13*(2), 268–289.

Couillard, V. (2007). The Nairobi Declaration: Redefining reparation for women victims of sexual violence. *International Journal of Transitional Justice, 1*(3), 444–453.

Dr. Denis Mukwege Foundation. (2018a, June 20). In Geneva, sexual violence survivors lobby international community for recognition and reparations. Retrieved from http://www.mukwegefoundation.org/2018/06/20/in-geneva-sexual-violence-survivors-lobby-international-community-for-recognition-and-reparations/. Accessed on August 29, 2018.

Dr. Denis Mukwege Foundation. (2018b, April 26). More than 800 rape survivors protest against increasing violence, following latest mass rapes in Congo. Retrieved from http://www.mukwegefoundation.org/2018/04/26/ 600-rape-survivors-protest-violence-mass-rapes-congo/. Accessed on August 29, 2018.

Freizer, S. (2016). Reparations after conflict related sexual violence: The long road in the Western Balkans. *Security and Human Rights*, 27, 5–13.

Herman, J. (2003). The mental health of crime victims: Impact of legal intervention. *Journal of Traumatic Stress*, 16(2), 159–166.

Kelly, J. T., Betancourt, T. S., Mukwege, D. M., Lipton, R., & Van Rooyen, M. J. (2011). Experiences of female survivors of sexual violence in eastern Democratic Republic of the Congo: A mixed-methods study. *Conflict and Health*, 5(25).

Klenke, K. (1996). *Women and leadership: A contextual perspective.* New York, NY: Springer Publishing Company.

La Prunelle RDC. (2018, June 19). Sud-Kivu: les survivant(e)s des violences sexuelles réclament plus d'action de la part de l'État. Retrieved from http:// www.laprunellerdc.info/2018/06/19/sud-kivu-les-survivantes-des-violences-sexuelles-reclament-plus-daction-de-la-part-de-letat/. Accessed on July 21, 2019

Leatherman, J. (2011). *Sexual violence and armed conflict.* Cambridge: Polity Press.

McCarthy, J. D., & Zald, M. N. (1987). Resource mobilization and social movements. In M. N. Zald & J. D. McCarthy (Eds.), *Social movement in an organizational society: Collected essays.* New York, NY: Taylor and Francis.

Ní Aol'ain, F., O'Rourke, C., & Swaine, A. (2015). Transforming reparations for conflict-related sexual violence: Principles and practice. *Harvard Human Rights Journal*, 28, 97–146.

Rubio-Marín, R. (2006). The gender of reparations: Setting the agenda. In *What happened to the women? Gender and reparations for human rights violations*. International Center for Transitional Justice. New York, NY:

Social Science Research Council. Retrieved from https://s3.amazonaws.com/ssrc-cdn1/crmuploads/new_publication_3/%7BD6D99C02-EA4A-DE11-AFAC-001CC477EC70%7D.pdf. Accessed on August 27, 2018.

Snow, D., Soule, S., & Kriesi, H. (2004). *The Blackwell companion to social movements*. Hoboken, NJ: Blackwell Publishing.

Soh, C. S. (2000). Human rights and the 'comfort women'. *Peace Review*, *12*, 123–129.

Staggenborg, S. (2016). *Social movements*. Oxford: Oxford University Press.

Ten Bensel, T., & Sample, L. (2017). Collective sexual violence in Bosnia and Sierra Leone. *International Journal of Offender Therapy and Comparative Criminology*, *61*, 1075–1098.

Tilly, C. (1978). *From mobilization to revolution*. New York, NY: McGraw-Hill.

United Nations. (2014, June). Guidance note of the Secretary-General: Reparations for conflict-related sexual violence. Retrieved from http://www.ohchr.org/Documents/Press/GuidanceNoteReparationsJune-2014.pdf. Accessed on August 17, 2018.

United Nations Office of the High Commissioner for Human Rights. Reparations for acts of sexual violence committed in conflict. Retrieved from https://www.ohchr.org/EN/NewsEvents/Pages/DisplayNews.aspx?NewsID=14685&LangID=E. Accessed on August 27, 2018.

United Nations Security Council S/2018/250. (2018, March 23). Report of the Secretary-General on conflict-related sexual violence. Retrieved from https://www.passblue.com/wp-content/uploads/2018/04/sexual-violence-in-conflict.pdf. Accessed on August 23, 2018.

United Nations Security Council S/2004/616. (2004, August 23). Report of the Secretary-General: The rule of law and transitional justice in conflict and post-conflict societies. Retrieved from https://digitallibrary.un.org/record/527647/files/S_2004_616-EN.pdf. Accessed on August 17, 2018.

Vergara-Camus, L. (2016). Why social movements matter for addressing inequalities and ensuring social justice. World Social Science Report. Retrieved from http://unesdoc.unesco.org/ulis/cgi-bin/ulis.pl?catno=245825&gp=1&mode=e&lin=1

Walker, M. U. (2016). Transformative reparations? A critical look at a current trend in thinking about gender-just reparations. *International Journal of Transitional Justice, 10*(1), 108–125.

Yepes, R. U. (2009). Transformative reparations of massive gross human rights violations: Between corrective and distributive justice. *Netherlands Quarterly of Human Rights, 27*(4), 625–647.

17

CONFLICT MANAGEMENT IN EXTRACTIVE INDUSTRIES IN INDONESIA: LEADERS–FOLLOWERS DYNAMIC TO ACHIEVE PERCEIVED SOCIAL JUSTICE IN COMMUNITIES

Josephine R. Marieta, Bagus Takwin and Corina D. Riantoputra

ABSTRACT

In Indonesia, the usage of natural resources is one of the three main conflict issues (Directorate General of Politics and Public Administration, Ministry of Home Affairs, 2016; Habibie Center, 2013). Forty-Seven percent of the conflicts are between communities and the extractive companies (Agrarian Reform Consortium, 2014). Many of these extractive companies choose to implement a short-term conflict management approach, which include charitable programs or the usage of security, as a way to interact with the locals. However, they do tend to ignore the local wisdom of the community in resolving the issues, or even apply a different parameter to acknowledge the developmental progress in the community. Due to their short-term, unsustainable approach, the communities' trust in these extractive companies is very low, perceiving that the companies are treating them unfairly. To cultivate trust in the community, an integrative stakeholder engagement process must be implemented by the extractive company through concrete actions for the community. These actions should involve the active participation of the communities from time to time, not only in times of crisis. This chapter argues that to be able to handle external conflicts, the extractive company must first resolve its internal conflicts by adjusting its perspective, orientation, and mindset between its leaders and followers. Another important aspect is that the companies need to develop an understanding regarding the cultural diversity and customs in Indonesia. The extractive company should implement an integrated stakeholder engagement approach which provides a platform for followers and leaders in the company to be able to work together in managing the conflict in the community. This chapter proposes the principles underlying the dynamics of the relationship between the management and staff in the field during the stakeholder engagement process to achieve perceived social justice in society.

Keywords: Conflict management; extractive industries, leaders–followers; internal conflict, stakeholder engagement; perceived social justice

INTRODUCTION

As a country that is rich in natural resources, Indonesia has attracted various large multinational mining companies. The presence of these companies results in conflict-prone situations. Conflicts especially arise between the companies and the surrounding communities. For quite some time, the usage of natural resources has always surfaced on the top three conflict issues in Indonesia (Directorate General of Politics and Public Administration, Ministry of Home Affairs, 2016; Habibie Center, 2013). The manner in which natural resources are managed is considered as one of the contributors to inequality among the members in communities. Reeson and Hosking (2012) in their research on extractive industries stated that although the contribution of extractive companies is very significant at the macro-level, their impact at the local scale is more complex. This statement is backed by the findings of the National Team for Poverty Prevention and Control in Indonesia that shows that regions which produce oil and gas have more poor people (Irfanny, 2015).

Because of the aforementioned conditions, there exist marginal groups in a community that experience structural injustice. The injustices arise because the resources are not distributed fairly among the existing groups.

The World Bank (2013) explained that inequality results in injustice, slows economic growth, and increases the risk of conflict. It is found that in regions in Indonesia with higher-than-average levels of inequality, the conflict ratio is 1.6 times greater than regions with lower levels of inequality. In fact, inequality has become a global phenomenon, having a negative impact on relations between groups, especially among those who are disadvantaged. Kemp, Owen, Gotzmann, and Bond (2011) have stated that inequitable distribution of risks, impacts, and benefits are the key drivers of resource conflict. In an interview with a local in a remote area in Indonesia, the local stated: "[...] it was more convenient to ask for (employment, educations, health services) to the extractive company because it was more likely to be heard than to the local government" (Y. K., personal communication, January, 18, 2013). With the issue of inequality, especially in developing countries such as Indonesia, it is quite a common practice for communities to often look to the extractive companies to provide what governments are not able to provide (e.g., infrastructure, education, health services, economic development initiatives, and employment). The expectation is so because the people in these regions feel that they are treated unfairly and consider one of the sources of injustice to be the presence of the extractive industries; therefore, the communities put pressure on the extractive company to meet their needs.

The relationship between extractive industries in Indonesia and the local communities that surround them is extremely complex. These industries experience a lot of pressure from the central and regional governments, the security forces, and other local stakeholders such as the local community and non-governmental organizations (NGOs). On an international scale, the pressure can be exerted by the head office of the extractive company, shareholders, global institutions, and financial and investment agencies that fund these companies. Consequently, there is a high level of mistrust by the local community toward these industries. Therefore, the perception and attitude of the local communities toward the oil, gas, and mining companies present in their regions tend to be negative (Erwiantono & Saleha, 2012). Findings from other research also demonstrate that the impacted communities have a low acceptance toward these companies (Environment Energy Bulletin, 2015). But at the same time, these communities develop high expectancies toward the extractive companies. There is a tendency for the impacted community to put pressure on the extractive company, even resorting to the usage of violent action such as protests, demonstrations, or even damaging the company's facilities. In such regions, the role of the local government to provide various developmental actions in the area has been replaced by the extractive companies. However, when the companies are not able to meet the requests, the community develops negative perceptions of injustice and prejudice toward the extractive company.

These growing tensions between the extractive companies and the impacted communities is reflected in the data of the Agrarian Reform Consortium (2014) which shows that 47 percent of the conflict actors in Indonesia are the local communities and their association with the extractive companies. These conflicts range from minor disagreements to violent conflicts (Kemp et al., 2011). Kemp et al. (2011) described these conflicts as a "battleground" where the extractive companies' interest and activities are questioned or even rejected by the community. In the face of such a negative discourse, many extractive companies are trapped into solving the community's problems with quick-fix solutions. These companies implement short-term conflict management approaches such as charitable programs or the use of a security-based approach as a way of interaction with the locals (Adnan et al., 2008). With the aim of improvising public acceptance toward the extractive company, various approaches have been implemented by the companies. These range from conducting fire-fighting programs and providing financial support to the local leaders to repressive policies or security-based approaches such as the deployment of officers to secure the extraction process (Yanuarti, Marieta, Yusuf, & Tryatmoko, 2003). Humpreys (2005) states that to resolve natural resource conflicts, the military approach is considered to be more effective than the negotiation approach.

Previous research tended to focus on explaining the conflict in the context of the relationship between communities and the extractive company. For example, the social license to operate (SLO) by Boutilier and Thomson (2011) conceptualizes the communities' perception regarding the acceptability of a company. However, Bulzomi (2013) explains that the continuing conflict between extractive industries and the local community was due to the lack maintaining strategic stakeholder relations by the company. Strategic stakeholders' relations need to take into consideration the role of the staff of the company, especially the field representatives who deal with the community on a daily basis, because their interaction with the community plays a vital role in the community's acceptance of the company

(Moffat, 2015). Knowledge regarding the community's perception of procedural and interactional injustice, as obtained through interviews conducted by the field representatives of the company, plays a major role in escalating or de-escalating the conflict (Kemp et al., 2011). Thus, one of the important aspects that needs to be considered while managing conflicts in an extractive industry is the relationship between the leaders and followers. The corporate entity that holds executive, management, or superior positions, sets the strategic goals, and makes decisions regarding the operation of the extractive company are considered as leaders. In contrast, followers are the staff who work in the field to implement the policies of the company; they represent the extractive company in the area/field of operation. Difference in perspectives, orientations, and mindsets between these two entities has increased the complexity involved in the conflict handling programs and policies.

Through an analysis of cases in Indonesia, this chapter shows how the extractive company's internal conflicts can contribute to the escalation of conflicts between companies and communities. Describing the dynamics of leaders (corporate entities) and followers (field representatives) of a company could help contribute to an integrative conflict management handling process. Although many conflicts related to natural resources in the world would rely heavily on the political or economic approach (such as in the African region), Indonesia as the second largest democracy in the world has raised several more complex social challenges for its conflict management approach. Moreover, the findings regarding the dynamics between the two entities could be applied to the dynamics of group interactions in another industry or in other regions as well.

To overcome internal and external conflicts, an understanding regarding the relationship between leaders and followers is a must. In addition, there must be adequate instructions as to how the relationship should interact and how to maintain a harmonious association. This chapter offers a theoretical framework on the relationships between leaders and followers, emphasizing the importance of adjusting the perspective, orientation, and mindset between the leaders and followers. Such an outlook stresses on the importance of understanding the cultural diversity and customs in Indonesia. Moreover, an integrated stakeholder involvement process is needed, especially for followers, to be able to work together with leaders for preventing and handling conflicts.

LESSONS FROM INDONESIAN THROUGH CASES

Indonesia is a vast archipelago of 17,000 islands and has the fourth largest population in the world (250 million people) with its 1,340 tribes and 650 local dialects. This country is also blessed with abundant natural resources – it possesses the second largest oil reserves in Southeast Asia, is the eighth largest gold producer in the world, and is the fifth largest producer of copper and nickel. Many natural resource conflicts in the world rely heavily on the political or economic approach (such as in the African region) for resolving its situation; however, Indonesia as the second largest democratic country in the world raises several complex social challenges for its conflict management approach.

Unique Corporate Culture

The multinational companies have dominated the extractive industries in Indonesia. Their corporate culture becomes a very unique blend of the culture from the country of origin and that of the local area where it operates. The nature of conducting business, the work system, and the leadership style in the management process of the extractive company are influenced by the culture of the home country, including the United States, Canada, Britain, France, and many others. Along with local tradition, custom plays an important role while the field representative of the company interacts with the community, as many of the field representatives belong to the local area. However, their actions in the field are regulated by the extractive company's regulations; nevertheless, the work environment and patterns of social relations are heavily influenced by the local nuances of the many areas in Indonesia (Java, Sumatra, Papua, and many other places).

As the headquarters and the local representatives are making contact in the daily business process, an interaction of a low context and high context culture occurred. The corporate entity dominated by the low context culture where communication was explicit, and the needs were articulated in the communication. And the field representatives were influenced by high context culture, where communication is not direct, accentuate by symbols and heavy in context. In such a situation, misunderstandings are common and problems arise because of the differences in perception. An example can be drawn from some of the routine incidents that occur in the field, such as during the death of a member in the community. In many areas in Indonesia, it is the custom to show one's support for the family of the deceased by giving donation. Most field representatives usually urge the extractive company to take part in this practice as they understand that this act can also be interpreted as honoring the community's tradition; however, the extractive company's regulation views such practices as negative. The field representatives would like the extractive company to be more flexible or to conform to local tradition, but the extractive company views such practices otherwise and do not take steps to participate.

Several of such misunderstandings may result in polarization of the leaders and followers. Leaders view the followers as not complying to the extractive company's regulations and the followers view the leaders as not being sensitive to the local customs. With this gap created in the association between leaders and followers, the corporate entity thinks that the field representative tends to lean toward the community instead of the extractive company while the field representative thinks that the leader is too rigid and does not show empathy toward the community. Understanding of the geographical conditions and regional issues and developing a corporate culture that is acceptable to both sides and serves as a melting pot from the high- and low-context culture becomes an important step for developing an integrated conflict management approach.

Consistency, Capacity, Competency, and Capability

The issues of consistency on policies, capacities in understanding the locals, competency and capability of leaders and followers become central issues in providing a perceived justice in the communities. Another important aspects is the consistency of policy implementation which directly affect the local people. Various extractive companies failed to be consistent in the implementation of their programs as they could not withstand the pressure from the parent extractive company. During the fall in oil prices, many companies choose to lay off workers; such approaches were rejected by locals who failed to notice the impact on the extractive companies because of the global policies. Consequently, locals began to raise their concerns through demonstrations. Many of the leaders chose a short-term approach and began re-hiring people as the demonstrations could affect the image of the companies.

Competency and capability has created other issues as well. To address those condition, several extractive companies provided an affirmative action program for the locals. Scholarships were initiated by the extractive company so that locals could get better education; many of them who graduated aspired to work with the company once they finished their education. The government too supports such programs and regulates the hiring process of locals. However, the implementation of these programs is complex, as many of the locals (due to the quality of their education) can only hold a blue-collar position but several of them think that their educational background should provide them a white-collar position.

Another problem that arises is with regard to the relationship between the leader and the follower while understanding the condition and way of life of the local people, because, as already stated, Indonesia is a country of 250 million people with 1,340 tribes and 650 local dialects. Most of the extractive industries (onshore and offshore) are located in remote areas, which has its own uniqueness and challenges. The issues observed in one area would be totally different from that of another. Many of the people involved in the extractive industries failed to understand this complexity. Leaders usually do not belong to the area of the extractive industries and so have limited or basic knowledge about the local issues and also the local actors. Moreover, even the field representatives belong to the big cities in Indonesia and so do have a complete understanding of local issues but sometimes neither a proper understanding regarding the company's vision and mission.

Differences in Views, Orientations, and Mindset between Leaders and Followers

Leadership is a relationship process whereby leaders influence the followers to achieve common goals (Northouse, 2010). Leaders can adopt different leadership styles in their role depending on the followers' abilities, role complexity and structure, environmental situation, member relations, and, most importantly, the leader's personal ability. There is a gap existing between the corporate entity (leaders) and the field representative (staffs) on the issue of community acceptance. In several companies, the perception of community acceptance can be totally different between the leaders and followers. It is quite common that the management level view that their company's relationship with the community tended to be in a neutral toward poor condition. However, the field representatives viewed it differently, stating that the relationship was in a relatively good condition.

In the face of certain issues, the field representatives often feel that the management is not able to support them and vice-versa. The leaders feel that the mindset of the followers is trapped in a narrow perspective and is not inclusive. Though the leaders usually have a more global mindset, they tend to ignore the local issues. These differences have resulted in a difference in approaches and views when faced with problems in the community. While the corporate entity will consider a broader perspective and approach for the problem, the field representatives will consider a more localized one. For example, during an unrest situation wherein the community is protesting against the extractive company on certain issues, the management will respond to such incidents taking into consideration how the situation will affect the position of the extractive company globally (such as the shares of the extractive company in the stock markets or from a human rights' angle). Nevertheless, the field representatives tend to approach such incidents differently (that is, how the incidents will affect their safety). Different mindsets will result in different approaches while handling the incidents and, thereby, the settlement process will not be an integrative one but a compartmentalized problem-solving mechanism.

The danger of such an approach is that it will produce a low level of trust between the two groups as the management/corporate entity will think that the staff in the field have taken sides with the community, especially as many of them are locals, and the field representatives will think that the management does not support them in times of crisis, especially during risky events such as during protests or demonstrations where the lives of the field representatives may sometimes be at stake.

OVERCOMING THE DIFFERENCES BETWEEN LEADERS AND FOLLOWERS

Through an analysis of cases in Indonesia, one can see that the internal conflicts between the corporate entity and the field representatives are generated by differences in views, orientation, and mindset. The corporate entity applies a broader perspective during social construction that tends to be abstract, ignoring details and concrete features; however, those who work in the field tend to view the issues in a more detailed manner, particularly while construing those aspects that tend to be plainly visible. There is a difference in the kind of thinking applied: those in leadership positions use an abstract thinking process while those in follower positions use concrete-level thinking. Each one's meaning-making is different, which ultimately produces differences in attitudes and actions taken.

Differences are also seen in the leaders and followers work orientation. The leaders are oriented toward the interest of the extractive company, while the followers are more community-oriented. Leaders focus on achieving the goals and interest of the extractive company, while the followers think about increasing the community's acceptance toward the extractive company. There is also a difference in the mindsets of both. The management behind the desk uses a rule-based mindset, which is the tendency to always stick to the rules that have been determined by the extractive company, while the implementers in the field use an outcome-based mindset, namely the tendency to obtain outcomes and positive consequences even though the acquisition process is not in accordance with the rules.

To bridge these differences, a form of relationship between leaders and followers is needed to enable them to work together and complement each other's views, orientation, and mindset. For this reason, an "integrative stakeholder engagement" process is needed. The first step that needs to be done is to bring together corporate leaders and followers (field representatives) to face the reality that exists within the extractive company and in the field. This step can provide knowledge about what actually happened, resulting in a more comprehensive and realistic view.

The second step is to transform both leader and follower orientation into an orientation that transcends importance to all stakeholders. In it, both the interests of the extractive company and the interests of the community are considered important. With this orientation, leaders and followers can have a common vision and seek the same interests.

The third step is to jointly find possible rules to produce the best outcome and allow them to find the best solution for conflict prevention and resolution. A condition should be created to facilitate the mindset of leaders and followers that should prioritize ethical rightness not rigid rules or justify means to an end (Table 1).

The lack of consistency, capacity, competency, and capability that appears among the leaders and followers in an extractive company is an

Table 1. Integrative Stakeholders Engagement Process.

Leaders	Integrative Stakeholder Engagement Process	Followers
Abstract construal level	Comprehensivse-realistic knowledge	Concrete construal level
Company oriented	Stakeholder oriented	Community oriented
Rule-based mindset	The-right-and-the-good-based mindset	Outcome-based mindset

indication of the differences that exist in regard to views, orientation, and mindset. Each individual focuses on only certain issues, thereby failing to have a detailed picture of the overall reality. As mentioned in the previous section, leaders tend to focus in more generalized manner whereas followers concentrate more specifically on issues. The cultural diversity among them may also contribute to the complexity in their relations. Efforts must be made to adjust and foster good relations through the establishment of a common ground between them; only then will they be able to overcome these shortcomings. Many extractive companies have set up conflict management training for all their staff in charge of the stakeholder engagement process. In several instances, this capacity building is mandatory for management and staff of the extractive company.

Internal conflict resolution would form the basis for a more adequate resolution of external conflicts. A more comprehensive-realistic view with respects to all stakeholders, and the-right-and-the-good-based mindset are expected to function in resolving external conflicts in order to create a perception of social justice for all stakeholders. With the ongoing integrative stakeholder engagement process, the perception of social justice for community members can be generated and community acceptance for extractive companies can be obtained.

Implication for Conflict Management Practice

Natural resource conflict in Indonesia is often protracted, and it can be latent or manifest itself in open conflict. Even though the issues of the conflict are often overlapping, the extractive company should be able to identify these issues in detail, differentiate the structural aspects, and identify the accelerators or triggers of its reality in the field.

The process of conflict handling in each condition, whether latent or manifest, should also be differentiated. For the latent stages, a conflict early warning and early response (CEWERS) must be conducted whereby conflicts are monitored regularly, and issues and actors are mapped; this process should be conducted as completely as possible. This conflict monitoring program should be led by the field representatives and they should report their findings to the corporate entity or the management, periodically. If the situation manifests into a critical situation or open conflict, the management should take the lead by activating and forming a conflict management team and determining the main direction of conflict resolution.

This conflict team should be a cross-departmental team, which includes representatives from leaders and followers, to carry out a rapid response to the crisis situation. The main function of the team is to perform strategic, communication, and operational duties. The strategic team is tasked with formulating the extractive company's direction on the general description of handling critical situations and the process of conflict resolution that must be carried out. They then translate the direction into a more operational form in the context of strategies, procedures, and methods and develop a success criterion. The communication team translates the routine operational activities for a condensed period. In addition, this team also makes plans that include the techniques and tools that would be used to achieve the goals. This team also acts as a bridge for internal and external communication. The third team is the operational team that is tasked with the implementation of activities based on a specific work plan. This operational group will have a lot to do with parties outside the extractive company.

Some of the criteria that are needed to manage conflict well include the ability to think analytically, creatively, and strategically. In addition, it requires self-confidence, communication skills, and the ability to adapt as per the changes that develop. In relation to outside parties, skills are also needed to build networks and focus on stakeholders. Another important entity pertains to developing effective leadership, with the ability to manage differences and handle conflicts.

CONCLUSION

This study intends to contribute to the field of conflict management and the literature on leader and follower relations in three ways. First, as has been pointed out, handling internal extractive company conflicts is a very important aspect in resolving conflicts between companies and communities. An analysis of cases in Indonesia helps to provide an explanation with regard to this. These findings should be able to be implemented in other regions as well where circumstances for the extractive industries in other part of the world are similar to the ones in Indonesia. Second, we have introduced a theoretical framework that provides explanation as to how internal conflicts in extractive industries occur because of differences in views, orientation, and mindset between leaders and followers. These differences can be bridged by developing a common language of conflict resolution through an integrative and comprehensive conflict management program directed at the leaders in the head office (in Indonesia or overseas) and the followers in the area. Third, we have outlined clear implications that would unfold if the extractive companies would fail to understand the importance of involving and allowing followers to play an active and proactive role in conflict management in extractive industries.

REFERENCES

Adnan, H., Tadjudin, D., Yuliani, L., Komarudin, H., Lopulalan, D., Siagian, Y. L., & Munggoro, D. W. (Eds). (2008). *Belajar dari Bungo: mengelola sumberdaya alam di era desentralisasi* [Learn from Bungo: Managing natural resources in the era of decentralization]. Bogor: CIFOR.

Boutilier, R., & Thomson, I. (2011). Modelling and measuring the social license to operate: Fruits of a dialogue between theory and practice. *Social Licence to Operate*. Retrieved from http://socialicense.com/publications/Mod ellingandMeasuringtheSLO.pdf

Bulzomi, A. (2013). *Practice what you preach: Theory and practice of Chine National Petroleum Corporation (CNPC)'s stakeholder engagement plan in Chad*. Antwerp: IPIS.

Direktorat Jenderal Politik dan Pemerintahan Umum Kementrian Dalam Negeri RI. (2016). Directorate General of Politics and Public Administration, Ministry of Home Affairs Republic of Indonesia.

Environment Energy Bulletin. (2015). *Impatient communities' protests put more pressure on platinum producers*. Retrieved from https://www.business live.co.za/bd/companies/mining/2017-06-13-impatient-communities-protests-put-more-pressure-on-platinum-producers/

Erwiantono & Saleha. (2012). *Persepsi & ekspektasi pembangunan masyarakat terhadap pemerintah daerah dan perusahaan migas* [Perception and expectations of the community development towards local governments and oil and gas companies]. *Makara Sosial Humaniora, 16*(1), 57–67.

Habibie Center. (2013). *Peta Kekerasan di Indonesia* [Map of violence in Indonesia]. Kajian Perdamaian dan Kebijakan the Habibie Center. Retrieved from https://www.habibiecenter.or.id/wp-content/uploads/2016/10/THC-Violence-Intensity-Index-2015_Bahasa.pdf

Humpreys, M. (2005, August). Natural resources, conflict, and conflict resolution. *Journal of Conflict Resolution, 49*(4), 508–537.

Irfanny, R. (2015). *Riset: Daerah kaya migas punya warga miskin lebih banyak* [Research: Oil and gas-rich regions have more poor people]. Tempo. Retrieved from https://m.tempo.co/read/news/2015/09/25/092703910/riset-daerah-kaya-migas-punya-warga-miskin-lebih-banyak

Kemp, D., Owen, J. R., Gotzmann, N., & Bond, C. J. (2011). Just relations and company–community conflict in mining. *Journal of Business Ethics, 101*, 93–109.

Konsorsium Pembaruan Agraria [Agrarian Reform Consortium]. (2014). *Membenahi Masalah Agraria: Prioritas Kerja Jokowi-JK Pada 2015* [Fixing the agrarian problem: Jokowi-JK work priority in 2015]. Jakarta: KPA.

Moffat, K. (2015). The social licence to operate: A critical review. *Forestry*, 1–12.

Northouse, P. G. (2010). *Leadership: Theory and practice* (5th ed.). Thousand Oaks, CA: Sage Publishers.

Reeson, A. M., & Hosking, K. (2012). Mining activity, income inequality and gender in regional Australia. *Australian Journal of Agricultural and Resource Economics*, 56(2), 302–313.

World Bank. (2013). *Humanity divided: Confronting inequality in developing countries*. New York, NY: World Bank.

Yanuarti, S., Marieta, J., Yusuf, & Tryatmoko, M. W. (2003). *Konflik di Maluku tengah: penyebab, karakteristik dan penyelesaian jangka panjang* [Conflict in Central Maluku: Causes, characteristics and long-term solutions]. Jakarta: Lembaga Ilmu Pengetahuan Indonesia.

EPILOGUE

DEMOCRATIZING LEADERSHIP: PRE-CONFLICT PREVENTATIVE PEACEBUILDING

Mike Klein

ABSTRACT

Peacebuilding is often premised on international intervention in post-conflict situations. This epilogue extends the concept to address preventative peacebuilding in pre-conflict societies. Social movement organizations that spring from democratically oriented movements can either reproduce dominant and dominating leadership styles, or they can cultivate democratizing leadership (Klein, 2016) by developing democratic practices, structures, and cultures within and between organizations. Democratizing leadership promotes leadership as a verb more than a noun: as the operation of power in relationship between people, rather than as positional power grounded in an authority figure. In democratizing leadership, democratic decision-making is preceded by the development of individual and collective voice and followed by responsible collective action. In addition to these processes, democratic values are also essential, including: freedom (differentiated from autonomy), justice (procedural, social, and restorative justice), and equity (more than equality), which underlie structural processes and inform practices. When social move-ment organizations find creative tension between ad hoc leadership and the tendency toward bureaucratization, they can cultivate a dem-ocratic culture through organizational practices and structures for preventative peacebuilding work. Leadership in such organizations recognizes and utilizes creative conflict to sustain agonistic pluralism and promote conflictual consensus (Mouffe, 2013). This epilogue provides examples of democratizing leadership from social movement organizations, including: In the Heart of the Beast Theater, Minnesota Alliance of Peacemakers, Neighborhood Leadership Program, and the Higher Education Consortium for Urban Affairs, that illustrate how democratizing leadership can be developed in pre-conflict preventative peacebuilding organizations by integrating democratic practices, structures, and cultures.

Keywords: Democratizing leadership; pre-conflict countries; preventative peacebuilding; social movement organizations; democracy; agonistic pluralism

The chapters in this volume present case studies with profound implications for peace, reconciliation, and social justice leadership across the globe and in our own communities. Together, these stories weave a complex narrative of reconciliation, peacemaking, community peacebuilding, international law, and social justice that helpfully complicate our notions of leader and follower. The encompassing category of "peacebuilding" is often premised on international intervention in post-conflict situations, primarily by countries of the Global North in countries of the Global South. How might we expand the focus of peacebuilding leadership to include local, conflict-prevention work in our home societies? Just as Ira Chaleff's chapter on interracial healing exemplifies this "turn to the local," I advocate for the importance of transforming notions of leader and follower in our own societies, in addition to – and as a complement to – transnational peacebuilding. Given the rising tides of populist nationalism and intra-national political polarization, how do we learn from post-conflict countries to conduct peacebuilding work in our own societies and communities? And how do we cultivate mutuality in our understanding and practice of leadership and followership to acknowledge the problematics of colonialism, patriarchy, white supremacy, heteronormativity, and other forms of domination, while promoting inclusivity and equity across the complicated dynamics of power?

Our normative frameworks for peacebuilding – often unacknowledged – might be critically examined to help us question the presumptive roles of leaders and followers. One approach to this critical examination is unsettling the typical focus of peacebuilding work on "post-conflict" countries, to look for a more mutual and interconnected approach to peace, reconciliation, and social justice leadership. The "Hourglass Model of Conflict Resolution Responses" by Miall, Ramsbotham, and Woodhouse (2011, p. 13) describes the transition of post-conflict countries through categories of: war, ceasefire, agreement, normalization, and reconciliation. But just as true to this model, we may describe other countries as "pre-conflict" societies, defined by the Hourglass Model as transitioning through categories of: difference, contradiction, polarization, violence, and war. Is there any doubt that internal polarization grips the politics of many countries? Some of these same countries advocate transnational peacebuilding and yet also promulgate transnational violence and war. How might we move beyond an apparent bifurcation between transnational post-conflict peacebuilding and domestic pre-conflict peacebuilding? Social justice leadership is required at both ends of the peacebuilding spectrum. To be effective and ethical in this work, we need to identify and work across the normative differences in our conceptual frameworks.

By conceiving of all countries as existing somewhere on the range of "pre-conflict" or "post-conflict" we might recognize mutual concern and interdependence. And by conceptualizing peacebuilding work across these categories, we might also recognize that lessons from post-conflict societies can hold wisdom for pre-conflict societies engaging in preventative peacebuilding. Developing this sort of mutuality in leadership across pre- and post-conflict societies is rooted in humility; to listen carefully and with respect to people who have experienced violence, domination, and oppression. As evidenced by the preceding chapters, survivors of injustice and marginalization have the most to teach us about social justice and about leadership and followership that is marked by solidarity. Our search for peace, reconciliation, and social justice – in pre- or post-conflict countries – can bind us across peacebuilding work in global solidarity, given that our conflicts and struggles are rarely confined to national boundaries and have much to teach and learn from one another.

I encountered a striking example of social justice leadership that transcended normative categories of post-conflict and pre-conflict countries in November 2014, as protestors gathered for the twenty-fifth year of a campaign to close the School of the Americas (renamed Western

Hemispheric Institute for Security Cooperation in 2001) outside of Fort Benning Military Base in Columbus, Georgia, USA. At a conference connected to the vigil, a Colombian delegation introduced their presentation with this stark assessment:

> We have come to the United States to teach you how to resist neo-liberal domination. We have been subject to it, and resisting it, for decades through Plan Colombia, through militarization, through the mechanism of debt, through growing economic inequality, through the privatization of public infrastructure like prisons and utilities; all for the profit of a few over the good of the people. But the ever-increasing hunger of neo-liberal domination has expanded beyond the resources of the Global South and now turns to feed upon itself. Now you are beginning to feel the violence and know the pain of the dominating hegemony that has ravaged our country for decades. Over this time, we have learned much about resistance and now we have come to teach you so that you may learn to resist and grow in solidarity with the vast majority of the world who suffer under this system. (Klein, 2016, p. 61)

At an event premised on US citizens protesting *for* human rights in Latin America, we were educated *by* Latin American social justice leaders to work *with* each other. These little words — *for, by, with* — have big implications for the way we understand and practice leadership and followership for social justice. How may we identify the best approach to the role of leaders and followers by attending to the dynamics of power enacted by, for, or with each other across our understandings of pre- and post-conflict societies?

Creative engagement between leaders and followers depends on this normative approach to social analysis in addition to more typical descriptive analysis through the social sciences. For example, the normative values underlying many cultures and religious traditions refer to something like the Golden Rule: do unto others as you would have others do unto you. What if we extend that presumed normative grounding to a more empathetic perspective, one that was introduced to me as the Platinum Rule (in 2008 by Phyllis Braxton of Pink Consulting LLC). How might leader and follower dynamics change if we: do unto others as *they* would have *us* do unto *them*? Rather than presuming that followers want the same thing as leaders, or that the subjects of peacebuilding have the same goals as the agents of peacebuilding, what if we began with a more relational rather than transactional approach? What if we practiced empathetic listening to raise the voices and agency of people on the receiving end of peacebuilding to make it a more mutual process rooted in solidarity and collective agency? This is a significant shift in normative perspective – evident in the preceding chapters – that questions power and privilege. It requires critical reflection on the positionality of leaders and followers that promotes a more rigorous reflexivity integrated into peacebuilding culture, structure, and practice.

In addition to normative analysis, mutuality in relationship between leaders and followers relies on sustaining rather than resolving creative tensions within peacebuilding organizations, and between peacebuilding organizations and those impacted by their work. If we can conceive of leadership as more verb than noun, we can actively shape the dynamics of power to promote more democratic organizational structures and practices. When we presume leadership to be a noun – for example the "great-man" model of unique and rare traits and qualities, or on authoritative and hierarchical positions of power – individual and collective agency is diminished in deference to the charismatic few. But when leadership is conceived as a verb, it functions more situationally and contextually; ascribing the dynamics of power between individuals, groups, and organizations, rather than proscribing power in static relationships of domination and subordination. Leaders of one moment might be followers of the next, as new situations arise, and different skills are required. This is not to advocate for completely ad hoc leadership or the lack of any defined roles in organizations, but to find creative tensions between hierarchical bureaucratic leadership, and the unwieldly direct democracy practiced unevenly in social movements. So, how do we create democratizing practices, structures, and cultures that promote peace, reconciliation, and social justice leadership?

I have found remarkable examples of social movement organizations that cultivate what I term *democratizing leadership* (Klein, 2016) by developing democratic practices, structures, and cultures within and between organizations. When social movement organizations sustain creative tensions between ad hoc leadership and the tendency toward bureaucratization, they can model and cultivate preventative peacebuilding work, promoting problem-solving across differences to avoid contradiction and polarization that leads toward political violence. In dynamic examples of democratizing leadership, I found that power sharing through democratic decision-making is preceded by the development of individual and collective voice, and it is followed by responsible collective action. As difficult as it might be for leaders to share power, it can be even more difficult for followers to receive and use power. To make decisions and to take action democratically, there must be opportunities for followers to find voice and use it, then use it together. Therefore, rather than leadership directed *at* or *for* people, democratizing leadership is enacted *by* and *with* people: developing practices that promote finding and using voice and creating structures that facilitate shared decision-making and collective action.

Democratic structures and practices support the processes of democratizing leadership, and they require a foundational democratic culture rooted in values, including: freedom (differentiated from autonomy), justice (procedural, social, and restorative justice), and equity (more than simply equality). These democratic values, integrated into organizational cultures through democratizing structures and practices, not only support democratizing leadership, but they also guard against the potential excesses of a nominally democratic process, such as the silencing of minority voices or the tyranny of the majority in decision-making. This is the very heart of the work for leadership in preventative, pre-conflict peacebuilding: promoting conflict resolution across political differences to avoid social divisions that lead to contradiction, polarization, and political violence.

I have found dynamic examples of practices, structures, and cultures in democratizing leadership through my research on social movement organizations. For example, In the Heart of the Beast Theater Puppet and Mask Theater hosts an annual May Day Parade for an audience of 50,000 in Minneapolis, Minnesota, USA. They structure their community-building democratic engagement around shared decision-making that begins with ritual practices for all voices to be heard, and proceeds through structured decision-making toward collective action with a May Day deadline (Klein, 2009, 2016). Yet even this consensus-based community art process leaves room for the freedom of dissenting and conflicting voices by reserving an agonistic space − a "free speech section" − at the end of their otherwise coherent parade narrative. The result is an annual democratic ritual that gives voice to the hopes and concerns of the community and points toward solutions through collective action.

In another example of creative organizational tensions between hierarchical authoritarianism and ad hoc improvisation, the Minnesota Alliance of Peacemakers (Klein, 2016) governs bimonthly meetings of 72 peacebuilding organizations through a democratically elected coordinating team, rather than a single executive leader. And a structured democratic facilitation process utilizing Open Space Technology (Owen, 2008) creates a dynamic structure for voice, decision-making, and collective action. The alliance seeks to balance the freedom of a broad-based association with a structured approach to equity that recognizes and accommodates power differentials between small community-based organizations and large well-funded nonprofits. The result is alignment between the cultural values of the organization, and its structures and practices. Neither of these organizations utilize direct democracy for most decisions – leaving some participants to decry too little democracy, while others complain of too much – however both organizations judiciously and selectively incorporate democratizing leadership to fit their goals and to reflect their values. Social justice leadership in pre-conflict preventative peacebuilding should experiment with processes that promote voice, decision-making, and collective action to find appropriate practices and structures that reflect and enact a democratic culture.

Peacebuilding organizations may ground their democratic cultures in normative commitments to democratizing leadership in the principles and documents of international entities such as the United Nations Universal Declaration of Human Rights, Sustainable Development Goals, or Declaration on Rights of Indigenous Peoples; or in national constitutions; or in social movement manifestos that articulate a culture of democracy as grounding for the cultivation of democratic structures and practices. This is no easy process, but one fraught with disagreement over the appropriate grounding and over the level and extent of democratic process. Yet these creative tensions are just what democracy is intended to sustain; a way to work together across our differences without insisting on conformity to the will of authoritative and authoritarian leadership.

Democratizing leadership can recognize and utilize creative tensions in organizations to sustain agonistic pluralism and promote a contingent conflictual consensus (Mouffe, 2013) to avoid the extremes of authoritarian control or unsustainable ad hoc leadership. Maintaining creative tensions between the improvisational nature of social movements and the formalized structure of institutions can produce a dynamic third way through democratizing leadership. A democratic commitment to agonistic pluralism acknowledges the importance of creating and sustaining space for dissenting and conflicting voices while also recognizing the need for consensus at crucial moments of democratic decision-making.

Social movement organizations located in my community illustrate how leaders and followers can cultivate an agonistic culture of democracy in addition to democratic structures and practices. The Neighborhood Leadership Program (NLP, 2019) organizes diverse, capacity-building cohorts of community leaders to learn approaches to freedom, justice, and equity through processes of voice, decision-making, and collective action. More than a skill-building program, NLP develops leadership around commitments to equity and social justice by engaging local issues and institutions, and by assembling a cohort of diverse leaders across intersectional categories of race, class, gender, ability, age, nationality, and other identifiers (Klein & Shoholm, 2017). Another local organization with an international focus, the Higher Education Consortium for Urban Affairs (HECUA, 2019), provides local, national, and international study-away experiences for a consortium of colleges and universities. Such international education can be seen as peacebuilding work, yet HECUA's approach goes further to practice what it teaches. HECUA is in the midst of an organizational-level truth and reconciliation process to address racial disparities within this educational social movement organization. Their internal review of structures and practices is guided by a commitment to supporting a culture of justice and equity for the students and communities they serve, and for the professional staff of the organization. Such work tends to raise conflicts over differential ideas about equality and equity and in agonistic disagreements over justice that acknowledges past wrongs reproduced in present structures and practices. It is fraught work, and all the more admirable for the tensions it produces above and beyond the daily work of the organization. But these are creative tensions inherent in democratizing leadership for preventative pre-conflict peacebuilding organizations.

This volume is replete with powerful examples like these. Given this, an epilogue might be a late moment to suggest that the title of the book might be out of temporal order: that instead, social justice leadership leads toward reconciliation in the pursuit of peace. Perhaps this is an appropriately reflective way to conclude this volume and send us into the next chapters of peacebuilding work? In my ongoing learning from local indigenous peoples, I have come to recognize the importance of decolonizing our thinking that is essential to unsettling settler-society conceptions of leaders and followers. Dr Waziyatawin — a voice of the Dakota people from my own pre-conflict society in Minnesota, USA — describes the order of decolonizing operations as: truth-telling, historical re-interpretation, reparations, economic justice, and ending the oppression of white supremacy to promote mutual-respect (Waziyatawin, 2008). Only after these steps are taken, reconciliation can be considered if and when those who were harmed are ready to proceed. My own academic institution is taking its first steps on a path toward truth-telling about the Dakota land we occupy. And we are taking these first steps on a critically reflective journey with the local Dakota tribal community knowing that we are sure to stumble along the way, but seeking freedom in relationship, justice in historical context, and equity through social justice leadership in pursuit of reconciliation and peace.

Democratizing leadership, as one approach to pre-conflict preventative peacebuilding, distributes power through organizational structures and practices to promote voice, decision-making, and collective action, while democratizing organizational culture to promote freedom, justice, and equity. Other remarkable approaches are evident throughout the chapters of this book. Our challenges, as we close this volume, are: to learn the lessons from these particular examples, to encourage their application in post-conflict societies, and to adapt them to pre-conflict societies. Peacebuilding work across pre- and post-conflict societies may help us learn more effective strategies for addressing violent conflict and promoting nonviolent political approaches to living together across our differences, through mutually supportive leadership that begins in our own social contexts and extends toward each other. As the chapters of this book demonstrate, the work of peace, reconciliation, and social justice leadership in the twenty-first century is dynamic, evolving, and challenging: calling on all of us as activists, academics, artists, advocates, and researchers to engage across our differences to develop practices, structures, and cultures of mutuality and solidarity.

REFERENCES

HECUA. (2019). Anti-racism efforts: The higher education consortium for urban affairs. Retrieved from https://hecua.org/about/anti-racism-efforts/

Klein, M. (2009). *Raising hands: Ritualizing leadership for democratic decision-making and action*. Phd thesis, University of St. Thomas, St. Paul, MN.

Klein, M. (2016). *Democratizing leadership: Counter-hegemonic democracy in organizations, institutions, and communities.* Charlotte, NC: Information Age Publishing.

Klein, M., & Shoholm, D. (2017). *Neighborhood leadership: Celebrating twenty years of the Amherst H. Wilder Foundation's Neighborhood Leadership Program (NLP).* St. Paul, MN: Praxia Books.

Miall, H., Ramsbotham, O., & Woodhouse, T. (2011). *Contemporary conflict resolution.* Cambridge: Polity Press.

Mouffe, C. (2013). *Agonistics: Thinking the world politically.* London: Verso.

NLP. (2019). The neighborhood leadership program. Retrieved from https://www.wilder.org/what-we-offer/community-leadership-programs/neighborhood-leadership-program

Owen, H. (2008). *Open space technology a user's guide* (3rd ed., rev. and expanded ed.). San Francisco, CA: Berrett-Koehler.

Waziyatawin. (2008). *What does justice look like?: The struggle for liberation in Dakota homeland* (1st ed.). St. Paul, MN: Living Justice Press.

INDEX